Russia's Turn to Persia

Iran has remained one of the most effective tools in Russia's foreign policy towards the West for more than two hundred years. Drawing on previously unpublished and recently declassified sources which change the established wisdom on many aspects of the history of Russia and Iran, Denis V. Volkov examines this relationship and situates it within the broader context of Oriental studies.

With a particular focus on the activities of scholars-diplomats, as well as scholars involved in academia, missionary activities and the military within their own professional domains, Volkov analyses the interaction of intellectuals with state structures and their participation in the process of shaping and conducting foreign policy towards Iran. This work explores the specific institutional practices of Russia's Oriental studies, including organisation of scholarly intelligence networks, taking advantage of state power for the promotion of institutional and individual interests, and profound engagement with Russia's domestic and foreign policy discourses of its time.

DENIS V. VOLKOV is Assistant Professor in Middle Eastern History at the University of Manchester. He spent almost fifteen years in Iran, working in the field of interstate economic cooperation between Russia and Iran. His research interests include the history and the present of Russo–Iranian relations, Russia's Oriental studies, intellectual history, Russian and Iranian nationalism, and, particularly, Russian émigré Orientalists. His most recent publications are "Vladimir Minorsky (1877–1966) and the Iran–Iraq War (1980–1988), or The Centenary of 'Minorsky's Frontier',", in *Russians in Iran: Diplomacy and Power in Iran in the Qajar Era and Beyond*, ed. Rudolph Matthee and Elena Andreeva, and "War and Peace in the Other and the Self: Iran through the eyes of Russian spies" *Cahiers de Studia Iranica* 62 (2018): 225–60.

Russia's Turn to Persia

Orientalism in Diplomacy and Intelligence

DENIS V. VOLKOV
University of Manchester

CAMBRIDGE
UNIVERSITY PRESS

University Printing House, Cambridge CB2 8BS, United Kingdom

One Liberty Plaza, 20th Floor, New York, NY 10006, USA

477 Williamstown Road, Port Melbourne, VIC 3207, Australia

314-321, 3rd Floor, Plot 3, Splendor Forum, Jasola District Centre, New Delhi - 110025, India

79 Anson Road, #06-04/06, Singapore 079906

Cambridge University Press is part of the University of Cambridge.

It furthers the University's mission by disseminating knowledge in the pursuit of education, learning and research at the highest international levels of excellence.

www.cambridge.org
Information on this title: www.cambridge.org/9781108446693
DOI: 10.1017/9781108645270

© Denis V. Volkov 2018

First published 2018
First paperback edition 2020

A catalogue record for this publication is available from the British Library

Library of Congress Cataloging in Publication data
Names: Volkov, Denis V., author.
Title: Russia's turn to Persia : orientalism in diplomacy and intelligence / Denis V. Volkov.
Description: Cambridge, United Kingdom; New York, NY: Cambridge University Press, 2018. | Includes bibliographical references and index.
Identifiers: LCCN 2018014863 | ISBN 9781108490788 (hardback)
Subjects: LCSH: Russia – Foreign relations – Iran. | Iran – Foreign relations – Russia. | Soviet Union – Foreign relations – Iran. | Iran – Foreign relations – Soviet Union. | Middle East – Study and teaching – Russia – History. | Middle East – Study and teaching – Soviet Union – History. | BISAC: HISTORY / Middle East / General.
Classification: LCC DK68.7.I7 V64 2018 | DDC 327.47055–dc23
LC record available at https://lccn.loc.gov/2018014863

ISBN 978-1-108-49078-8 Hardback
ISBN 978-1-108-44669-3 Paperback

To the memory of my parents
To the love of my wife and son

Contents

Figures

Acknowledgements

This book is based on extensive research conducted at the archives of Russia (Moscow and St Petersburg) and Georgia (Tbilisi), which would have been almost impossible had I not received the generous support of the British Institute of Persian Studies (BIPS), the British Society for Middle Eastern Studies (BRISMES) and the British Association for Slavonic and East European Studies (BASEES). My deep gratitude also goes to the staff of the ten Russian archives in which I had the pleasure of working for their sincere and efficient help, while I am similarly grateful to the employees of the Georgian National Centre of Manuscripts for their warm hospitality and expert cooperation. Further thanks are due to colleagues at the Universities of Oxford, Yale, St Andrews and San Diego, at CEELBAS, and at the Hokkaido Slavic Research Centre who invited me to present papers, thereby enabling me to successfully test the interim results of the research that underpins this book.

I hereby express my whole-hearted gratitude to Professor Oliver Bast for his academic and research advice that combined the best features of the West-European German/British and Russian/Soviet scholars of all generations, along with his profound expertise on the Middle East and Russia, and Russo-Iranian relations in particular, which played such a crucial role in my research. Furthermore, I am immensely grateful to Professor Vera Tolz for guiding me into the enchanted forest of Russian thought on national identity and for her expert advice on methodological technicalities. My thanks also go to all my colleagues at the University of Manchester, particularly to Siavush Randjbar-Daemi, who has never tired of sharing his academic know-how with me and on whose help I have always been able to count. My research for this book benefited enormously from the professional and friendly support and the invaluable comments of Edmund Herzig, Ali Ansari, Abbas Amanat, Matthew Jeffries, Adeeb Khalid, Dominic Parviz Brookshaw, Stephanie Cronin, Touraj Atabaki, Charles and Firuza Melville, Lana

Ravandi-Fadai, Douglas Streusand, Norihiro Naganawa, Babak Rahimi, and many others.

These acknowledgements would be incomplete without mentioning the empathy and whole-hearted support of my uncle Viktor and my brother Pavel. However, first and foremost, my greatest thanks go to my beloved wife, Mozhgan, and to my dear son, Dmitry-Omid, who have been the main source of my inspiration and motivation throughout this process, and without whose self-sacrificing care and unwavering moral support this book would not have seen the light of day. I dedicate this work to them.

Note on Transliteration

The language of the major part of primary source material used in this monograph is Russian. The transliteration of Russian names (personal names, book titles, journals, newspapers and organisations) is provided in accordance with the Sixteenth Edition of the Chicago Manual of Style. Bibliographical references also comply with the same style. Unless otherwise stated, all translations from Russian are by the author.

Abbreviations and Acronyms

ARAN (Arkhiv Rossiiskoi Akademii Nauk) – Archive of Russia's Academy of Sciences;

AV (Arkhiv Vostokovedov) – Archive of Orientologists (St Petersburg);

AVPRF (Arkhiv Vneshnei Politiki Rossiiskoi Federatsii) – Archive of the Foreign Policy of the Russian Federation;

AVPRI (Arkhiv Vneshnei Politiki Rossiiskoi Imperii) – Archive of the Foreign Policy of the Russian Empire;

Cheka (Chrezvychainaia Komissiia po Bor'be s Kontrrevoliutsiei i Sabotazhem) – Extraordinary Commission for Combating Counter-Revolution and Sabotage;

DST (La Direction de la Surveillance du Territoire) – French Counterespionage Service;

FSB (Federal'naia Sluzhba Bezopasnosti) – Federal Security Service of the Russian Federation;

GARF (Gosudarstvennyi Arkhiv Rossiiskoi Federatsii) – State Archive of the Russian Federation;

GNCM – Korneli Kekelidze Georgian National Centre of Manuscripts;

GPU (Gosudarstvennoe Politicheskoe Upravlenie) – State Political Directorate;

GRU (Glavnoe Razvedovatel'noe Upravlenie) – Chief Intelligence Directorate of the Army;

GULAG (Glavnoe Upravlenie Ispravitel'no-Trudovykh Lagerei) – Chief-Directorate of Corrective Labour Camps and Labour Settlements of the OGPU/NKVD;

INO OGPU (Inostrannyi Otdel Gosudarstvennogo Politicheskogo Upravleniia) – Foreign Department of the United State Political Directorate;

IRGO (Imperatorskoe Russkoe Geograficheskoe Obshestvo) – Imperial Russian Geographical Society;

IVRAN (Institut Vostokovedeniia Rossiiskoi Akademii Nauk) – Institute of Oriental Studies of Russia's Academy of Sciences;

Abbreviations and Acronyms

KGB (Komitet Gosudarstvennoi Bezopasnosti) – State Security Commitee;

KIPS (Komissiia po izucheniiu plemennogo sostava naseleniia Rossii) – Commission for the Study of the Tribal Composition of the Population of Russia;

KUTV (Kommunisticheskii Universitet Trudiashikhsia Vostoka) – Communist University of the Toilers of the Orient;

MID (Ministerstvo Inostrannykh Del) – Ministry of Foreign Affairs;

MIV (Moskovskii Institut Vostokovedeniia) – Moscow Institute of Oriental Studies;

Narkomnats (Narodnyi Komissariat Natsional'nostei) – People's Commissariat of Nationalities;

Narkomvneshtorg (Narodnyi Komissariat Vneshei Torgovli) – People's Commissariat of Foreign Trade;

Narkomvoendel (Narodnyi Komissariat Voennykh Del) – People's Commissariat of Military Affairs;

NEP (Novaia Ekonomicheskaia Politika) – New Economic Policy;

NKID (Narodnyi Komissariat Inostrannykh Del) – People's Commissariat of Foreign Affairs;

NKVD (Narodnyi Komissariat Vnutrennikh Del) – People's Commissariat of Internal Affairs;

NKVT (Narkomvneshtorg, i.e. Narodnyi Komissariat Vneshei Torgovli) – People's Commissariat of Foreign Trade;

OGPU (Ob'edinennoe Gosudarstvennoe Politicheskoe Upravlenie) – United State Political Directorate;

PGU KGB (Pervoe Glavnoe Upravlenie Komiteta Gosudarstvennoi Bezopasnosti) – First Chief-Directorate of KGB (external intelligence);

Politbiuro (Politicheskoe Biuro) – Political Bureau of the Communist Party;

Polpred (Polnomochnyi predstavitel') – Plenipotentiary;

Razvedupr (Razvedovatel'noe Upravlenie) – Intelligence Directorate of the Red Army;

Revvoensovet (Revoliutsionnyi Voennyi Sovet) – Revolutionary Military Council;

RGALI (Rossiiskii Gosudarstvennyi Arkhiv Literatury i Iskusstva) – Russia's State Archive of Literature and Arts;

RGASPI (Rossiiskii Gosudarstvennyi Arkhiv Sotsial'no-Politicheskoi Istorii) – Russia's State Archive of Socio-Political History;

RGVA (Rossiiskii Gosudarstvennyi Voennyi Arkhiv) – Russia's State Military Archive;

RGVIA (Rossiiskii Gosudarstvennyi Voenno-Istoricheskii Arkhiv) –
Russia's State Military Historical Archive;
RKISVA (Russkii Komitet dlia Izucheniia Srednei i Vostochnoi Azii) –
Russian Committee for the Study of Central and Eastern Asia;
RKKA (Raboche-Krestianskaia Krasnaia Armiia) – Red Army of
Workers and Peasants;
RSFSR (Rossiiskaia Sovetskaia Federativnaia Sotsialisticheskaia
Respublika) – Russian Soviet Federative Socialist Republic;
Sovnarkom (Sovet Narodnykh Komisarov) – Council of the People's
Commissars;
SVR (Sluzhba Vneshnei Razvedki) – External Intelligence of the
Russian Federation;
VeCheka (Vserossiiskaia Chrezvychainaia Komissiia po Bor'be
s Kontrrevoliutsiei i Sabotazhem) – All-Russia Extraordinary
Commission for Combating Counter-Revolution and Sabotage;
VNAV (Vsesoiuznaia Nauchnaia Assotsiatsiia Vostokovedov) – All-
Union Scientific Association of Orientologists;
VTsIK (Vserossiiskii Tsentral'nyi Ispolnitel'nyi Comitet) – All-Russia
Central Executive Committee of the Communist Party;
ZVORAO (Zapiski Vostochnogo Otdeleniia Russkogo
Arkheologicheskogo Obshestva) – Proceedings of the Eastern Branch
of the Imperial Russian Archaeological Society.

Archives Used for Research (Russia and Georgia)

Russia (Moscow)

ARAN (Arkhiv Rossiiskoi Akademii Nauk) – Archive of Russia's Academy of Sciences (Moscow Branch);

AVPRF MID RF (Arkhiv Vneshnei Politiki Rossiiskoi Federatsii) – Archive of the Foreign Policy of the Russian Federation;

AVPRI MID RF (Arkhiv Vneshnei Politiki Rossiiskoi Imperii) – Archive of the Foreign Policy of the Russian Empire;

GARF (Gosudarstvennyi Arkhiv Rossiiskoi Federatsii) – State Archive of the Russian Federation;

RGALI (Rossiiskii Gosudarstvennyi Arkhiv Literatury i Iskusstva) – Russia's State Archive of Literature and Art;

RGASPI (Rossiiskii Gosudarstvennyi Arkhiv Sotsial'no-Politicheskoi Istorii) – Russia's State Archive of Socio-Political History;

RGVA (Rossiiskii Gosudarstvennyi Voennyi Arkhiv) – Russia's State Military Archive;

RGVIA (Rossiiskii Gosudarstvennyi Voenno-Istoricheskii Arkhiv) – Russia's State Military Historical Archive;

Russia (St Petersburg)

ARAN (Arkhiv Rossiiskoi Akademii Nauk) – Archive of Russia's Academy of Sciences (St Petersburg Branch);

AV (Arkhiv Vostokovedov) – Archive of Orientologists of the Institute of Oriental Manuscripts;

Georgia (Tbilisi)

GNCM – Korneli Kekelidze Georgian National Centre of Manuscripts.

Introduction

In today's Social Sciences and Humanities few, if any, scholars would deny that there is a strong correlation between scientific and scholarly knowledge and the social context within which this knowledge is produced. In Europe, scholarly contemplation of this topic dates back to the end of the nineteenth century – a period which saw the genesis of various social theories and the first attempts at conceptualising the nation-state.[1] Naturally, while these developments shared a number of common features across all the Western states in which they occurred, there were also marked differences and characteristics that were specific to each individual country. In this regard, Russia, which had always been distinct from both Europe and Asia, is a case in point. Thus, emphasising the importance of these distinctions in his substantial work *Science in Russia and the Soviet Union*, Loren Graham wrote in 1993: 'No one will deny that Russian society and culture have in the thousand years of Russian history differed from society and culture in Western Europe, where modern science was born. Russia has followed a different economic path from that of Western Europe, and it has religious political and cultural traditions quite unlike those of its Western neighbors.'[2] Although these words were said at a time when few could even imagine that Russians would soon be cherishing an authoritarian

---

[1] See Francine Hirsch, *Empire of Nations: Ethnographic Knowledge and the Making of the Soviet Union* (Ithaca, NY: Cornell University Press, 2005): 25, 26–30, 44. See also Ilya Gerasimov, Jan Kusber and Alexander Semyonov, eds, *Empire Speaks Out: Languages of Rationalization and Self-Description in the Russian Empire* (Boston: Brill, 2009): 3–23, 229–72; Alexander Vucinich, *Science in Russian Culture 1861–1917* (Stanford, CA: Stanford University Press, 1970): xiv, 5–14, 30–4; Yuri Slezkine, *Arctic Mirrors: Russia and the Small Peoples of the North* (Ithaca, NY: Cornell University Press, 1994): 388–90; Nikolai Krementsov, *Stalinist Science* (Princeton, NJ: Princeton University Press, 1997): 13–16.

[2] Loren Graham, *Science in Russia and the Soviet Union* (Cambridge: Cambridge University Press, 1993): 1.

state model having had the chance to roll back to the totalitarian state so familiar to them, Putin's present-day Russia with its omnipresent power of intelligence apparatus continues to serve as a partial illustration of the words of this celebrated scholar of Russia.[3]

However, the issue of distinctions between possible modes of social development directly influencing all other spheres within different nation-states had already been considered by intellectuals at the end of the nineteenth and the beginning of the twentieth century. A good illustration of this can be found in the words of Bogdan Kistiakovskii (1868–1920), a renowned social philosopher and legal scholar in late Imperial Russia, of Ukrainian origin, who stated as early as 1909: 'No one, single idea of individual freedom, of the rule of law, of the constitutional state, is the same for all nations and all times, just as no social and economic organisation, capitalist or otherwise, is identical in all countries. All legal ideas acquire their own peculiar coloration and inflection in the consciousness of each separate people.'[4] However, against the backdrop of various kinds of national specificity, there were common, general tendencies and factors, namely at the social, economic and political levels, in all Western societies which were considered by many historians to be major influences on science and scholarly knowledge and their development, and they were clearly apparent in Russia throughout the pre- and post-1917 periods.[5]

---

[3] See Kimberly Marten, "The 'KGB State' and Russian Political and Foreign Policy Culture," *Journal of Slavic Military Studies* 30/2 (2017): 131–51; Aaron Bateman, "The KGB and Its Enduring Legacy," *Journal of Slavic Military Studies* 29/1 (2016): 23–47; Aaron Bateman, "The Political Influence of the Russian Security Services," *Journal of Slavic Military Studies* 27 (2014): 380–403.

[4] The English translation is given according to Laura Engelstein, "Combined Underdevelopment: Discipline and the Law in Imperial and Soviet Russia," in *Foucault and the Writing of History* ed. Jan Goldstein (Oxford: Blackwell, 1994): 225. The Russian original is 'Нет единых и одних <и> тех же идей свободы личности, правового строя, конституционного государства, одинаковых для всех народов и времен, как нет капитализма или другой хозяйственной или общественной организации, одинаковой во всех странах. Все правовые идеи в сознании каждого отдельного народа получают своеобразную окраску и свой собственный оттенок.' Bogdan Kistiakovskii, "V zashitu prava. Intelligentsiia i pravoznanie," in *Vekhi: Sbornik statei o russkoi intelligentsii* (Moscow, 1909), www.vehi.net/vehi/kistyak.html (accessed 25 September 2013).

[5] See Graham, *Science in Russia*, 1. See also Vera Tolz, *Russia's Own Orient: The Politics of Identity and Oriental Studies in the Late Imperial and Early Soviet Periods* (Oxford: Oxford University Press, 2011): 6; Hirsch, *Empire of Nations*, 7, 25–30; Daniel Beer, *Renovating Russia: The Human Sciences and*

Introduction   3

Twentieth-century European thought engaged with major international debates on the philosophy and social history of scientific and
scholarly knowledge. Since the beginning of the century, humanities
scholars studying the history and present of science, and scientists
themselves, particularly in those countries which were in the vanguard of the rapid development of science, had been paying further
attention to questions such as the social effects of this process on societies, the role that science and scholarly knowledge play in a particular
country or society and for mankind in general. In the second half of
the twentieth century, the issue of the relationship between scientific
and scholarly inquiry and their social context and, especially, the role
of state power in this relationship became subject to the scrutiny of
social philosophers and historians. They also pondered the question of
the place of scientists and scholars in the complex and entangled grid
of multi-branch, reciprocal influence between individuals and various
forms of knowledge, social institutions and state power.[6]

Among them, Michel Foucault's (1926–84) work is of particular
interest. His ideas on power relations within the power/knowledge
nexus, the notion of discourse deeply influencing the process of sci-
entific/scholarly knowledge production and the perception of various
truths by society, the role of intellectuals and the phenomenon of resistance are the most pertinent to the subject of this study.[7] Foucault's
work is characterised by a high level of inherent inconsistency and a
lack of theoretical totality and cohesion, but especially by its icono-
clastic and challenging nature. However, what goes without saying is
that 'his influence is clear in a great deal of post-structuralist, post-
modernist, feminist, post-Marxist and post-colonial theorizing. The

the Fate of Liberal Modernity, 1880–1930 (Ithaca, NY: Cornell University
Press, 2008): 3–8; Slezkine, Arctic Mirrors, 388–90; Krementsov, Stalinist
Science, 13–16; Stephen Kotkin, Magnetic Mountain: Stalinism as a Civilization
(Berkeley: University of California Press, 1995): 14, 21–3.
[6] In this context, the names of the prominent intellectuals who in this or that way
touched upon these issues such as Pierre Bourdieu (1930–2002), Gilles Deleuze
(1925–95), Jacques Lacan (1901–81), Louis Althusser (1918–90), Jean-Paul
Sartre (1905–80), Simone de Beauvoir (1908–86) and Martin Heidegger (1889–
1976) are worth mentioning.
[7] See the works by Michel Foucault, such as: The Order of Things: An
Archeology of the Human Sciences (London: Routledge, 1989),
The Archaeology of Knowledge and the Discourse on Language
(New York: Pantheon, 1972), Power/Knowledge: Selected Interviews and Other
Writings, 1972–1977 (Brighton: Harvester, 1980).

impact of his work has also been felt across a wide range of disciplinary fields, from sociology and anthropology to English studies and history'.[8]

Indeed, the Foucauldian theoretical legacy contains a much vaster spectrum of historically and philosophically important ideas; however, many of them, including those concerning the history of sexuality and Western societies' perception of madness, are mostly irrelevant to my topic and will not be touched upon here. Those of Foucault's ideas on which I am going to rely can be used separately as basic theoretical tools for studying societies such as late Imperial and early Soviet Russia – societies which, at first glance, may not fully correspond to Foucault's focus on late European juridical monarchies and liberal states but which, on the contrary, being different, prove the wider international universality of the Foucauldian ideas on power relations.

Equally, it must be noted that the applicability of these theoretical notions to the analysis of late Imperial and early Soviet Russia has been questioned, since Foucault arrived at his conclusions through the study of the late European juridical monarchies and liberal states, a grouping to which Russia arguably did not belong.[9] However, more recently, scholars have argued convincingly in favour of the Foucauldian approach to the study of Russian history, emphasising the universality of Foucault's thoughts on power relations.[10] Drawing on the insights provided by these scholars, the theoretical framework of my research will be informed by the above-mentioned Foucauldian notions.

The research presented in this book is situated within the above-mentioned two periods as they are the most crucial phases in the modern history of both Russia and Iran. In addition to their above-mentioned historiographical importance, explained by the character of large-scale developments in both countries and Russia's intense

[8] Sara Mills, *Michel Foucault* (London: Routledge, 2005): 1.
[9] For the debates on the feasibility of applying Foucauldian ideas and notions to the Russian case, see Engelstein, "Combined Underdevelopment." See also Beer, *Renovating Russia*, 3–8, 16–26, 202–8; Kotkin, *Magnetic Mountain*, 21–3. This will also be touched upon further in this chapter.
[10] In the first instance, such scholars can be named as including Nikolai Krementsov, Loren Graham, Alexander Vucinich, Vera Tolz, Michael Kemper, Daniel Beer, Peter Kneen, Nathaniel Knight, Stephen Kotkin, Jeffrey Roberg, Stephen Fortescue, Francine Hirsch, Ilya Gerasimov, Vadim Birstein and Yurii Slezkine.

activities in Persia/Iran, it is precisely during these periods that Russia's Persian policy was seriously affected by the perceptions which circulated within the prevailing field of Russia's Orientological knowledge of the time, namely Persianate studies. The scholars and experts engaged in this field constituted the core of late Imperial and early Soviet Russia's Oriental studies – the field that exerted its intellectual influence far beyond its professional precincts in Russia.[11] This, of course, is also explained by the protracted, crucial importance of the multifaceted perceptions of the East and the West and their correlation within the context of various interpretations of Russia's national identity during the two periods in question.

Though the depth of academic and practical training varied in different domains, late Imperial Russia's Orientologists,[12] as well as scholars within Persian studies, in its narrow sense, were expected to study the history, culture and languages of a broader region embracing the territories of modern Turkey, Afghanistan, Pakistan, India, the Central Asian states and further to the borders of China – the region which is now subsumed under the classification of the Persianate world.[13] The scholarly interests of late Imperial Russia's mature academics, and the practical assignments received by the military officers, diplomats and missionary clergymen lay within the same broad geography. For example, Vasilii Barthold can equally be regarded as an Iranist, a Turcologist and an expert on the interaction of Central Asia with Chinese culture.[14] The future acting Head of the Russian Legation in Persia, later Professor of Persian studies in SOAS, Vladimir Minorsky served and gathered scholarly material in Turkey and Central Asia, in addition to his substantial Persian record

---

[11] See Chapters 2 and 4 for analysis of Tolz's *Russia's Own Orient*. On the term Persianate, see Marshall Hodgson, *The Venture of Islam: The Expansion of Islam in the Middle Periods* (Chicago: Chicago University Press, 1974): 293–4.

[12] In order to avoid the unnecessary Saidian connotation and to preserve the neutral epistemological denotation of the term, I henceforth am using the noun Orientologist and the adjective Orientological throughout the manuscript, thus imitating Tolz and Schimmelpenninck van der Oye. Whenever the term is used with the Saidian connotation or in the context of the debates related to Said's concept, the words Orientalism and Orientalist are used, except for direct quotations.

[13] See RGVIA, f. 400, op. 1 'The Asiatic Section of the General Staff', d. 3522 (1907), l. 38–41 (Colonel Iagello's report on teaching Oriental languages); l. 50–2 (Head of the General Staff's instructions on Orientological training).

[14] See Appendix (Barthold).

of service and scholarly activities.[15] The future Lieutenant-General of the Russian Imperial Army, later founder of the Military Academy of the RKKA, Andrei Snesarev also spoke Hindi and Chinese and studied these regions, in addition to Iran and Afghanistan.[16] Such an approach was underpinned by the Russian scholars' thesis regarding the role of Iranian culture as a binding agent for a region spreading 'far beyond the linguistic Iran – from Constantinople to Calcutta and the towns of Chinese Turkestan'.[17] Moreover, this approach was also demanded by the political situation in the region, which was profoundly influenced by the underlying unity of historical and cultural commonalities of the peoples inhabiting those areas. Therefore, all the individuals studied in this research can also be subsumed under a broader definition of Persian studies, namely Persianate studies.

This research also proves that Russia's Persianate studies, as well as Persian studies therein – a field that became more narrowly defined as the study of Iran and Afghanistan along with the further development and specialisation of Oriental studies in Russia – consisted of four main domains for the production of scholarly knowledge during the late Imperial period, namely academic scholarship, the military, the diplomatic service and the Russian Orthodox Church's missionary institutions, whereas the early Soviet period can be characterised by the presence of three main domains capable of contributing to Orientological knowledge, namely academic scholarship, and the military and diplomatic domains. The analysis of the activities undertaken within the above-mentioned Orientological domains during the two periods which is carried out in this research at institutional and individual levels clearly reveals the interplay of diverse multi-vector power/knowledge relations between the equipotent players, namely institutions, individuals, state, discourses and knowledge. This research, hence, also questions the Saidian Orientalist concept of two-vector relations between state power and scholarly knowledge, as well as any kind of argument on the inapplicability of the Foucauldian concept to the Russian case.

---

[15] See Appendix (Minorsky).

[16] See Appendix (Snesarev); RGVIA, f. 409, op. 2, p/s 338–604 (Snesarev's Record of Service), l. 3 (2 June 1899).

[17] Vasilii Bartol'd, "Iran: Istoricheskii obzor," in *Sobranie sochinenii*, vol. 7 (Moscow: Nauka, 1977): 232. On the place and influence of Iranian culture on neighbouring regions, see ibid., 237.

In addition, regarding the activities of the institutions and individuals involved in Persian studies during the two periods, this book presents ample historiographical information on the technicalities of Russia's dealings with Persia/Iran and illuminates some developments in the modern history of Russo-Iranian interaction from an entirely new angle. In doing so, and given the manifold interactions between Russia and Iran during the two periods in question, the undertaken research necessitated applying to a range of archives and, as a result, draws on documents from the eleven main political, socio-historical, academic and military archives of Russia and Georgia,[18] hence putting into scholarly circulation recently declassified and unpublished documents on Russo-Iranian relations. The book also engages with the most recent and relevant Russian-language literature, still unused in English-language scholarship. In Western scholarship, there are few works on the Russo-Iranian nexus[19] and no book-length works whatsoever with specific focus on Russia's Persian studies, or Iranology, and its involvement in Russia's foreign policy towards Persia/Iran. Therefore, the study also aims at filling this lacuna by means of shedding new light on Russian Orientology through the prism of Foucauldian power/knowledge relations.

Statement of Method

By means of the analysis of institutional and individual activities within the domains in question, the research aims to trace the manifestations of the mutual influences of the main above-mentioned components of power/knowledge relations. This is done by drawing on Foucault's

---

[18] During the two periods, Tiflis played a strategic role in both political and military terms in the context of Russia's Persian policy. Georgian archives contain a significant number of valuable documents on the issue, including the safekeeping of Konstantin Smirnov's collection at GNCM.

[19] In this respect, the most recent significant work that can be named is Stephanie Cronin, ed., *Iranian–Russian Encounters: Empires and Revolutions since 1800* (London: Routledge, 2013), which contains insightful articles on the history of Russo-Iranian relations in multiple dimensions, namely from the political, military and economic to the two countries' mutual cultural perceptions of each other. Another is Elena Andreeva, *Russia and Iran in the Great Game: Travelogues and Orientalism* (New York: Routledge, 2007), which presents analysis of the travelogues, authored by all sorts of Russians who travelled to Persia during the nineteenth century, from the angle of Said's Orientalism.

theoretical postulations regarding notions such as society, truth, knowledge, the intellectual, discourse and others which are rather general in their essence. In order to receive more detailed answers on the technicalities of the interactions of the Foucauldian agents of power and among them, particularly, of intellectuals with state power, it is necessary to additionally employ the following more specific approach.

It is difficult to evaluate, let alone measure, the influence of intellectuals on actions of state power, in general, and on foreign policy, in particular. There is an abundance of works concerned with state control over scholarship and, especially, with the influence of the Communist Party of the Soviet Union on scholarly knowledge and intellectuals.[20] Though it is hardly possible to overestimate this influence, more recently some researchers, such as Robert Dahl, Dean Schooler, William Gamson and Jeffrey Roberg, have argued that most of the older scholarship tended to view this influence as being unidirectional, whereas according to them it should be viewed as, at least, bi-directional or indeed multi-directional, involving not only the relationship between scientific/scholarly knowledge and state power but also between intellectuals themselves, knowledge, social institutions and the society in which all of them operate.[21] Examining and questioning two earlier attempts that had been made at identifying and measuring this influence,[22] Jeffrey Roberg proposed his own approach.[23] He advocates a synthesis of these earlier approaches, concluding:

> influence can be gauged by distinguishing among presence, attempt, and outcome. By dividing influence in this manner, we must seek to answer three questions: First, does the potential influencer have access to the

[20] In this sense, the following work, for instance, could be pointed out as the most representative: Stephen F. Cohen, *Rethinking the Soviet Experience: Politics and History since 1917* (New York: Oxford University Press, 1985).

[21] Jeffrey L. Roberg, *Soviet Science under Control: The Struggle for Influence* (London: Macmillan, 1998): ix, 1–17. See also Krementsov, *Stalinist Science*, 3–4; Kotkin, *Magnetic Mountain*, 2–9, 14, 21–3; Slezkine, *Arctic Mirrors*, 388–95, 221–64.

[22] As Roberg classifies them, the first is *outcome-dependent* and is associated with Robert Dahl's work, while the second is *process-oriented* and was initially offered by Dean Schooler.

[23] See Roberg, *Soviet Science*, 5–9.

decision-making arena, that is, can he/she be present to put forward policy options? Second, if the influencer gained access, what did he/she do while in the decision-making arena? And third, what was the actual outcome, that is, did the actor achieve the outcome that he/she wanted, or at least modify the outcome?[24]

Thus, according to Roberg, the response to all these questions will give a complex vision of how this influence has emerged. At this stage, the analysis should be completed by exploring the personal characteristics required by an actor in acquiring this influence.[25]

While I intend to partly draw on this approach too, it must be pointed out that it pays attention mainly to the practical or even physical access of the actors to the decision-making arena. It underestimates the intentional and unintentional, indirect influence of intellectuals and their communities whose scholarly and professional activities influenced decision-makers and those very actors, through both generating the relative discourses (in the case of academic scholars) and through operating at a level that affected the very execution of policies (in the case of experts). Therefore, in order to make up for that, the above-mentioned approach will be enriched by studying various manifestations of the influence being exerted by scholars and state experts in the field of the foreign policy of late Imperial and early Soviet Russia towards Iran. This, of course, should be done cautiously since it is important to recognise that these kinds of influence have often tended to be exaggerated by other intellectuals.

In so doing, the research will draw on the personal archival files of scholars and experts, as well as on their public (published) or official written record, i.e. books, articles, reports, memos, notes, etc. This will be supplemented by analysis of the institutional activities of the Orientological structures in which they were involved. The necessary data will be obtained from the relevant Russian- and English-language secondary sources but mostly from archival documents and the writings authored by the individuals in question. In addition, the study of inner Russian discourses which existed at the time and influenced contemporary activities within Persian studies will help identify whether this or that action was undertaken by an individual because of his

---

[24] Ibid., 6–7.
[25] Ibid., 7.

susceptibility to a particular discourse or whether he was motivated mainly by personal/institutional interests, or by a combination of these influences. The analysis of the archival sources containing private diaries and correspondence, combined with the available scholarship on the issue, will secure the retrieval of the necessary answers.

At the same time, in order to provide an answer to my overarching question, namely to gauge the influence of academic Orientologists, as well as of scholarly trained experts, being practitioners working for political or military organs of the state, in the field of the Russian state's foreign policy towards Iran, my book will address the following eight sub-questions.

1   What were the institutional structures for the involvement (to differing degrees) of academically trained and scholarly active Iran experts, both ("pure") academics and experts directly employed by state organs (ministries, military, party apparatus, commercial entities), in the process of policy formulation, decision-making and conducting Russia's/the USSR's policy towards Iran?

The answer to the above-mentioned question will mainly be given in Chapters 2 and 3, which will deal with the history of the institutional organisation of Russian/Soviet Oriental studies, in particular Persian studies, or, as it was later called, Iranology. Besides an examination of the scholarly activities in this field, there will be a brief analysis of the historical context of Russo/Soviet–Iranian relations. The answer will also be supplemented by information retrieved from the biographies of the scholars and experts under study.

2   What was the nature of this involvement, e.g. written and/or verbal advice and consultancy (scholarly publications, memoranda, membership in committees, hearings, formal consultations, informal involvement through personal acquaintance with decision-makers, etc.), teaching/training/instructing of personnel, (secret) missions and expeditions, official postings as working on Iran for various state entities inside/outside Russia?

According to Roberg, asking these questions provides valuable data for defining the influence of scholars and experts on state policy and is very important for identifying the internal mechanisms of their interaction during both general periods under study.[26] The archival

26 Ibid., 15.

record will enable me to analyse the technicalities of the cooperation imposed by the state on these scholars and experts or chosen by them consciously or unwittingly. From there I will be able to deduce the patterns that were characteristic of each particular state power of the time (late Imperial Russia, the early Soviet state). This question will be dealt with mainly in Chapters 4 and 5.

3   In the case of policy advice on specific issues in Russo/Soviet–Iranian relations, what exactly was suggested by the experts and based on what grounds? What kind of personal impact, expressed in what forms (endorsement or criticism of past/current government policies, other forms), was there?

The personal archival files and the written works by the scholars and experts being studied will be examined in order to find the answer to this question. It is in this context that I will explore their participation in creating and developing professional discourses, as well as their personal views and the correspondence of these views with actual actions.

4   Is there congruence between the expert advice provided and the policies that were actually pursued in the end?
5   Is it possible to trace instances of direct impact of individual scholars and experts on the course of shaping and/or execution of policies? If so, how significant was it?

For its part, the received answer will logically lead us to the following question, namely:

6   How effectively did the state bring into play scholarly and expert knowledge, as a whole, and the expertise of individuals, in particular?
7   What motivated scholars and experts in their cooperation with the state? What was the character of their relationship with the state (smooth or conflict-ridden, etc.)?

The last five questions will be tackled throughout the whole book.

8   In relation to the above seven questions, what are the common features and specific differences of the three periods under consideration (1863–1917, 1917–21 and 1921–41)?

The answer to this question will comprise the statement of the distinctions and the common features of the two general periods under study, late Imperial and early Soviet Russia – in other words, from the second half of the nineteenth century to 1941. This will be addressed in General Conclusions.

The above-mentioned time frame is mainly based upon events in the two countries' political history and Russia's activity in Iran. The first period comprises the establishment of the Asiatic Section of the General Staff in Russia and the Persian Cossack Brigade in Persia, the peak events of the Great Game and the Anglo-Russian Convention of 1907, Russia's participation in cracking down on the Persian Constitutional movement, and Russia's assistance to the Persian central government to quell tribal separatist activities, fighting the German and Turkish influence and securing the Persian front during World War I. Then, in the course of and after the 1917 developments in Russia, comes a period of considerable unilateral changes in Russia's policy towards Persia, including "exporting revolution" and urging Persia to fully recognise the new Soviet state. The years after the conclusion of the 1921 Soviet–Iranian treaty can be characterised as a time of relatively mutually beneficial cooperation of the two states when Soviet Russia was trying to conduct its interests on the basis of the outward respect of Iran's territorial integrity and using mainly conventional diplomatic methods – a period that lasted until 1941, the year of the second Soviet military invasion of Iran. In further substantiation of the time frame, it should be noted that by the late 1930s all the individuals who were the main representatives of Persian studies within their domains, and are thus studied in this research, had died or, rather, predominantly had been executed by the state.

The book studies the involvement of scholars who were mostly engaged in professional academic activities on the one hand (including such prominent figures as Vasilii Barthold, Valentin Zhukovskii and Vladimir Gurko-Kriazhin), as well as that of experts who had received the relevant Orientological training but pursued careers in the state (or party) bureaucracy or in the military/intelligence on the other hand (including such individuals as Vladimir Kosagovskii, Konstantin Smirnov, Vladimir Minorsky, Andrei Snesarev, Nikolai Bravin, Pavel Vvedenskii, Vladimir Osetrov (pseudonym Irandust), Sergei Pastukhov (pseudonym S. Iranskii) and Konstantin Chaikin). Documents on the activities of the above-mentioned individuals and of the institutions with which they had been involved were consulted from the eleven main Russian and Georgian archives.

This book consists of seven main parts, namely the Introduction, five chapters and Conclusions. The current section highlights the context in which the subject of the research is problematised, and the research rationale. It also presents the outline of the book and its research methodology. It does not include a conventional literature review since the secondary sources relevant to a particular chapter are analysed in that chapter. Some short sections of this book, in one way or another, were used by the author for articles published in peer-reviewed journals and edited volumes. Chapter 1 contains the theoretical framework and substantiates the employment of this framework for the study of the power/knowledge nexus in the Russian case and for Oriental studies therein. It draws on English-, Russian- and French-language scholarship on the issue. Chapter 2 explains why this monograph mainly deals with Persian studies, or Iranology, and contains analysis of its organisational set-up during the late Imperial period in the context of contemporary discourses. It also touches upon the activities of a broader number of the representatives of late Imperial Russia's Oriental studies than those earmarked for detailed case study in Chapters 4 and 5. Work similar to Chapter 2 is conducted in Chapter 3, but for the early Soviet period. It also analyses the continuities and shifts which took place over the 1917 watershed. Chapters 4 and 5 contain case studies of the individuals most representative of their Orientological domains during the late Imperial and early Soviet periods, respectively. Chapters 2, 3 and, particularly, 4 and 5, predominantly draw on archival sources, in addition to the relevant literature.

1 *Foucauldian Notions and Their Applicability to the Russian Case*

Introduction

As was mentioned before, the theoretical framework of the manuscript draws on Foucault's conceptualisation of the interplay of power relations, where individuals (in this case – the intellectual), institutions and discourses situated within the power/knowledge nexus are the main players. Therefore, from the outset, it is necessary to define which notions are expected to be implemented as theoretical tools for this study and how they can be situated in their application to the Russian context which is performed in this chapter. So the first part of the chapter will be dedicated to the introduction of the Foucauldian concept of scholarly knowledge and its correlation with society. Then, I will briefly introduce the debate on the applicability of Foucault's ideas and notions to the case of late Imperial and early Soviet Russia. Further on, while surveying the development of scientific and scholarly knowledge during these two historical periods, in general, and in Russia's Oriental studies, in particular, I will trace the presence of Foucauldian power relations in the context of Russian society at the time. Thus, I will demonstrate the validity of Foucault's relevant concepts for the student of Russian history. After that, I will explore the following notions in application to my research in more detail: the power/knowledge nexus, discourse, resistance and the role of the intellectual. At the beginning of each section there will be a brief general introduction of the particular Foucauldian notion, which will then be linked to the Russian historical context.

Foucauldian Concepts and Russia

Foucault's concepts of power, knowledge and discourse caused heated debates in the 1960s and 1970s and had a considerable impact on the further development of critical thinking at the end of the twentieth and the beginning of the twenty-first century. Among Foucault's main concepts, his insistence on the absence of an absolute and pure truth is most noteworthy. Taking an approach to the study of the production of knowledge that he conceives of as archaeology,[1] he argued that the process of striving for ultimate truths through conventional scholarly activities throughout the course of human history had always been subject to the influence of a vast range of factors, which led him to conclude that all truths are conceived or, to be more precise, constructed rather than being absolute and ultimate. Therefore, according to Foucault, there are no objective, constant and independent truths within the system of human knowledge, especially in the human and social sciences.[2]

But, what is Foucault's notion of truth? One answer to this question can be found in an interview that Foucault gave in 1976 and which was later labelled "Truth and Power":[3]

Truth is to be understood as a system of ordered procedures for the production, regulation, distribution, circulation, and operation of statements. Truth is linked in a circular relation with systems of power that produce and sustain it, and to effects of power which it induces and which extend it – a 'regime' of truth. This regime is not merely ideological or superstructural; it was a condition of the formation and development of capitalism. *And it's this same regime which, subject to certain modifications, operates in the socialist countries.*[4]

However, some researchers working on Foucault, such as Laura Engelstein, adhere to the opinion that when Imperial Russia reached the epoch in which some of the Foucauldian modern mechanisms of social control and social self-discipline that had originated from Western practices had begun to develop in Russia, the old regime and Russian

---

[1] In brief, it can be defined as analysing scientific and scholarly notions and the process of their production in the social context of a particular historical period within a certain society.

[2] See Foucault, *Order of Things*; Foucault, *Archaeology of Knowledge and the Discourse on Language*; and Foucault, *Power/Knowledge*.

[3] The interview was conducted in June 1976. Michel Foucault, "Truth and Power," in *Microfisica del potere: Interventi politici*, eds, Alessandro Fontana and Pasquale Pasquino, trans. C. Lazzeri (Turin: Einaudi, 1977): 3–28.

[4] Michel Foucault, *Power*, ed. James D. Faubion (New York: New Press, 2000): 132 (emphasis added).

society still remained largely unchanged. She contrasts the Russian situation with that of other European countries which, she maintains, had already passed the two formations of the juridical monarchy and the *Polizeistaat*, having reached the status of the modern Foucauldian disciplinary regime.[5] Developing this idea, Engelstein argues, in her article "Combined Underdevelopment: Discipline and the Law in Imperial and Soviet Russia", 'Where monarchies once imposed order by brute force, through the coercive instruments of the state, Foucault observed, liberal capitalist societies exercise control through the gathering and production of information, the surveillance associated with these scientific projects, the imposition of categories derived from such investigation, and by inculcating mechanisms of self-censorship and self-restraint that compel people to police themselves.'[6]

Moreover, somewhat overstating the Russian case's "otherness", Engelstein comes to conclusions which might also partially reflect a residual Cold War mentality. She emphasises that Foucault stresses the underlying difference between the so-called Old Regimes, where the state is the sole source of power, and liberal societies in which power regulates activities, based on scientific/scholarly knowledge, and is realised by means of disciplinary practices permeating society.[7] She, therefore, concludes that in the Russian case, 'although Western culture penetrated the empire's official and civic elites, and the model of Western institutions to a large extent shaped the contours of state and social organization, the regime of "power/knowledge" never came into its own in the Russian context.'[8]

It appears that Engelstein's reasoning takes into consideration only the general organisational modes of modern Western society, as discussed by Foucault, and operates with very narrow definitions of structures when exploring the applicability of the power/knowledge nexus to late Imperial and early Soviet societies. Her focus is on the outward appearance and the concrete shape of structures. However, I would argue that what are really at stake here are not structures but principles. Indeed, although in terms of social organisation Russia was considerably different from its Western contemporaries, the principles

---

[5] See Engelstein, "Combined Underdevelopment," 225.
[6] Ibid., 221.
[7] Ibid., 224.
[8] Ibid., 225.

according to which power relations operated and permeated the whole society were quite similar.[9]

Of course, it is rather difficult to deny the specificity of these relations in Russian society and, consequentially, in Russian science and scholarship, in comparison with Western societies. As Graham states: 'Imported initially from Western Europe, it [science] took root and developed in distinct ways [...] The variations that arose were not only organizational and economic, but cognitive. The intellectual pathways of many areas of Russian and Soviet science are dissimilar from those in Western Europe and America.'[10] However, taking into consideration the place of modern Russian culture as part of a pan-European endeavour, the basic principles are common. Thus, no scientist or scholar nowadays would argue with the fact that a utilitarian quality has become inherent to modern knowledge. Equally, it would be absolutely wrong to expect scientific/scholarly knowledge to only deal with the problems of the day.[11] Although, in addition to this, a historian of Russian science, Alexander Vucinich, asserts that 'The inner logic of social development and the inner logic of scientific development are different',[12] he immediately gives a quotation from a world-famous scientist: 'Science is more than a unique mode of inquiry. It is also, to use an expression of Niels Bohr, an endeavor to reduce knowledge to order – to subsume an increasing flow of knowledge under a decreasing number of general laws.'[13]

However, it goes without saying that "reducing" or "ordering" are the same as "editing" or "policing", which implies a great deal of regulating mechanisms, which tend to be personified by individuals, various institutions and/or, finally, by society itself, all of which are guided by certain combinations of specific rules and regulations. In this sense, Foucault aptly shows us that the whole system of human thought and the totality of its achievements are 'knowledge invested in the complex system of institutions'.[14] Thus, knowledge is embodied not only in theories or experiments, which are also subject to influence,

[9] See Beer, *Renovating Russia*, 205–9. See also Kotkin, *Magnetic Mountain*, 21–3.
[10] Graham, *Science in Russia*, 1.
[11] See Vucinich, *Russian Culture*, xii.
[12] Ibid.
[13] Ibid.
[14] Chris Horrocks and Zoran Jevtic, *Introducing Foucault* (New York: Totem Books, 1998): 37.

but in a whole body of practices and institutions.[15] Indeed, the various factors comprising this influence may consist of both those on the highest level of structures organising human societies (for instance, state power, social and cultural structures, academic and other communities) and those of less complexity (relations between individuals, their personal viewpoints, endeavours and passions). All these shape or indeed construct knowledge, which therefore cannot be considered truly impartial, constant and objective.

Imperial Russia

Dwelling on this topic, Vucinich ultimately accepts the validity of the above-mentioned ideas:

Yet a given society can influence the development of science in many ways. A society's needs may emphasize some sciences at the expense of others,[16] or stimulate the rise of new sciences. A society's dominant philosophic traditions may interact with scientific theory in different ways, and different kinds of relations may be worked out between science and various non-scientific modes of inquiry. The society of Imperial Russia influenced Russian scientists in these ways and many more.[17]

Thus Vucinich cannot but explain the early success of Russian scientific and scholarly knowledge at the end of the nineteenth century by historical, geographical and economic features. He stresses, for instance, that Russia's place in the vanguard of the world's soil sciences relates to the vital importance of the issue to Russians, while the early blooming of Russian geography, ethnography and comparative linguistics is explained by Russia's vast areas and profuse ethnic variety, etc.[18]

It is clear that the scientific activities in these fields would have been impossible without "state order", another component of Foucault's power grid. The above-mentioned breakthroughs took place precisely

---

[15] Ibid., 85.
[16] The most eloquent case in this context is the attitude of early Soviet state power to science. For example, see Tolz, *Russian Academicians*, 183–4. Also, see Appendix (Beneshevich).
[17] Vucinich, *Russian Culture*, xiii–xiv.
[18] Ibid., xiv.

in those areas that were crucial for state viability and development of the then Russian Empire. For instance, the activities concerning geographic, ethnographic and linguistic research date back to the beginning of the eighteenth century, the time of Peter the Great, when Russia had to compete with other countries for the last lands that remained unclaimed and non-appropriated, especially the vast areas lying to the east and south of the Imperial centre. Of course, initially such activities were directed not by "pure" scientific necessity but by strategic, military, political and economic (trade expansion) purposes,[19] though these aims were attained with the help of particular scientific individuals and institutions.

Indeed, for this period of Russian history, the interplay between power and knowledge in a Foucauldian sense with its entanglement of social, state and individual factors[20] is clearly discernible. In this same vein, Graham concludes that

the fact that Russia's early brilliant achievements in scientific explorations were prompted by a mixture of political and scientific motivations simply illustrates what already should be clear, that science never proceeds in a political and economic vacuum. The introduction of science to Russia in the early eighteenth century was a part of Westernization, and Russia adopted the motives as well as the science of its powerful neighbours.[21]

However, in this context it is important to bear in mind Vucinich's qualifier that 'the Russian government – and the guardians of the official ideology – accepted science as a part of Russian civilization but had grave doubts about its worth as a part of Russian culture.'[22] By the 1880s, the challenging spirit of science, implying unconstrained inquiry and a critical attitude towards literally everything, including even the most cherished values of the Russian society – traditional orthodox consciousness, justifying the institutions of autocracy – brought the so-called "freethinking" (*vol'nodumstvo*) and, ultimately,

---

[19] See Graham, *Science in Russia*, 26.
[20] See Pasquale Pasquino, "Michel Foucault (1926–84): The Will to Knowledge," in *Foucault's New Domains*, ed. Mike Gane and Terry Johnson (London: Routledge, 1993): 46–7.
[21] Graham, *Science in Russia*, 27.
[22] Vucinich, *Russian Culture*, 184.

political revolt to Russian universities. Naturally, the regime identified
them first as centres of proliferation of political unreliability.[23]

In the Imperial Russia of the second half of the nineteenth century and the beginning of the twentieth, the overwhelming majority
of intellectuals considered science as a natural ally in securing political changes and in the struggle against Russia's authoritarian regime
and the backward religious orthodoxy that was hampering progress.[24]
Thus it was quite natural that many immediately found themselves in
trouble with the state. Therefore, in comparison to the West, the interaction between science and the state in Russia has been, on the whole,
conflict-ridden throughout its whole history and even dramatically so
during certain periods (such as the Soviet one).

It follows that 'the troubled relationship between knowledge and
power did not begin in the Soviet period, but can easily be found in
tsarist history. The root of the problem was the inherent contradiction that arises when a state tries both to modernize and to remain
authoritarian.'[25] Among the most representative examples are the
cases of Lobachevskii and Mendeleev[26] – the former protested against
the administration of the university promoting religious orthodoxy and the latter was opposed to absolutist monarchy and, eventually, was fired from the university and banned from teaching for
supporting students' protests. However, later both of them were given
a much higher position and more serious responsibilities within the
government structures.[27]

Soviet Russia

It is, however, also true, as Graham states, that 'Despite the fact that
the tsarist regime was oppressive, it still allowed considerable working
room for independent-minded people. There is no known case under
tsarist rule of the execution of a scientist or engineer merely because
of his or her political views.'[28] Indeed, this changing pattern in the
Russian state's attitude towards its scientists and scholars has been a

[23] Ibid., 184.
[24] See Graham, *Science in Russia*, 58.
[25] Ibid., 157.
[26] See Appendix (Lobachevskii, Mendeleev).
[27] See Graham, *Science in Russia*, 157.
[28] Ibid., 158.

continuous feature of the history of Russian science. The ambiguity of encouragement and acknowledgement that is followed by rejection and persecution and then again encouragement and acknowledgement has haunted not only scientists but also various kinds of intellectuals and experts in tsarist Russia, the Soviet Union and even present-day Russia.[29] What varied over time was the intensity of the persecution. Here it is necessary to mention one of those historical moments when Foucault's discontinuity took place, that is the years after 1917, when state policy towards science and its representatives changed considerably, not only in terms of Foucault's *epistème* and discourse, but transforming in a way that was ultimately problematic, and even tragic.[30]

In other societies, the relationship between support for scientific activities and the scientific position of intellectuals was, most of the time, relatively stable even in times of economic and political crisis, whereas in late Imperial Russia individuals engaged in scientific activities experienced dismissal from their positions and social and political ostracism, and, in early Soviet Russia, in addition to all that, they might be imprisoned, exiled or executed.[31] It was also highly likely that their next of kin would be deprived of basic social and political rights. In Soviet Russia 'a scientist could be an adviser to the highest state bodies one day and an "enemy of the people" the next, and vice versa. Scientists conducted research in the well-equipped institutes of "Science Cities" with the levels of comfort unattainable for ordinary Soviet people, and in gloomy starveling *sharashki* prison camps.'[32]

---

[29] See Krementsov, *Stalinist Science*, 3–9. See also Graham, *Science in Russia*, 158.

[30] On epistèmatic changes and discourses, see later in the chapter.

[31] See Graham, *Science in Russia*, 156. See also Vadim J. Birstein, *The Perversion of Knowledge: The True Story of Soviet Science* (Cambridge, MA: Westview Press, 2001), 32, 35, 39.

[32] Krementsov, *Stalinist Science*, 3. *Sharashka* was an informal name for secret research and development laboratories in the Soviet Gulag labour camp system. Etymologically, the word *sharashka* is derived from a Russian slang expression *sharashkina kontora* ("Sharashka's office", possibly from the radical meaning "to beat about"), an ironic, derogatory term to denote a poorly organised, impromptu or bluffing organisation. The scientists and engineers at a *sharashka* were prisoners picked from various camps and prisons and assigned to work on scientific and technological problems for the state. Living conditions were usually much better than in an average taiga camp, especially bearing in mind the absence of hard labour. The results

Simultaneously with the 1917 Bolshevik coup d'etat and the events of the Civil War, there took place a shift in perceptions of not only the role of science in society but of the role of a human being himself and the value of his life. Naturally, all that had an enormous impact on scientific and scholarly knowledge in "new" Russia, as Engelstein points out in her article "Combined Underdevelopment":

In contrast to the imperfect world of capitalist liberalism, which both extends and violates the promise of rights, the Soviet regime long offered discipline without rights. This was not merely the old Polizeistaat under new ideological auspices [...] but its refurbishment with new tactics, by which society was enlisted to do its own policing but in which the discursive authority of the professional disciplines, speaking in the name of 'science', functioned only as a dependency of the state.[33]

What sort of a "dependence" that was, what content and characteristics it had, and whether there was a reciprocal dependence and of what kind – all these issues comprise a part of the questions this research aims to answer. For, 'exploring the social context of scientific activity, a historian is able to identify the peculiar combinations of social factors which effect it and it is the extent and nature of these effects that the specific characteristics of science of the given period depend on'.[34] Hence, it is important to study the dynamics of science development not only in terms of its continuity and the inner logic of scientific/scholarly disciplines but also in terms of the place they occupy in a particular society within a particular period of history. And the relationships between science and state, science and scientists as a part of power are among the main components of these combinations, according to Foucault.[35]

of the research in *sharashkas* were usually published under the names of prominent Soviet scientists without credit given to the real authors, whose names frequently have been forgotten (see Krementsov, *Stalinist Science*, 3; see also Eduard Galein, "Reabilitatsiia stalinisma kak sredstvo utverzhdeniia putinskoi diktatury," https://petrimazepa.com/stalinrehab.html, accessed 20 November 2017).

[33] Engelstein, "Combined Underdevelopment," 236.
[34] Vladimir Kelle, "Introduction," in *Nauka i tekhnika v pervye desiatiletiia sovetskoi vlasti: sotsiokul'turnoe izmerenie, 1917–1940*, ed. Elena Muzrukova and Liudmila Chesnova (Moscow: Academia, 2007): 7.
[35] See Foucault, *Power*, 130–40.

Foucauldian Power/Knowledge

In order to better analyse these relationships, the relevant Foucauldian conceptual notions will be used in this research. In his work *Power/Knowledge*, Foucault describes knowledge as being a conjunction of power relations and information-seeking, which he terms 'power/knowledge'. He states, in an essay entitled "Prison Talk", that 'it is not possible for power to be exercised without knowledge, it is impossible for knowledge not to engender power'.[36] Foucault emphasises that knowledge is not neutral but rather an integral part of struggles over power. According to him, in producing knowledge, one is always making a claim for power. Therefore, Foucault coins the compound 'power/knowledge', allowing him to emphasise the way that these two elements are intertwined with one another.[37]

Furthermore, for Foucault, power as such is also an entanglement of relations and interconnections, something much more abstract than a certain specifically defined tool, which 'is not conceived of as something to be possessed, the attribute of a subject, but as a relation, the site of a constant tension which sometimes assumes the form of a collision'.[38] Foucault's main concepts are mostly related to the interplay between social structures, various social and political institutions, and individuals. 'It is in the relationship between the individual and the institution that we find power operating most clearly.'[39] Thus, Foucault emphasises the analysis of the effects of various institutions on separate individuals or groups of people. However, this influence is not unidirectional. In the process of a complex entangled interaction, people play their own role in accepting and developing or transforming and rejecting those effects. And that also generates new processes, leading to changes and transformations in cognitive domains.

However, nowhere in Foucault's writings is there a clear and straightforward definition of his notion of power. Four years after his death one of his contemporaries, Gilles Deleuze, tried to sum up Foucault's main ideas and presented the following succinct definition of power in his book *Foucault*: 'Power has no essence; it is simply operational.

---

[36] Michel Foucault, "Prison Talk," in *Power/Knowledge*, ed. Colin Gordon (Brighton: Harvester, 1980): 52.
[37] Mills, *Michel Foucault*, 69.
[38] Pasquino, "Michel Foucault," 42.
[39] Mills, *Michel Foucault*, 33.

It is not an attribute but a relation: the power-relation is a set of possible relations between forces, which passes through the dominated forces no less than through dominating, as both these forces constitute unique elements.'[40] This is elaborated in Foucault's own words from his interview "Truth and Power":

What makes power hold good, what makes it accepted, is simply the fact that it doesn't only weigh on us as a force that says no; it also traverses and produces things, it induces pleasure, forms knowledge, produces discourse. It needs to be considered as a productive network that runs through the whole social body, much more than as a negative instance whose function is repression.[41]

At this point it becomes necessary to consider Foucault's view of power as being productive. Foucault moves away from simplistic perceptions of power in which power is conceived of in only two dimensions: people and state institutions, the oppressed and the dominating, the constrained and the constrainers. Thus, in contrast, according to his notion, power is a substance which permeates all social environments with its multi-branched and multi-directional interconnections and creates new forms of behaviour, relationships and, finally, new forms of itself, which is seen equally well not only in Western societies but in the Soviet case, too.[42]

Foucault is strongly opposed to the opinion that conceptualises power as the ability of certain powerful agents to impose their will on individuals or groups of people in terms of obeying what they do not want to. He challenges the perception of power as something which is exercised by those in power towards those who are weaker and who try to avoid it. According to him, power is something that cannot be possessed. It is more like a process and a system of relations spread throughout the society, rather than simply the application of a power vector towards the oppressed on behalf of the oppressors. Another important point is the role of individuals, which is conceived of as active and creative, not as passive and oppressed. Individuals are not

---

[40] Gilles Deleuze, *Foucault*, trans. Sean Hand (Minneapolis: University of Minnesota Press, 1988): 27.
[41] Foucault, *Power*, 120.
[42] See Kotkin, *Magnetic Mountain*, 22.

only the places of power application but the sources of resistance; they are not only, and even not so much, the recipients of power, but rather its conductors and transformers within the system of their relations with others and with institutions. Power needs to be seen as something that is constantly performed, rather than achieved.[43]

In addition, Foucault's perception of the relation between power and the state is much wider than commonly adopted notions of that relationship and even lies in another coordinate system. He argues:

I don't want to say that the state isn't important; what I want to say is that relations of power, and hence the analysis that must be made of them, necessarily extend beyond the limits of state [...] because the state, for all its omnipotence of its apparatuses, is far from being able to occupy the whole field of actual power relations. The state is superstructural in relation to a whole series of power networks that invest the body, sexuality, the family, kinship, knowledge, technology, and so forth.[44]

Thus, truth or knowledge, being a part of power, is being influenced and is exerting influence; hence the importance and regulating character of power relationships in every social environment. In this respect, Foucault explains:

Each society has its regime of truth, its 'general politics' of truth – that is, the types of discourse it accepts and makes function as true; the mechanisms and instances that enable one to distinguish true and false statements; the means by which each is sanctioned; the techniques and procedures accorded value in the acquisition of truth; the status of those who are charged with saying what counts as true.[45]

Indeed, in the interview "Truth and Power", Foucault outlines the following five traits, characterising Western, or democratic, societies:

Truth is centered on the form of scientific discourse and the institutions that produce it; it is subject to constant economic and political incitement (the demand for truth, as much for economic production as for political power); it is the object, under diverse forms, of immense diffusion and consumption

---

[43] See Mills, *Michel Foucault*, 34–9.
[44] Ibid., 122–3.
[45] Foucault, *Power*, 131.

(circulating through apparatuses of education and information whose extent is relatively broad in the social body, notwithstanding certain strict limitations); it is produced and transmitted under the control, dominant if not exclusive, of a few great political and economic apparatuses (university, army, writing, media); finally, it is the issue of a whole political debate and social confrontation ('ideological' struggles).[46]

I would argue that these five features also apply to the cases of Imperial and Soviet Russia. In order to demonstrate this it is necessary to analyse the institutional organisation of the power/knowledge nexus and its inner power relations within the late Imperial Russian and early Soviet contexts.

Organisational Arrangement of Science and Scholarly Knowledge in Late Imperial Russia

By the middle of the 1910s there were ten universities in Russia, including the oldest of them, Moscow University,[47] which was established in 1755 by a Russian scientist, Mikhail Lomonosov – the architect of Russian science, whom Russian society would later assign an important discursive role[48] and who, in fact, as Barthold put it as early as 1915, 'was the first among scholars to point out the necessity of the organisational establishment of Oriental studies in Russia'.[49] In addition to Moscow University, Russia had the Imperial Academy of Sciences, founded in 1725, which

continued to sponsor valuable research throughout the nineteenth and early twentieth century. If nineteenth-century Russia was often thought of in the West as a country outside of the scientific tradition, a nation where forms of Slavic mysticism and Orthodox Christianity not conducive to science were the principal intellectual trends, it is quite clear, to the contrary, that by the end of that century Russia possessed a developing and capable scientific community already rooted in an institutional base.[50]

---

[46] Ibid., 131.
[47] See Graham, *Science in Russia*, 80.
[48] See Appendix (Lomonosov).
[49] Vasilii Bartol'd, "Vostok i russkaia nauka," in *Sobranie sochinenii*, vol. 9 (Moscow: Nauka, 1977): 539.
[50] Graham, *Science in Russia*, 80.

At the same time, by the turn of the twentieth century it had become obvious that Russia was well behind the leading countries of the West and that this could not be tolerated in the context of upholding international prestige and proving the sustainability of the Russian absolutist polity against the backdrop of increasing domestic, unauthorised "freethinking attitudes". The country badly needed modernisation and the ruling establishment finally realised that, in the process of economic and military development, it could not do without the promotion of science. Gradually, science became one of the main components of Russian society and its culture, to an extent resulting in Russia occupying leading positions in some scientific and scholarly areas by the first decade of the twentieth century.[51]

However, as already mentioned, the regime increasingly perceived intellectuals as a threat and therefore became highly suspicious of university communities and other centres of scientific and scholarly activity.[52] For this reason, the government's policy towards intellectuals and the scientific institutions to which they were affiliated contained a great amount of political ambiguity. The tsarist authorities had to combine punitive measures with actions aimed at the encouragement of scientific and scholarly knowledge – wishing them to develop, but in the direction that the authorities believed to be in their interest. 'Their confidence in performing this difficult balancing act varied greatly with the political times, resulting in contradictory policies. Russia's greatest scientists [...] were affected both by periods of reform and periods of reaction. Their educations and even their research were intimately tied to the political, economic, and intellectual milieux of their times.'[53] For instance, it would be pertinent to refer to the example of Mendeleev, who was oppressed because of his political views and support of students' protests and, soon after, in the context of the 1860s–1870s' liberal political changes, was appointed an advisor to the reformist minister of the tsarist government and was in charge of supervising many state scientific programmes.[54]

Another distinctive example that lies in the field of the interaction of state power and scientific institutions is the relationships between

[51] Ibid., 3.
[52] See Vucinich, *Russian Culture*, 63.
[53] Graham, *Science in Russia*, 32.
[54] Ibid., 157.

the Russian Imperial Academy of Sciences and the tsarist regime. The
content of these relationships considerably distinguished the situation
in Russian science from that in the West. Contrary to Lomonosov's
perception of the national roles of the Academy and the universities,
which defined the task of the Academy as an institution that would
bring science into Russia from the West with a simultaneous rooting
in Russian culture and the task of universities as the cultivation of
national scientists and the further development of national scientific and scholarly knowledge,[55] the Academy still strove to preserve
its leading administrative and scientific roles in the development of
national science. On the other hand, in the political unrest of the time,
'the tsarist government distrusted the politicised university professors
more than it did the members of the Academy, and the latter institution benefited from this distrust'.[56]

Naturally, being organisationally an organic part of state power and
financially totally dependent on it, the Academy retained a much more
conservative position in comparison with the universities, which were
more subject to the direct influence of a traditionally defiant younger
generation. In response, it received more state support and capacities,
including financial ones. This status quo was also maintained by the
underdeveloped character of Russian capitalism, which could not provide sufficient funding for independent scientific activities. This factor
enhanced the dependence of science on the state, which itself could
hardly afford to fund scientific research after the war with Japan
and during World War I. All those factors influenced the relations
between scientific institutions and seriously affected the development
of Russian science itself.[57]

As far as Russian Oriental studies are concerned, it was institutionally
much younger than other Russian academic disciplines but by the turn
of the century it had gained a significant position within the national
scientific and scholarly community, particularly in such an important
Russian institution as the Imperial Academy of Sciences. Compared
to Oriental studies, only Slavonic studies was represented by a greater
number of scholars who were full members of the Academy. Another
remarkable feature that distinguished this discipline from its Western

[55] See Vucinich, *Russian Culture*, 196–7.
[56] Graham, *Science in Russia*, 81.
[57] Ibid., 81.

counterpart was that all of its scholars were partly or entirely engaged in studying Russia's so-called "own" Orient – the Caucasus, Central Asia and the Far East – the regions which were within the borders of the Russian Empire itself.[58] This situation also reflects the strong interdependency between scholarly knowledge and state priorities that existed at that time in the context of Imperial national state building.

In addition to that, the history of the inception of Oriental studies in Russia itself illustrates the close relation that the development of this discipline had with its utilisation for the purposes of the state. The organisation of teaching Oriental languages at the beginning of the nineteenth century coincided with the increasing activity of Russian foreign policy in the Orient.[59] In 1804, the chairs of Arabic and Persian were established at Moscow University as well as two others – in Kazan' and in Kharkov. The choice of languages is also characteristic.[60] From the outset, the teaching of Oriental languages and cultures at Russian universities was aimed at preparing expert cadres, who were needed for ministries of foreign affairs and military entities. Sometimes even the curriculum would become a tool in diplomatic rivalry between Russia and other countries. For instance, the teaching of Dari started in Russian universities during the Crimean War in order to send a diplomatic message to Britain regarding Russia's possible increase of interest towards the area, which was the last frontier between Russia and the most valued British colonial possessions.[61]

In this respect, in his work "The Imperial Roots of Soviet Orientology", Schimmelpenninck van der Oye provides a very telling testimonial, quoting the rector of St Petersburg University, who wrote to the Russian Minister of Education in 1888: 'Our civilizing mission in the East and the political confirmation of our power and influence in all corners of Asia will not succeed unless we carefully prepare for it, unless along with military measures we train men who

---

[58] Vera Tolz, "Russia: Empire or a Nation-State-in-the-Making?" in *What Is a Nation? Europe 1789–1914*, ed. Timothy Baycroft and Mark Hewitson (Oxford: Oxford University Press, 2006): 302.

[59] The most important events of this period are the 1804–13 Russo-Persian war and the 1806–12 war between Russia and the Ottoman Empire, which included vast Arabic-speaking areas.

[60] David Schimmelpenninck van der Oye, "The Imperial Roots of Soviet Orientology," in *The Heritage of Soviet Oriental Studies*, ed. Michael Kemper and Stephan Conermann (Abingdon: Routledge, 2011): 31–2.

[61] Ibid., 37.

know these regions, their way of life, beliefs and languages.'[62] On the other hand, the reciprocal influence exercised by scholars by creating certain "discursive priorities" was also at play. In this regard it is worth mentioning Aleksandr II's order to keep the Oriental Languages Faculty open when, during the students' unrest of 1861, he urged that the rest of the St Petersburg University be shut down.[63] All the above-mentioned concrete examples illustrate both the state's aspirations in the field of science and its attitude towards scholarly knowledge, and the interplay of relations between scholars and academic institutions, amongst themselves and in their relations with the state.

A very pertinent characterisation of the ambiguous nature of this web of interdependent relations can be found in Vucinich's work *Science in Russian Culture 1861–1917*: 'On the one hand, the government saw science as indispensable to the modernization of Russia's economy, armed forces, and public services; on the other, it distrusted the scientific spirit, with its critical attitude towards authority, its relativistic interpretation of nature and social institutions, its individualistic approach to problems, and its belief in the supreme wisdom of man's rational capacities.'[64] This ambiguity, which was so characteristic of late Imperial Russian society, remained right up until 1917, when the new polity brought a type of relations which were considerably different in their content but which saw similar inner mechanisms at work.[65]

Organisational Arrangement of Science and Scholarly Knowledge in Early Soviet Russia

Having seized state power as a result of the October 1917 coup, the Bolsheviks encountered strong opposition from many, including the overwhelming majority of intellectuals. Russian intellectual society was deeply ideologically divided. Naturally, against the backdrop of internal resistance and external threats and engaged in the struggle to retain power, the Bolsheviks elevated utility and usability of scientific and scholarly knowledge to the highest rank among the state scientific

---

[62] Ibid.
[63] Ibid.
[64] Vucinich, *Russian Culture*, xi.
[65] See Kotkin, *Magnetic Mountain*, 9–14.

priorities. 'Immediately following the October Revolution, the new authorities began to distinguish between fields of research regarded as important for socialist construction and others deemed of lesser or no importance. This division determined not only the distribution of funding but also whether certain academic posts and disciplines would exist at all.'[66] Here, a case in point is the fate of Vladimir Beneshevich, a corresponding member of the Academy, whose scholarly discipline – Byzantine Church Law – was abolished like many others that were classified as "reactionary sciences".[67]

Thus, the Russian scientific community found itself facing the question of survival, not only of disciplines and scientific activities but also the physical survival of scientists and scholars themselves. In addition to the difficulties of the Civil War, such as famine and anarchy, the Russian scientific community, being an organic part of the Russian society of the time, encountered the mass terror of the Bolsheviks. Scientists and scholars were exiled abroad, imprisoned and executed without any investigation, and subjected to legal proceedings, particularly during the War Communism of 1918–21.[68] In his substantial work about the post-revolution persecution implemented by the Bolsheviks towards scientists and scholars, Vadim J. Birstein quotes a letter sent by the Permanent Secretary of the Academy, Prince Ol'denburg, to Lenin on 21 November 1921, where he appealed to the Head of *Sovnarkom* to intervene against 'uncontrolled mass execution' of scientists who had not been involved in any political activity.[69] Apparently, Lenin did not even let this letter leave his office, therefore no due measures were undertaken. The only resolution regarding the letter was to put it into the archive, so the executions continued.[70] During this period the state's attitude towards intellectuals could often be characterised by Lenin's eloquent quotation: 'The intellectual forces

---

[66] Vera Tolz, *Russian Academicians and the Revolution: Combining Professionalism and Politics* (London: Macmillan, 1997): 183–4. See also Kelle, "Introduction," 8, 10; Iurii Krivonosov, "Partiia i nauka v pervye gody Sovetskoi vlasti," in *Nauka i tekhnika v pervye desiatiletiia sovetskoi vlasti: sotsiokul'turnoe izmerenie, 1917–1940*, ed. Elena Muzrukova and Liudmila Chesnova (Moscow: Academia, 2007): 14.

[67] See Appendix (Beneshevich). Also see Tolz, *Russian Academicians*, 183–4; Krivonosov, "Partiia i nauka," 13, 16.

[68] See Birstein, *Perversion of Knowledge*, 28–33.

[69] Ibid., 32.

[70] Ibid., 32.

of the workers and peasants are growing and gaining strength in the struggle to overthrow the bourgeoisie and its henchmen, the intellectual lackeys of capital, who imagine they are the brains of the nation. Actually, they are not brains, but shit.'[71]

Thus, the regime of fear, uncertainty and snitching was being inculcated in the whole society and, respectively, in the Russian scientific community. The demolition of the main moral standards was being encouraged. In these circumstances, for those who were, for some reason, not capable of active armed resistance or leaving the country, the only way out was to compromise through conformism and demonstration of outward loyalty towards the new polity. Moreover, taking into consideration the Bolsheviks' interest in maximising the usability of science and achieving immediate results, in order to save and develop the remains of scientific and scholarly knowledge it was necessary to initiate research and programmes which were vitally important, first of all, for the state itself and which promised quick practical implementation of scientific outcomes. This interplay of scientific and state interests and their institutional relations was most representative in the case of the Academy of Sciences.[72]

While depicting the early post-revolution history of the Russian Academy of Sciences, Graham writes:

> It is one of the paradoxes of the history of science in early Soviet Russia that the scientific institution that was generally acknowledged as being the most conservative, the Academy of Sciences, met the Bolshevik revolution with less overt resistance than did the universities and other scientific institutions. Indeed, the Academy not only refrained from the hostile declarations and acts that were characteristic of many learned organizations and professional societies immediately after the October Revolution, but cooperated with the Soviet government from a fairly early date.[73]

However, it is hardly possible to find something surprising or inexplicable about it – not only because of the arduous conditions, which have just been mentioned, and the prevailing instinct of self-preservation but also because of the fact that during the final years of Imperial

[71] Vladimir Lenin, *Sobranie sochinenii*, vol. 44 (Moscow: Progress Publishers, 1970): 284, in Birstein, *Perversion of Knowledge*, 35.
[72] See Krivonosov, "Partiia i nauka," 13–14.
[73] Graham, *Science in Russia*, 82.

Russia, the Academy disapproved of the conservative policy of the tsarist government. It reckoned it to be incompetent in almost all fields, particularly in that of scientific and scholarly knowledge.[74]

Besides that, judging by the almost two-hundred-year history of the Russian Academy of Sciences, it had always been totally dependent on the state (except for a very short period between the two revolutions in 1917 when, after the February Revolution, the Academy was legislatively granted organisational autonomy).[75] In fact, it had institutionally been part of the state power and exercised power itself: 'The Academy was from the very beginning treated as a branch of the government and subject to imperial command.'[76] So, it had already been part of the institutional practices of the Academy to find ways of getting on with the central governing institutions, which supports Foucault's concept of the active interaction between all components of his power/knowledge compound.

Almost all academicians took the Bolsheviks' coming to power as a catastrophe on a national scale and, in December 1917, after two emergency meetings, adopted a strong anti-Bolshevik resolution. However, on the following day, they were informed that if they refused to acknowledge the authority of *Sovnarkom*, the Academy would not be subsidised. Thus, in January 1918, the President of the Academy, Karpinskii, and the Permanent Secretary, Ol'denburg, entered the first round of negotiations with the Commissar of Education, Lunacharskii, about the future of relationships with the new authorities.[77]

Naturally, the Bolsheviks were also interested in the full cooperation of scientists and scholars for the purpose of solving further issues of national state building. 'They worked on three fronts: adapting the traditional scientific institutions to modern conditions, creating new institutions to respond to previously unattended needs, and building a bridge between science and ideology.'[78] Therefore, in this context, scientists gained a remarkable opportunity to defend their own personal and professional interests. While describing the situation of the time, Graham points out:

---

[74] See Birstein, *Perversion of Knowledge*, 20.
[75] See Graham, *Science in Russia*, 18–20.
[76] Ibid., 19.
[77] See Birstein, *Perversion of Knowledge*, 22.
[78] Vucinich, *Empire of Knowledge*, 72.

The permanent secretary of the Academy in the years after 1904, Prince S. F. Ol'denburg, dreamed of a renaissance of Russia, a blooming of its scientific and cultural potential, with the Academy of Sciences playing the leading role. When the Communist leaders inherited this extraordinary institution they faced a decision – abolish it … or build a structure of scientific research in which it would be the central and critical element. They decided to adopt the last choice.[79]

At the beginning of 1918 Karpinskii had already promised that 'the Academy, in keeping with its tradition of service to the state, would help develop the productive forces for national needs. In response the government began to release funds for the Academy's operations.'[80]

Here, it is worth referring to the Foucauldian notion of the productivity of power and the creative role of power relations. Wherever new forms of power are exerted, new forms of resistance and power relations emerge. The components of the Foucauldian power grid never tend to self-destruction; they produce new relations, often directly resulting in increasing national economic and cultural product.[81] The Bolsheviks' government 'was the first in the world to recognize the now common notion of science as a powerful instrument in national development'.[82] It employed utilitarian usage of scientific and scholarly knowledge on a wide scale, pursuing its immediate goals of securing power and constructing a new state. And the Russian scientific community, namely the Academy, having overcome, at least outwardly, its initial hostility towards the new polity, began constructing new structures of relations which led to its benefiting from the state's active science policy. Partly in spite of, but, perhaps, more due to new circumstances, Russian scientists and scholars managed to recover and considerably develop their institutions and activities. The situation that emerged after 1921, in the relatively liberal context of the NEP, provided them with a previously unknown level of autonomy in their internal affairs and created real opportunities for exerting influence on state scientific policymaking.[83]

[79] Graham, *Science in Russia*, 81.
[80] Ibid., 84.
[81] See Jon Simons, *Foucault and the Political* (London: Routledge, 1995): 82.
[82] Krementsov, *Stalinist Science*, 11.
[83] Ibid., 29.

Having carefully analysed the 1920s–1930s' history of Russian science in terms of its power/knowledge relations, Nikolai Krementsov distinguishes a phenomenon that was characteristic only of Soviet science, namely the emergence of so-called 'spokesmen' and 'patrons'. He asserts that the scientific and scholarly communities gradually 'produced spokesmen able and willing to undertake the "dirty" job of representing their disciplinary and institutional interests to the control apparatus and trying to persuade the decision makers to serve their particular agendas and the development of various Soviet scientific disciplines was greatly influenced by the personal relations between particular disciplinary spokesmen and their powerful party patrons'.[84] At the beginning, the spokesmen belonged to the same scientific circles (such as Ol'denburg), and the patrons were reputable influential individuals, for example, among writers (such as Gor'kii who played the role of one of the most influential patrons for Oriental studies, biology and medicine),[85] or politicians (such as Lunacharskii (1875–1933) – linguistics; Bukharin (1888–1938) – history, philosophy; Krzhizhanovskii (1872–1959) – economics, mathematics),[86] but later, as the intergrowth of state political structures and scientific institutions gradually advanced, these two groups mixed, simultaneously occupying posts both in scientific institutions and party/government/security services structures.[87]

Therefore, 'As official policies became gradually more assertive, academicians were left with less and less room to maneuver.'[88] 'In the early days of the New Economic Policy, the weight of scientific opinion, heir to the disciplinary authority of the bourgeois professions, reinforced the official project of social control and social engineering. Later, as Stalin consolidated his hold on power, science itself fell under the domination of political orthodoxy.'[89] New forms of regulation of scientific and scholarly activities kept emerging. Control over scientists and scholars tightened. All of which created new forms of interaction between the components of the extended power grid – the

[84] Ibid., 5.
[85] Ibid., 35.
[86] Ibid., 31–9.
[87] Mark Popovskii, *Science in Chains*, trans. Paul S. Falla (London: Collins and Harvill Press, 1980): 72–84, 77, 111, 134–5, 198.
[88] Tolz, *Russian Academicians*, 183.
[89] Engelstein, "Combined Underdevelopment," 233.

interplay of spokesmen, patrons, scientists and scholars and the state bureaucracy.

It was natural that Soviet Oriental studies shared the destiny of the Soviet scientific community, being equally subject to the entangled interplay of institutional and individual relationships. Oriental studies were of particular interest to the new government, especially in the early post-revolution years.[90] In the heat of revolutionary and war victories inside Russia, the Bolsheviks saw great revolutionary potential in the Orient and were firmly resolved to export revolution to the countries of the "oppressed Orient". Oriental studies were the scholarly discipline that could provide immediate practical results. Orientalists were expected to concentrate on political and socio-economic aspects, to "find" uncompromising class struggles and irreconcilable contradictions which would substantiate further Soviet military and, later, ideological expansion to the Orient.[91]

The Foucauldian *Episteme*

However, the above-mentioned features do not constitute the full content of power/knowledge relations. There are also other very important components pointed out by Foucault; *episteme* and discourse are among them. In fact, they are among the most essential Foucauldian notions because of their capability to vector and to shape the process of knowledge development. Having studied three of the main historical periods that shaped the system of cultural values of contemporary Western civilisation (the European Renaissance of the sixteenth and the first half of the seventeenth century, the 'classical era' of the seventeenth and eighteenth century, the 'modern era' of the nineteenth and twentieth century) he reached the conclusion that what took place was not actually the creation of objective knowledge but the emergence of regulatory practices; that the very beginning of the process of scientific research was initiated by certain circumstances or social

[90] See Michael Kemper, "Integrating Soviet Oriental Studies," in *The Heritage of Soviet Oriental Studies*, ed. Michael Kemper and Stephan Conermann (Abingdon: Routledge, 2011): 2–3.
[91] See Wayne S. Vucinich, "The Structure of Soviet Orientology: Fifty Years of Change and Accomplishment," in *Russia and Asia: Essays on the Influence of Russia on the Asian People*, ed. Wayne S. Vucinich (Stanford, CA: Hoover Institution Press, 1972): 52.

and political institutions and relationships which subsequently would strongly influence or even fully determine its general trends, methods, technicalities, ultimate results and their interpretation.

This process can be characterised as discontinuous "community" activities aimed at constructing truth.[92] So, according to Foucault, his study demonstrates that during certain periods of human history there was something which would allow thought to form and organise itself. This something, being a sort of invisible grid or network, would limit and determine experience, knowledge and the very activity aimed at achieving truth; it would govern the sciences or other areas of human knowledge and activities in one way or another in each period. Initially, Foucault called it *épistème*.

Épistème in Russia

From the very outset, in the Russian case, there is reason to point out the *épistème* that throughout the whole three-hundred-year period, since the time of Peter the Great to nowadays, has remained steady and without any considerable changes or shifts – namely the idea of catching up with the West by means of the scientific and scholarly development of Russian society. The initiating and regulating role of state supreme authority (with the top-down vector) has never been contravened in this process, though the methods of science promotion were authoritarian. Another discursive component of this *épistème* was the pronounced national trend and the preservation of its own cultural and political identity.[93] At first, the task consisted of domesticating science and scholarly knowledge and cultivating Russia's own Platos and Newtons.[94]

As has already been mentioned, Lomonosov saw the role of the Academy of Sciences as importing Western science to Russia, while universities would proliferate it and produce a native scientific and scholarly community. As time passed, the task became more complex. Since the second half of the nineteenth century, the initial notion of the nationalisation of science as the emergence of the nation as the

[92] Horrocks and Jevtic, *Introducing Foucault*, 19.
[93] Graham, *Science in Russia*, 2.
[94] Ibid., 24.

structuring unit and the principal arena of scientific activity'[95] was
supplemented by national state building.

Nationalization, above all, was reflected in the emergence of the (nation-)
state as a structuring unit and a funding agent of scholarship and science.
It was also manifested in the belief that scholarship should contribute to
nation-building (through offering scientific definitions of a nation and a
justification of the historical presence of a nation on a particular territory,
thereby helping to forge close links among members of the national communities and individuals' loyalty to these communities).[96]

A similar situation could also be found during the post-1917 decades.[97]
Therefore, the *épistème* of "catching up with the West" has remained
essentially unchanged since the time of Peter the Great.

The Foucauldian approach does not imply that these constructed
or modified "truths" are necessarily lies. Rather, it demonstrates that
there is simply no truth or knowledge which would not depend on
the society or state where it is generated. The difference is only in the
extent to which it is subject to this influence and its intensity. Thus, the
idea of discourse comes into being. The *épistème* gradually generates
Foucault's discourse, which comes to the fore as the omnipresent and
determinative component of human knowledge; however, as something less overwhelming in terms of time and space but more specific
in terms of the social and professional groups within which it is spread.

The Foucauldian Discourse

In his *Archaeology of Knowledge*, Foucault himself defines the term
"discourse" as 'the general domain of all statements, sometimes as an
individualisable group of statements, and sometimes as a regulated
practice that accounts for a number of statements'.[98] Sara Mills, in

[95] Vera Tolz, "European, National, and (Anti-)Imperial: The Formation
of Academic Oriental Studies in Late Tsarist and Early Soviet Russia,"
Kritika: Explorations in Russian and Eurasian History 9/1 (Winter 2008): 53.
[96] Ibid., 62.
[97] See Hirsch, *Empire of Nations*, 25, 26–30, 62–101. See also Kemper,
"Integrating Soviet Oriental Studies," 4–8; Vera Tolz, "Orientalism,
Nationalism, and Ethnic Diversity in Late Imperial Russia," *Historical Journal*
48/1 (2005): 127–50.
[98] Michel Foucault, *The Archaeology of Knowledge* (London: Routledge,
1972): 80.

her book *Michel Foucault*, presents the following definition of the Foucauldian notion of discourse, based upon Foucault's influential lecture "The Order of Discourse" (1981) and his other main works: 'A discourse is a regulated set of statements which combine with others in predictable ways. Discourse is regulated by a set of rules which lead to the distribution and circulation of certain utterances and statements. Some statements are circulated widely and others have restricted circulation.'[99]

Indeed, by discourse Foucault means groups of statements which deal with the same topic or issues and which seem to produce a similar effect. They may be grouped together under some institutional pressure, or on the basis of origin or usage, or in view of their operational similarity.[100] However, other Foucault scholars go beyond the two components of utterances and statements in their understanding of discourse. They point to conventional, prevailing practices as a third constituent of discourse, which sometimes even plays a more determining role in the process of forming a discourse than semantic structures. In their opinion, it often happens that these practices generate the character of statements and even statements themselves. Accentuating this in their book *Introducing Foucault*, Chris Horrocks and Zoran Jevtic characterise Foucauldian discourse in this way: 'Discourses are not linguistics systems or just texts – they are practices, like the scientific discourse of psychoanalysis and its institutional, philosophical and scientific levels.'[101]

Following on from this premise, discourse is understood to be governed by the three interlinked structures:

Surfaces of emergence: social and cultural areas through which discourse appears, e.g. the family, work group or religious community.

Authorities of delimitation: institutions with knowledge and authority, like the law or the medical profession.

Grids of specification: a system by which different kinds of madness, say, can be related to each other in psychiatric discourse.[102]

It is obvious that the emergence of certain structural systems which deal with the activities of human thought is possible only within social

---

[99] Mills, *Michel Foucault*, 54.
[100] Ibid., 53–66.
[101] Horrocks and Jevtic, *Introducing Foucault*, 86.
[102] Ibid., 86.

environments, involving people and forms of interaction between them. As a result of the process of human activities taking place in such environments, various forms of institutions tend to emerge. They regulate relations in such vital domains as knowledge and authority, thereby constituting the above-mentioned second main determinative of discourse. The process of interaction between individuals, various groups and communities, and social and political institutions results in the generation and development of specification grids, which arrange the components of discourse.

Scrutinising the nature of Foucauldian discourse and its correlation with conventional notions of the 'world thought order', Mills comments:

So Foucault is not denying that there are physical objects in the world and he is not suggesting that there is nothing but discourse, but what he is stating is that we can only think about and experience material objects and the world as a whole through discourse and the structures it imposes on our thinking. In the process of thinking about the world, we categorise and interpret experience and events according to the structures available to us and in the process of interpreting, we lend these structures a solidity and a normality which it is often difficult to question.[103]

Indeed, functioning in that way, discourse tends to create its object and develop it, generating new discourses. These processes are caused by a set of rules and conditions, established between various social, cultural and political institutions, adopted practices and widely spread patterns of behaviour. Foucault writes:

There is in all societies, with great consistency, a kind of gradation among discourses: those which are said in the ordinary course of days and exchanges, and which vanish as soon as they have been pronounced; and those which give rise to a certain number of new speech acts which take them up, transform them or speak of them, in short, those discourses which, over and above their formulation, are said indefinitely, remain said, and are to be said again.[104]

---

[103] Mills, *Michel Foucault*, 56.
[104] Michel Foucault, "The Order of Discourse," in *Untying the Text: A Post-Structuralist Reader*, ed. Robert Young (London: Routledge, 1981): 48–78, 57.

Therefore, it is to be expected that there would be mechanisms for the regulation and control of these processes. And it is in these mechanisms that Foucault is particularly interested: 'In every society the production of discourse is at once controlled, selected, organised, and redistributed by a certain number of procedures whose role is to ward off its powers and dangers, to gain mastery over its chance events, to evade its ponderous, formidable materiality.'[105] So, Foucault ascertained that there were procedures which would constrain discourse, regulating its development and reproduction or ensuring its transformation or complete demise.

Among those procedures is the commonly acknowledged ability to distinguish the true from the false – the practice that determines the shaping of discourse and its place in the power/knowledge system proposed by Foucault. Analysing this constraining practice of Foucauldian discourse, Mills comments that

those in positions of authority who are seen to be 'experts' are those who can speak the truth. Those who make statements who are not in positions of power will be considered not to be speaking the truth. The notion of the truth must not be taken as self-evident; he shows in his work how truth is something which is supported materially by a whole range of practices and institutions: universities, government departments, publishing houses, scientific bodies and so on. All of these institutions work to exclude statements which they characterise as false and they keep in circulation those statements which they characterise as true. For Foucault, only those statements which are 'in the true' will be circulated.[106]

Thus, Foucault demonstrates how and under what conditions certain statements or practices can survive and develop but others not. They will be viable only if considered to be true according to the currently prevailing notions, and for that they should be in conformity with other statements and practices that have been authorised and adopted by a society. Simultaneously, the process of exclusion takes place. Thereby, this mechanism described by Foucault makes societies or certain environments reject and filter the statements and practices which are not in full conformity with the discourse. Hence, discourse

[105] Ibid., 52.
[106] Mills, *Michel Foucault*, 58.

occurs in an extremely complex and entangled system of interconnection, presented by Foucault as power/knowledge.

Discourse in Imperial Russia

Returning to the Russian societies of the late Imperial and early Soviet periods, initially it is necessary to refer to social and political discourses that existed in the nineteenth and early twentieth century regarding different modes of modernising Russia which should ultimately have led to achieving the Western model of society, while retaining essentially Russian features. So, each discourse of this kind would have emerged mainly based on the views of a particular monarch of the time and his advisors. It would have been shaped and imposed on Russian society according to the top-down vector and, at the same time, it would have been subject to the influence and even modifications of its executors – individuals and institutions. For their part, all these relations greatly influenced Russian scholarship.

This can be illustrated by national discourses that appeared in the periods of Tsar Alexander I (1801–25) and the activities of the so-called Private Committee; Tsar Nicholas I (1825–55) and the chief educational administrator, Count Sergey Uvarov; Tsar Alexander II (1855–81) and Dmitry Miliutin's slogans of *glasnost'* (openness), *zakonnost'* (legality) and *nauchnost'* (scientificity); and Tsar Nicholas II (1896–1917) and Count Witte.[107] For example, 'Uvarov promoted a renaissance of the Academy of Sciences and a new blossoming of scholarship in the universities. He created in Russia a tradition of excellence in Oriental studies and he strongly supported the existing one in mathematics.'[108] The reforms inspired by Miliutin had an enormous impact on scientific and scholarly knowledge, particularly on military Oriental studies – which will be studied in Chapter 2. Many restrictions, including those concerning caps for admission to universities, class privileges and bans on travel abroad for studying, were abolished. The appropriations for research activities, including those

---

[107] See Bartol'd, "Russkaia nauka," 541–2. See also David Schimmelpenninck van der Oye, *Russian Orientalism: Asia in the Russian Mind from Peter the Great to the Emigration* (New Haven: Yale University Press, 2010): 154–60; Graham, *Science in Russia*, 32–8.

[108] Graham, *Science in Russia*, 35.

of the Academy of Sciences, were considerably increased, and the freedom of forming scientific and scholarly communities and holding conferences was extended.[109]

At the level of the scientific and scholarly community, the above-mentioned discursive tendencies were being refracted and transformed. Thus, other discourses were produced. For example, it is necessary to mention the tightly entangled discourses of nationalisation and inter-nationalisation of Russian science and scholarship.[110] The issue of language – so important in this context – would also often come to the fore.

The debate was explicitly linked to the issue of nation-building and was influenced by the conflicting trends of nationalization and internationaliza-tion in science and scholarship. The advocates of using Russian argued that it would create a 'national community of academics' that would advance Russian science and scholarship internationally. Others, however, continued to argue that, because foreign scholars often knew little Russian, its use by academics served little purpose. Thus many academic works continued to be published in Russia in foreign languages until 1917 [when discontinuity led to the formation of a new discourse].[111]

It implied the constant endeavour of demonstrating and proving the authenticity and independence of the new Soviet scholarship. Shortly after, during the subsequent years, it also led to not only the virtual ban of using languages other than Russian, but to the emergence of a spe-cial 'Newspeak'[112] in humanities scholarship and even in the sciences, which seriously affected internationalisation of Russian scientific and scholarly knowledge.

There were other discourses in Russian society before and after 1917 that had strong distinctions. It is noteworthy that Russian Oriental studies, which originated as a tool for the practical applica-tion of scholarship in the fields of foreign and military affairs, later generated a discourse on pure scholarship within its own context.

---

[109] See Alex Marshall, *The Russian General Staff and Asia, 1800–1917* (London: Routledge, 2006): 21–6. See also Graham, *Science in Russia*, 37–8.

[110] See Bartol'd, "Russkaia nauka," 544–5. See also Tolz, "European," 62–3; Marshall, *Russian General Staff*, 167–8.

[111] Tolz, "European," 63.

[112] See Krementsov, *Stalinist Science*, 8.

Since the late 1850s there had been strong opposition at the Faculty of Oriental Languages of St Petersburg University towards the promotion of practical applicability.[113] Similar views were also propagated by the patriarchs of Russian Oriental studies, namely Viktor Rosen (1849–1908),[114] Vasilii Barthold, Sergei Ol'denburg (1864–1934) and Nikolai Marr (1864–1934), among others. As far as it was possible in tsarist Russia they tried to stay away from the utilitarian side.

However, they were deeply worried about the moral aspects of their scholarship. Paying much attention to the 'moral assessment of the connection between power and knowledge',[115] Russian Imperial Orientologists often criticised Western Oriental studies for its political and colonial over-engagement, and anticipated post-colonial debates long before Edward Said's work.[116]

Inspired by Rosen's belief in the need to question the prejudices of European scholars studying the 'Orient,' in 1905 Barthold began reading a university course on the historiography of Oriental Studies in Europe and Russia. First published as a book in 1911, the course aimed 'among other things, at dispelling various myths about the East in Russia and Europe.' In Barthold's writings, many European scholars were criticized for their 'biased views and prejudices' in a manner not entirely dissimilar to Said's critique of European Orientalism.[117]

Naturally, the general critical attitude of Russian scholarship towards the West was also enhanced by the events of World War I.[118]

Thus the post-1917 attacks by Marr and Ol'denburg on 'bourgeois scholarship' and its juxtaposition to Soviet scholarship about the 'East' with its own distinct profile were not simply a manifestation of political opportunism. To some extent they represented a further development of the views that had been forming among scholars both in Russia and elsewhere in Europe since the early twentieth century and became radicalized in the course of World War I as a result of wounded national pride and doubts about the moral values of 'European civilization'.[119]

---

[113] See Tolz, *Russia's Own Orient*, 69–84.
[114] See Appendix (Rosen).
[115] Tolz, *Russia's Own Orient*, 83.
[116] Ibid., 69–72.
[117] Tolz, "European," 73.
[118] Ibid., 76.
[119] Ibid., 76–7.

Discourse in Soviet Russia

All this became the prologue to both future radical changes in discourses under the mostly coercive ideological pressure of the Soviet epoch and, simultaneously, the preservation of some discursive manifestations – in other words, to continuities. 'Some Orientalists perished, while others left the country as refugees.'[120] Those who survived and remained in the country could hardly express and follow their personal and professional views if they were not in conformity with the new ideological postulates. After 1917 and the hardships of the Civil War, even during the still relatively diverse variety of opinions of the 1920s NEP, Russian "old" scholarship had to compromise with the new regime, adopting, although often only outwardly, the appropriate ideological structures along with the new rules of the game, and gradually giving way to new, Soviet Orientology. Simultaneously, a new generation of Russian Orientologists was being trained based on works by Marx and Engels, implementing a new methodology for the study of the Orient.[121] As Kemper concisely points out: 'Marxist Oriental studies in early Soviet Russia emerged in opposition to the "bourgeois" Russian tradition of classical Oriental scholarship; rather than studying texts and history, Bolshevik Orientalists saw their task in providing the Soviet government with the necessary political and socio-economic knowledge to support the liberation of the contemporary East from colonialism and imperialism.'[122]

This approach generated a new discourse on Islam among the early Soviet Orientological scholars. The Bolshevik state's attitude towards Islam, as well as that in early Soviet scholarship, was ambivalent. In the 1920s, there were plenty of often-contradictory perceptions of Islam and its role in world history. Naturally, most of them were based on Marxist interpretations and were after identifying the "class character" of Islam, locating it within Marx's notion of socio-economic formations, finding feudal and capitalist features in it.[123] One of the

---

[120] Vucinich, "Structure," 52.
[121] See Mikhail Rodionov, "Profiles under Pressure: Orientalists in Petrograd/ Leningrad, 1918–1956," in *The Heritage of Soviet Oriental Studies*, ed. Michael Kemper and Stephan Conermann (Abingdon: Routledge, 2011): 47–57. See also Vucinich, "Structure," 53–8; Beer, *Renovating Russia*, 202–4.
[122] Michael Kemper, "Red Orientalism: Mikhail Pavlovich and Marxist Oriental Studies in Early Soviet Russia," *Die Welt des Islams* 50 (2010): 435.
[123] See Kemper, "Integrating," 6. See also Kelle, "Introduction," 8.

revolutionaries wrote in his memoirs that, at the Fifth Congress of Soviets in 1918, there was even a decision taken on bringing pious Muslims into state power since experts argued that it would be feasible to make all Muslims convert to communists with the help of the Quran.[124]

Michael Kemper, in his article "The Soviet Discourse on the Origin and Class Character of Islam, 1923–33", writes on this issue:

After the October Revolution of 1917 the Bolsheviks did not yet have a clear strategy on how to deal with Islam. There was also a persistent uncertainty among the Bolsheviks [about] how to understand Islam on a theoretical level. Marx, Engels and Lenin did not provide a clear theoretical framework for a historical evaluation of Islam, and it took the Soviets more than a decade to explore the 'class character' of that religion. The central question of this discourse was how Muslim society would fit into the general development of human history – a process which Marx imagined as a sequence of specific socio-economic formations.[125]

All this was to answer the main question: how to treat Muslims living in the Soviet state.

It is necessary to point out that on the whole it was not the "old" scholars and specialists on Islam who regulated and defined the content and the character of this dispute. New individuals, professing significantly different views not only in terms of politics but also on scholarly methodology and activities, came to the fore. Among them were Mikhail Vel'tman (pseudonym Pavlovich; 1871–1927),[126] Sergei Pastukhov (Iranskii; 1887–1940), Vladimir Osetrov (Irandust; 1893–1938) and Vladimir Gurko-Kriazhin (1887–1931). So, it was not long before, in the early 1930s, the Soviet discourse on Islam was finally shaped. Islam was recognised as a feudal religion and solidly occupied its place in the row of other religions which were used by "exploiters" and "counter-revolutionary elements".[127] Thus, it became essentially anti-Soviet and deserved to be fought at all levels of society. Hence,

[124] RGASPI, f. 133, op. 1, d. 26 (Kobozev's memoirs. Not available for reading hall), l. 7–8.
[125] Kemper, "Soviet Discourse," 2–3.
[126] See Kemper, "Red Orientalism," 435–76.
[127] See Kemper, "Integrating," 7. See also Michael Kemper, "The Soviet Discourse on the Origin and Class Character of Islam, 1923–1933," *Die Welt des Islams* 49 (2009): 4; Kelle, "Introduction," 8.

based on the utilitarian priorities of the Soviet state's science policy, many Soviet Orientologists were assigned the role of anti-religious propagandists. They would be sent to various remote regions of the Soviet Union to carry out atheist activities. Such an attitude was also evident from the state persecution of the protagonists of Islam, including experts on Islam, historians, ethnographers and interpreters who were pulled to OGPU-NKVD organs. [128]

So, the general emphasis of the Bolshevik science policy on the practicality of knowledge led to a shift in scholarly activities in Oriental studies from studying and identifying relevant patterns to finding better ways of transforming the object of study itself. This resulted in drastically enhancing the individual impact of scholars and experts on scholarly, political and social activities which were taking place in Soviet society. At the same time, individuals, for their part, would form influential groups which started playing their own roles in this new complex of relations. Providing a general characterisation of these relations and supporting thereby Foucauldian notions of shaping discourse within scientific knowledge and the role of scientists and scholars in exerting influence, Peter Kneen classifies scientists within such relations as

the members of real groups which form around the research problems on which they are engaged. It is in this kind of group that problems are defined, results evaluated and professional recognition distributed. The direction and significance of scientific work, as well as the professional standing of scientists, are influenced by such groups, networks, or scientific communities, as they are sometimes called. The cognitive and social aspects of science can thus be seen to be intimately linked. [129]

As the character of these relations shows, the possibility of the existence of "pure" scientists and scholars is rightly questioned. [130]

---

[128] See Kemper, "Integrating," 7; Vucinich, "Structure," 52–8. OGPU (United State Political Directorate) existed in 1923–34 as a successor to GPU (1922–23; State Political Directorate), before that – VeCheka (1917–22; All-Russia Extraordinary Commission for Combating Counter-Revolution and Sabotage). NKVD (Peoples Commissariat of Internal Affairs) was formed in 1934 and existed until 1943, finally evolving into the widely known KGB (State Security Committee) in 1954, after some reorganisation, mergers and transformations.

[129] Peter Kneen, *Soviet Scientists and the State* (London: Macmillan, 1984): 1.

[130] See Foucault, *Power*, 130–1.

The Foucauldian Intellectual

On the role of intellectuals, Foucault writes in *Power/Knowledge*: 'Power must be analysed as something which circulates, or as something which only functions in the form of a chain ... Power is employed and exercised through a net-like organisation ... Individuals are vehicles of power, not its points of application.'[131] Emphasising the importance of the role of individuals in the context of power/knowledge, Foucault states: 'It seems to me that we are now at the point where the function of the specific intellectual needs to be reconsidered.'[132] At the same time, he argues against idealised and simplistic perceptions of independent "pure" scholars:

Reconsidered but not abandoned, despite the nostalgia of some for the great 'universal' intellectuals and the desire for a new philosophy, a new world-view [...] One may even say that that the role of the specific intellectual must become more and more important in proportion to the political responsibilities which he is obliged willy-nilly to accept, as a nuclear scientist, computer expert, pharmacologist, and so on. It would be a dangerous error to discount him politically in his specific relation to a local form of power, either on the grounds that this is a specialist matter that doesn't concern the masses (which is doubly wrong: they are already aware of it, and in any case implicated in it), or that the specific intellectual serves the interests of state or capital (which is true, but at the same time shows the strategic position he occupies); or, again, on the grounds that he propagates a scientific ideology (which isn't always true, and is anyway certainly a secondary matter compared with the fundamental point: the effects proper to true discourses).[133]

Commenting on Foucault's attitude towards the role of individuals in the context of the power/knowledge nexus, Herman Nilson, in his book *Michel Foucault and the Games of Truth*, writes:

Yet it is precisely to Foucault's credit that he showed through his work that knowledge alone does not suffice to change the world or one's own life; that what is important is to develop an attitude, a philosophical ethos. For

---

[131] Michel Foucault, "Two Lectures," in *Power/Knowledge*, ed. Colin Gordon (Brighton: Harvester, 1980): 98.

[132] Foucault, *Power*, 130.

[133] Ibid., 130–1.

Foucault, scientific work was not limited to an explanation of our development, but was based on the conviction that we should take an active and transforming role in fashioning the process of development through the example of our own existence.[134]

Given that 'power is not an institution, and not a structure; neither [...] a certain strength we are endowed with [...] [but rather] the name that one attributes to a complex strategic situation in a particular society',[135] the importance of how individuals conceive of their own place in this "situation", and of their intellectual and physical capabilities and to what extent they are concerned with that, drastically increases.

Thus, taking into consideration this complex entangled system of interconnections, Foucault puts forward new requirements on intellectuals operating in these conditions. He is strongly opposed to vesting contemporary intellectuals with obligations to adhere to "universal values". He considers it useless, as he believes in the "specificity" of intellectuals according to the place they occupy. Referring to the historical realities of his time, Foucault states ironically:

the intellectual has a threefold specificity: that of his class position (whether as petty-bourgeois in the service of capitalism or 'organic' intellectual of the proletariat); that of his conditions of life and work, linked to his condition as an intellectual (his field of research, his place in a laboratory, the political and economic demands to which he submits or against which he rebels, in the university, the hospital, and so on); finally, the specificity of the politics of truth in our societies. And it's with this last factor that his position can take on a general significance, and that his local, specific struggle can have effects and implications that are not simply professional or sectoral. The intellectual can operate and struggle at the general level of that regime of truth so essential to the structure and functioning of our society.[136]

Based on Foucault's above-mentioned dictum, it becomes evident that over the last few centuries intellectuals have played an increasing role in the context of that model of the world that mankind

---

[134] Herman Nilson, *Michel Foucault and the Games of Truth*, trans. Rachel Clark (London: Macmillan, 1998): 84.

[135] Michel Foucault, *The History of Sexuality: An Introduction*, trans. Robert Hurley (Harmondsworth: Penguin, 1978): 93.

[136] Foucault, *Power*, 132.

constructed and adopted for themselves; since, in society, where there is no objective and dispassionate knowledge and truths are available only in certain acceptable (for such a society) forms and always work in the interests of particular groups,[137] a formidable role accrues to intellectuals who are participating in the "battles" for or around constructing those truths. Thus, Foucault appeals for a radical re-assessment of the impact of intellectuals: 'it's not a matter of a battle on behalf of the truth but of a battle about the status of truth and the economic and political role it plays. It is necessary to think of the political problems of intellectuals not in terms of "science" and "ideology" but in terms of "truth" and "power".'[138]

So, according to Foucault, intellectuals are supposed to take an active stand, personifying that very resistance[139] in the nexus of power/knowledge. Considering resistance as an intrinsic part of power, Foucault asserts that there are no power relations without resistance. It emerges precisely when and where power is exercised. Applying this to the question of what constitutes appropriate conscientious social behaviour for the intellectual, Foucault argues that

the essential political problem for the intellectual is not to criticize the ideological contents supposedly linked to science, or to ensure that his own scientific practice is accompanied by a correct ideology, but that of ascertaining the possibility of constituting a new politics of truth. The problem is not changing people's consciousnesses – or what's in their heads – but the political, economic, institutional regime of the production of truth.[140]

Thus, Foucault sees the underlying task for intellectuals operating within the context of these "material processes" as follows:

It's not a matter of emancipating truth from every system of power (which would be a chimera, for truth is already power) but of detaching the power of truth from the forms of hegemony, social, economic, and cultural, within which it operates at the present time. The political question, to sum up, is not error, alienated consciousness, or ideology; it is truth itself.[141]

[137] See Mills, *Michel Foucault*, 79.
[138] Foucault, *Power*, 132.
[139] See Foucault, *History of Sexuality*, 12; Mills, *Michel Foucault*, 40–2.
[140] Foucault, *Power*, 133.
[141] Ibid., 133.

Based on Foucault's analysis of relations between individuals and a society which affects them through various institutions and state structures, subjectifying them and turning them into active agents operating within this vast net-like field of power relations, it can be concluded that, instead of being strongly limited to a high extent by multiple norms and regulations which are created by institutions and governments, in actual fact, individuals, especially intellectuals, have *more* opportunities, and even technical facilities, for exerting Foucauldian resistance, because they are an inherent part of these power relations and are endowed with additional opportunities by those very institutions. As espoused by Jon Simons, according to Foucault, 'all subjectifying power endows subjects with some capacities required to be agents, even when it is oppressive. As power in a positive sense enables subjects, one could not and would not wish to exist outside its limits.'[142]

This leads to the Foucauldian notion of governmentality, which deals with technologies of domination of others and those of the self. It demonstrates the tight interconnections and relationships between the power exercised towards individuals by institutions or a state and that which is exercised by individuals towards themselves. These processes imply interaction between aspects of politics and human ethics. There are conduct regulation rules and techniques in our society which are designed and applied from the top, but, simultaneously, there are also rules and techniques exercised by individuals in order to control and arrange their own conduct, and they are tightly entangled with each other.[143]

The Intellectual and Resistance in Imperial Russia

Naturally, the features of Foucauldian governmentality were significantly more characteristic of Soviet society than of late tsarist Russia. The evidence of relevant discourses – both imposed from the top and multiplied and developed by the appropriate self-control and adjustment of the conduct and scientific activities on behalf of intellectuals themselves – is much more clearly marked in the Soviet period.[144]

---

[142] Simons, *Foucault*, 82.
[143] See ibid., 36–41. See also Kotkin, *Magnetic Mountain*, 21–3.
[144] See Krementsov, *Stalinist Science*, 3–9; Kotkin, *Magnetic Mountain*, 21–3.

The pre-1917 Imperial scientists and scholars were subject to influence of a different kind. Though there were intellectuals who were still trying to comply with the idea of supremacy of the Orthodox Christianity and the essential role of absolutist monarchy in Russia, the overwhelming majority of Russian intellectuals saw their ultimate goal as being useful to the modernisation and renovation of Russia through their activities. They were united in acknowledging the necessity of transforming the polity of the time. In this respect they would have reckoned scientific and scholarly knowledge to have the appropriate qualities and the potential to help them realise their views.[145] 'By the end of the eighteenth century, the Russian intelligentsia has made the connection between scientific inquiry and political modernization, with the predictable response from the tsarist government and the Orthodox church.'[146]

This can be illustrated by mentioning the destinies of Lobachevskii and Mendeleev, who greatly contributed to the science nationalisation discourse and, while retaining their civil stands against state power, managed to influence not only scientific outcomes but also social and political ones.[147] 'The lives of Lobachevskii and Mendeleev are revealing illustrations of the influence of social and political circumstances on scientific creativity.'[148] Besides, it is appropriate to mention the case of the Academy of Sciences as the most representative part of the Russian scientific and scholarly community. Analysing the personal biographies and activities of its members, Vera Tolz points out that 'the academicians' characters and views had been formed under the influence of the great reforms of the 1860s. In the course of these reforms, a new "man of action" emerged, who thought independently and strove to apply his talents for the good of society.'[149] Thus, the attitude of mind among the intellectuals affiliated to the late tsarist Russia's science and scholarship can be characterised by the principle stressed by Vucinich: 'A scientist has obligations not only to his discipline as such and to the scientific community, but to society at large. He is not only a scientist but an American or German

---

[145] See Graham, *Science in Russia*, 57–8.
[146] Vucinich, *Russian Culture*, xv.
[147] See Graham, *Science in Russia*, 54.
[148] Ibid.
[149] Tolz, *Russian Academicians*, xi.

or Russian scientist.'[150] It is also quite natural that, for their part, the views of intellectuals, in particular academicians, were influenced by other factors, including, first of all, international ones. There had always been a tendency to look at the West and to compare processes in Russia with those which were happening or had happened in Western countries. It also influenced their behaviour. 'The uniqueness of the academicians' position is to be explained by the fact that they felt belonging to the international scientific community. Their international status gave the academicians a broader vision of their professional goals as well as a sense of greater political and social responsibility; it also increased their feeling of political security.'[151]

However, while striving to play a more socially and politically active role, the late Imperial intellectuals could not avoid some false perceptions and interpretations of processes in Western societies. For example, they wrongly appraised the relationship between scholars and state in the field of Oriental studies and ethnography. They overestimated the extent of scholars' involvement in state colonial projects in the West and the social and political influence of Western scholars and, hence, Russian scholars expected to be more involved in the relevant programmes and projects of the tsarist government, regarding both Oriental countries and Russia's 'own' Orient.[152]

The Intellectual and Resistance in Soviet Russia

As Francine Hirsch argues, surprisingly, after 1917, in terms of attitude towards knowledge, Russian academicians found more in common with the Bolsheviks, professing the principle *znanie-sila* (knowledge is power).[153] They were the first to identify knowledge as one of the mightiest tools for national development. Despite all the initial oppressiveness of the new polity during the initial post-1917 period, later, during the NEP, Russian science and scholarship were given much more professional autonomy and involvement in state programmes, though only for a short period of time. Ideas about the modernisation of Russia which had been professed by Imperial intellectuals formed

---

[150] Vucinich, *Russian Culture*, xiii.
[151] Tolz, *Russian Academicians*, ix–x. See also Beer, *Renovating Russia*, 18–19.
[152] See Hirsch, *Empire of Nations*, 34.
[153] See Tolz, "European," 71.

the basis of the new science policy, but its realisation was designed according to the Bolsheviks' rigid system of "usability" priorities.[154]

From the start, they found themselves relying on former imperial experts [...] who themselves looked to Europe for approaches to solving Russia's economic and social problems. Many of these experts had lived and studied in Europe. All were well versed in the politics of nationalism and the practices of empire. Like the Bolsheviks, these experts saw Russia's problems and potential through the prism of Europe's experiences, and like the Bolsheviks they had enormous faith in the transformative power of scientific government and in the idea of progress.[155]

Indeed, as far as the field of Oriental studies is concerned, it is necessary to mention that, in the late Imperial scholarly community and in 1920s society, each period being characterised by its own peculiarities, there was a strong belief that this field was one of the key scholarly disciplines that dealt with vitally important questions faced by Russia at that time.[156] In 1925, one of the leading Orientologists in both the late Imperial and early Soviet periods, Barthold precisely characterised the views of the scholars of that time: 'The fulfilment by Russian people of their historic missions in the West and in the East is in close dependence on the condition of Russian scholarship.'[157] According to these scholars, the nationalities question was central for the Russia of both periods. Tackling this question would allow Russia to achieve cultural unification and solve many internal problems, as well as demonstrate its power and success in dealing with the West.[158]

Conclusion

Thus, analysing pre- and post-revolutionary Russia, we come to the conclusion that "operational autonomy" in its Western form was not that developed and sophisticated in Russia, especially in the Soviet Union after the end of the 1920s, but it existed nonetheless, with the disciplinary mechanisms of self-control and self-regulation being of a

[154] See Krementsov, *Stalinist Science*, 11; Beer, *Renovating Russia*, 3.
[155] Hirsch, *Empire of Nations*, 7.
[156] Tolz, "European," 54.
[157] Bartol'd, "Russkaia nauka," 534.
[158] See Tolz, *Russia's Own Orient*, 5–6; Tolz, "European," 54.

different kind.[159] Soviet scientists and scholars acted not only under the pressure of various discursive and ideological stipulations, imposed by the party and creatively developed by some of their ideologically driven colleagues, but also under the vigilant control of special institutional structures (from the party committees – *partkomy* – at workplaces to the monitoring by political security entities – *Cheka*, GPU, NKVD, KGB). However, in spite of all that, scientists and scholars also managed to play their own game. 'While it was considered important to protect oneself as much as possible against ideological attack from philosophers or professional competitors, it was also recognized that party approval did not in fact depend ultimately on ideological factors, but rather on the ability of scientists to play politics.'[160]

Irrespective of the issue of the level of "individual operational autonomy", Foucault is particularly interested in power relations and how they influence the development of knowledge. These power relations can be equally found at work in late Imperial and Soviet societies. The technicalities of power/knowledge operation, discourse, the relationships between the intellectual and state power, and resistance – all the components, in other words, of the Foucauldian power relations grid – can be seen easily in the Russian case.[161] It might be argued that, in terms of the initial state power vector towards society in general (top down), relations were brutal in comparison with Western cases, but in the field of the multi-branch relations between intellectuals and state power (bottom up), the situation was much more entangled and complex. Thus Russian/Soviet scientists and scholars pursued their own personal and professional goals albeit while placed under rigorous constraints, imposed initially mainly by force.[162]

Therefore, in the Russian case also, the issue of intellectuals and resistance makes integral and complete the Foucauldian interplay of power relations, consisting of such main components as individuals,

---

[159] See Vucinich, *Empire of Knowledge*, 123; Krementsov, *Stalinist Science*, 31–6; Beer, *Renovating Russia*, 207; Kotkin, *Magnetic Mountain*, 23.

[160] Stephen Fortescue, *The Communist Party and Soviet Science* (London: Macmillan, 1986): 18.

[161] See Foucault, *Power*, 113–14. See also Kotkin, *Magnetic Mountain*, 21–3.

[162] The relevant material on the interplay between Russian/Soviet scientists and state power can be found in such works as Krementsov, *Stalinist Science*; Tolz, *Russian Academicians*; Tolz, *Russia's Own Orient*; Kemper, "Red Orientalism"; Kotkin, *Magnetic Mountain*, 21–3.

institutions, discourses, knowledge and power. Pasquale Pasquino writes in his overview of Foucault's ideas: 'It is on the basis of his analysis of these pivotal points of our culture, and of the concrete historical forms which the relations between them have assumed – exercises of government which accompany the production of discourses of truth and are founded on forms of conduct of life – that Foucault's work must be assessed.'[163] And, thus, Foucault's work is also useful for this research since in late Imperial and early Soviet Russia 'no less than in modern France, the state understood that its power rested on the characteristics and behaviour of the people'.[164] Hence, following the thesis that intellectuals, especially scientists and scholars, are the most influential and relatively integral part of a nation, it becomes clear what a great role the politics of their everyday life plays in this sense.[165]

[163] Pasquino, "Michel Foucault," 46–7.
[164] Kotkin, *Magnetic Mountain*, 23.
[165] Ibid., 6–14, 21–3.

2 | *Organisational Set-Up of Late Imperial Russian Oriental Studies*

Introduction

By the late nineteenth/early twentieth century Russian Oriental studies had evolved into a rather developed multi-branched system for the production of scholarly knowledge on the Orient. It comprised manifold Orientological scholarly (research-oriented) and academic (teaching-oriented) institutions as well as related structures in the Russian military and diplomatic services, and even within the Russian Orthodox Church. All of them were deeply intertwined in terms of both administrative organisation and the content and forms of the activities they carried out.[1] The critical analysis of their organisational set-up and of the modality of their functioning during the late Imperial period offered in this chapter is based on recent English- and Russian-language scholarship, as well as upon the relevant primary sources – the works of the individuals in question and archival documents. It also engages with the continuing debate about Orientalism and Russia, the genesis of which was signified by the discussion between Nathaniel Knight, Adeeb Khalid and Maria Todorova in the pages of the journals *Slavic Review* and *Kritika: Explorations in Russian and Eurasian History* precisely at the turn of the century.[2] In addition to the in-depth study

---

[1] See Kemper, "Integrating," 2; Schimmelpenninck van der Oye, "Imperial Roots," 31–42; Adeeb Khalid, "Russian History and the Debate over Orientalism," *Kritika: Explorations in Russian and Eurasian History* 1/4 (2000): 691–9; Vasilii Bartol'd, "Istoriia izucheniia Vostoka v Evrope i Rossii," in *Sobranie sochinenii*, vol. 9 (Moscow: Nauka, 1977): 418–19; Bartol'd, "Russkaia nauka," 537–40.

[2] See Nathaniel Knight, "Grigor'ev in Orenburg, 1851–1862: Russian Orientalism in the Service of Empire?" *Slavic Review* 59/1 (2000): 74–100; Nathaniel Knight, "On Russian Orientalism: A Response to Adeeb Khalid," *Kritika: Explorations in Russian and Eurasian History* 1/4 (2000): 701–15; Khalid, "Russian History," 691–9; Maria Todorova, "Does Russian Orientalism Have a Russian Soul? A Contribution to the Debate between Nathaniel Knight and Adeeb Khalid," *Kritika: Explorations in Russian and Eurasian History* 1/4 (2000): 717–27.

of the institutional set-up, emphasis will be placed upon the modality of the involvement of Russian Oriental studies in state politics and upon the main concomitant discursive manifestations, mostly drawing on the example of Persian studies in late Imperial Russia. The critical analysis in this chapter, performed in the light of Foucault's previously analysed postulates, will contribute to answering my research questions by clarifying the following issues.

First, what were the institutional structures for the involvement of the different kinds of Orientologists working on Persia and engaged in the four main domains of Russian Orientological knowledge production, namely academic scholarship, the military, the diplomatic service and Orthodox missionary activities? Second, what was the nature of the connection between the political context of the time and the emergence and development of this set-up in Russia, and how was it influenced by political and economic factors of Russo-Persian relations? The study of this second issue will lead to one of the key findings of this research, namely the pivotal role of Persian studies in late Imperial Russian Orientology. Third, what was the modality and the extent of the involvement of various entities and their personnel in the production of knowledge and in the process of political decision-making, and how effectively did the state use the results of their activities? Fourth, what were the main discourses within each of the above-mentioned domains and how did they influence the activities and outputs of the entities in question? And, finally, what were the similarities and differences between these four domains of Russian Iranology of the period?

The chapter begins with a discussion of essential political and economic background of the period in question – the late nineteenth century till 1917 – which includes the developments of the Great Game and the subsequent events concerning the stepping-up and retention of Russian influence in Persia during the Constitutional Revolution of 1905–11 and World War I. Thereupon, late Imperial Russian Oriental studies, in particular Persian studies, will be studied in terms of its organisational set-up and its modality of functioning within four domains: academic scholarship, the military, the diplomatic service and the Church. The chapter will finish with a comprehensive conclusion, summarising the key findings with reference to the scholarly debate about Orientalism and Russia and answering the above-mentioned questions.

Political Context of Russo-Persian Relationships in the Late Nineteenth and Early Twentieth Century

In the second half of the nineteenth century the struggle for influence in the Near and Middle East between the European powers intensified dramatically. Having been defeated by Russia in the wars of 1804–13 and 1826–8, and due to further developments in Persian domestic political and economic life, by the end of the century Persia had ceased to be any military threat whatsoever to its big northern neighbour and had turned into an arena of diplomatic rivalry, mainly between Russia and Great Britain. This very rivalry, solidly based on a sense of superiority towards the object of contest, shaped the nature of Russo-Persian relations during the latter part of the nineteenth and the beginning of the twentieth century.[3]

A reconnaissance mission carried out by staff officers of the Caucasus military district in 1889 reported extremely low combat readiness of the Persian troops and suggested that military confrontation with Persia would only occur if the country was to be pulled into war by other states. Further intelligence, collected ten years later and transferred to the Russian General Staff, confirmed the previous conclusions and noted further weakened capacity of the Persian military. The only forecasted threats were a risk of insurgence and the danger of Persia changing its political course under foreign influence, as well as foreign states, such as Great Britain and Ottoman Turkey, which were regarded as potentially being able to launch hostile operations from Persian territory.[4] Thus, the best way to counteract any such threats was deemed to be expansion and a strengthening of the Russian presence in the country. Thereupon, given its geographical location, the immediate proximity to neighbouring British India and the Ottoman Empire, the potential as a new trade area as well as its military weakness, Persia became the 'centre of constant fierce economic and political contest between Russia and Great Britain'.[5]

---

[3] See Andreeva, *Russia and Iran*, 1–2, 5–6, 59; Khalid, "Russian History," 691–9; Liudmila Kulagina, *Rossiia i Iran (XIX – nachalo XX veka)* (Moscow: Izdatel'skii Dom 'Kliuch-S', 2010): 128.

[4] See Marshall, *Russian General Staff*, 108–9; Nugsar Ter-Oganov, "Persidskaia kazach'ia brigada: period transformatsii (1894–1903 gg.)," *Vostok. Afro-aziatskie obshchestva: istoriia i sovremennost'* 3 (2010): 69–70.

[5] See Ter-Oganov, "Brigada," 69–70; Kulagina, *Rossiia i Iran*, 128.

In 1897, the Russian War Minister, Kuropatkin, submitted to Nicholas II a secret note entitled 'About our tasks in Persia' where he pointed out that, strategically, Russia had no need to annex new territories in Persia and, consequently, was in a favourable position to use this as a bargaining chip in its Western diplomacy, namely demanding that other states also keep their hands off Persia.[6] The then architects of Russia's foreign policy in Iran – Finance Minister Witte and Kuropatkin – considered Persia to be of vital importance as a place where Russian political and economic influence would be exercised for the pursuit of Russian national interests and in order to prevent the use of its territory for possible hostile operations against Russia by other states.[7] At the same time, having to put up with the fact that their country had become a playground for foreign states, the Persian ruling establishment resorted to playing their own game, sometimes very successfully playing rival powers off against each other.[8]

Though during the first three-quarters of the nineteenth century Great Britain had been considerably ahead of the Russian Empire in the field of economic influence,[9] this lag began to rapidly contract in the 1870s. In 1873, following a personal invitation from Tsar Alexander II, Naser al-Din Shah Qajar visited Russia. The trip deeply impressed the Shah and laid the ground for the consequent political and economic rapprochement of the two countries.[10] However, the main fruit of the Shah's trips to Russia (a second one took place in 1878) was the establishment of a Cossack Brigade in Tehran in 1879, on his request.[11]

It goes without saying that by establishing the Cossack Brigade in Persia, Russia was after enhancing its own influence over the Shah,

---

[6] AVPRI, f. 'Persian Desk', d. 2308, l. 115ob. See Appendix (Kuropatkin).

[7] AV, f.155, op. 1, d. 152, (The Humble Report of Lieutenant-General Kuropatkin on his trip to Persia in 1895). See also Andreeva, *Russia and Iran*, 5–6; Kulagina, *Rossiia i Iran*, 129.

[8] See Andreeva, *Russia and Iran*, 1; Saleh Aliev, *Istoriia Irana. XX vek* (Moscow: IVRAN – Kraft+, 2004): 36; Kulagina, *Rossiia i Iran*, 128–9.

[9] See Ter-Oganov, "Brigada," 69–70; Andreeva, *Russia and Iran*, 5–6; Kulagina, *Rossiia i Iran*, 130; Aliev, *Istoriia Irana*, 44.

[10] See Aleksandr Shirokorad, *Persiia – Iran: Imperiia na Vostoke* (Moscow: Veche, 2010): 98.

[11] The Shah was deeply impressed by the combat skills and the discipline of the Cossack guard of honour that convoyed him during his stay in St Petersburg and in the Transcaspian Region (see Kulagina, *Rossiia i Iran*, 136).

the court and the country in general.[12] In 1900, the War Minister mentioned the Cossack Brigade separately as a factor that allowed Russia, to a great extent, to govern the developments in Tehran.[13] Kuropatkin's words explicitly indicate the impact of the Cossack Brigade and Colonel Kosagovskii's activities on Imperial Russia's foreign policy towards Persia.[14] Kosagovskii, guided by personal Orientological expertise and his perception of the promotion of Russian national interests, succeeded in occupying an influential place in the Persian political establishment and, in fact, turned the Cossack Brigade into a powerful tool of Russian political influence in Persia as well as an abundant source of first-hand Orientological information.

Furthermore, along with its practical and potential influence on the ruling establishment and local political events, the presence and activities of such a unit in Persia created remarkable opportunities for gathering all kinds of information about the country – military, political, economic, social, geographic, ethnographic, historic, cultural, etc.; in other words, it assisted the production of scholarly knowledge. When recruiting officers to serve in the Brigade, the Russian General Staff, besides requiring experience of serving in the Caucasus or Central Asia, expected knowledge of Persian, French and another European language.[15] The Russian officers of the Persian Cossack Brigade became a powerful source of information for studying the country, especially after Colonel Kosagovskii became Chief-Commander in 1894, since he extended the activities related to gathering of such information to an unprecedentedly grand scale.[16]

The above-mentioned activities owed their success to the 1860s–1870s – the crucial period when underlying liberal reforms took place in practically all spheres of Russian society. The social, political and economic set-up of the whole Empire underwent serious modifications: the abolition of serfdom, the establishment of locally elected self-governments (*zemstva*), liberalisation of laws, court reform,

---

[12] RGVIA, f. 446, op. 1, d. 47, l. 27–30 (War Ministry correspondence with the MID).

[13] AVPRI, f. 144 'Persian Desk', d. 2308, l. 117.

[14] See Appendix (Kosagovskii).

[15] RGVIA, f.400 (Asian Section of the General Staff), op. 1, d. 3522 (Correspondence of the Head of the General Staff, 1907), l. 50–2.

[16] See Mikhail Baskhanov, *Russkie voennye vostokovedy* (Moscow: Vostochnaia literatura RAN, 2005): 126–7; Ter-Oganov, "Brigada," 69–79.

the considerable easing of political censorship and education reforms. This turning point also embraced critical changes in the perception of the role of the military, the necessity of which had been stipulated by the bitter defeat of the Empire in the Crimean War of 1853–6.[17] The new approach propagated by Miliutin, who was in charge of the War Ministry in the period 1861–81, changed views on the place of scholarly and scientific knowledge within the army, in general, and became the rich soil which fostered the future rapid development of Russian military Oriental studies, in particular.[18]

Progress in the turf war with Britain was also achieved through the year-on-year increase in military presence, underpinned by growing economic and financial influence at the end of the nineteenth and the beginning of the twentieth century. Russian economic penetration gained particular significance in the framework of Kuropatkin's policy, proclaimed by him after his trip to Tehran in 1895 and aimed at 'inconspicuous eliminating of the British influence in Persia'.[19] During the period between 1895 and 1910, Russia invested almost twenty-one million roubles in the construction of roads in Persia, and this while there was a lack of funding in this area in Russia itself.[20] By 1907, Russian companies were also implementing various projects in the south of Persia, the traditional zone of the British influence. Such a massive political and economic penetration demanded a related quantity of specially trained experts and the accelerated development of pertinent knowledge, which led to a considerable spree in Russian Imperial Iranology, of all domains.

Russian political influence in Persia, provided by various means including military presence in the country and close ties with the Persian court, was increasing year on year. Trying to use this influence against Western powers, Russia took steps which adversely impacted the development of Persia. Fearing the much more economically and industrially developed Britain and Germany – they could have built railways much faster, which would have facilitated their take-over of the Persian market and created the risk of potentially quick

---

[17] See Larisa Zakharova, "Autocracy, Bureaucracy, and the Reforms of the 1860s in Russia," *Soviet Studies in History* 29 (1991): 6–33.
[18] See Appendix (Miliutin).
[19] AVPRI, f. 144, d. 2308, l. 116.
[20] Ibid., d. 4021, l. 230–5.

redeployment of their troops in the proximity of Russian borders –
since 1873 Russia had been hampering the construction of railways
in Persia by every means available. In 1887, under Russian diplomatic
pressure, the Persian government juridically committed to refrain from
constructing railways and granting relevant concessions. In 1890,
Russia and Britain officially signed an agreement regarding the non-
construction of railways in Persia, renewed in 1900 for another ten
years.[21]

The Anglo-Russian convention of 1907 put an end to "free trade
competition" between the two powers and divided Persia into three
zones of influence (British, neutral, Russian). It can be argued that
the agreement benefited both sides. Nevertheless, in the short-term,
Russia benefited more than Britain, given her close geographical proximity. 'The treaty of partition [...] had turned the northern provinces
of Persia over to Russian rule, and during the pre-war years they were
not far removed from the status of an internal colony of the Russian
Empire.'[22] Thus, the previous more aggressive policies gave way to a
peaceful but powerful and relentless penetration orchestrated by Witte,
then a member of the State Council, who had previously occupied the
posts of Minister of Finance and Prime Minister. Having become economically stronger and, which was more important, having gained a
much more favourable military position in the country, in 1913 Russia
decided to obtain the concession for the construction of railways, by
that very act opening a similar opportunity to Britain.[23] In addition
to the fact that the Russian zone of influence – especially after enhancing the military, political and administrative institutions following
the revolutionary unrest of the years 1905–11 – had become a virtual Russian colony, Russia was both Persia's most important creditor
and its largest trade partner. The Russian Loan and Discount Bank
would finance not only large-scale local projects but would also allo-
cate funds to the Shah's court without any specific assignment.[24]

---

[21] See Dietrich Geyer, *Russian Imperialism. The Interaction of Domestic and
Foreign Policy, 1860–1914* (Oxford: Berg, 1987): 334–5; Kulagina, *Rossiia
i Iran*, 132–6; Aliev, *Istoriia Irana*, 46. Aleksandr Shirokorad, *Rossiia-
Angliia: Neizvestnaia voina, 1857–1907* (Moscow: AST, 2003): 402.
[22] Geyer, *Russian Imperialism*, 333.
[23] See ibid., 333–5.
[24] See ibid., 336.

From the above description of Russia's policy towards Persia at the
turn of the century, it becomes clear that the main feature of Russo-
Persian relations in this period was massive Russian penetration into
Persia carried out by versatile means: economic, political and military, where Russian economic weakness and non-competitiveness
were supposed to be compensated by political influence and military
presence.[25] This in turn meant that there was a great need for well-
trained experts in order to staff the manifold entities representing
the Russian state in Persia. It was, however, only belatedly that the
Russian Imperial establishment started paying significant attention to
the vital importance of this factor.

Intensive debate on the issue happened in the aftermath of Russia's
defeat in the war with Japan in 1904–5. A prominent role in this debate
was played by Russian scholars such as academician Barthold, who
sharply criticised the state's inadequate attention to Oriental studies
and its attitude to "the Orient", in principle.[26] The general character
of Russian activities in Asia and the condition of Oriental studies at
the turn of the century could be illustrated, in particular, by the ideological underpinnings, based on moral claims of the Imperial Russian
"civilising policy" towards Persia, which implied a strong feeling of
superiority, emanating from the sense of belonging to European civilisation which was inherent to the Russian elite.[27]

This sense of a civilising mission corresponds to one of the main
features of that very Western Orientalism described in Edward Said's
celebrated book.[28] Although in his work Said did not engage with
Russian Orientalism, contenting himself with the study of mainly
British and French cases, and his whole theoretical premise implied a
certain unified hostility of the West towards the Orient, his arguments
are not irrelevant to the study of Russian colonial policies, especially
when it comes to the arrogant and even contemptuous attitude of the

---

[25] Nugzar Ter-Oganov, "Zhizn' i deiatel'nost' Konstantina Nikolaevicha
Smirnova," in *Zapiski vospitatelia persidskogo shaha*, ed. K. N. Smirnov (Tel-
Aviv: Irus, 2002): 6. See also Kulagina, *Rossiia i Iran*, 157; A. A. Vigasin and
A. N. Khokhlov, eds, *Istoriia otechestvennogo vostokovedeniia s serediny XIX
veka do 1917 goda* (Moscow: Institut vostokovedeniia RAN, 1997): 142.
[26] See Bartol'd, "Russkaia nauka," 541–5. See also Marshall, *Russian General
Staff*, 167–70.
[27] See Tolz, *Russia's Own Orient*, 29.
[28] See Khalid, "Russian History," 691–9.

majority of Russian Imperial military officers and diplomats towards Persia.[29] This is well documented by Elena Andreeva in her work *Russia and Iran in the Great Game: Travelogues and Orientalism*, where she analyses more than two hundred travelogues and reports by Russian military officers, diplomats and scholars who had dealings with Persia during the second half of the nineteenth and the early twentieth century.[30] It could also be illustrated by Russia's forty-year inhibition of the construction of railways in Persia, which has already been mentioned.

However, in the Russian case the sense of superiority towards the Orient seems also to have been aggravated by the sense of inferiority towards Europe – to which Russians had compared themselves since the eighteenth century. This general feature of Russian popular perception became apparent in their relationship with the East – where, and only where, Russians could feel fully fledged Europeans, as if supporting Dostoevskii's thesis that Russians were Europeans in Asia and Tatars in Europe.[31] The same thesis is supported by Andreeva's book, which names it 'the East-West syndrome'.[32] It is also reflected in 'A Stereotype, Wrapped in a Cliché, inside a Caricature: Russian Foreign Policy and Orientalism' by James Brown, who made a succinct attempt to trace 'the troubled relations' in this triangle – the West–Russia–the East – until nowadays.[33] However, the study of the Russian juxtaposition of the Self with the Occident and the Orient appeared most distinctively in articles by the main participants in the debate on Russian Orientalism: Knight and Todorova.

Knight argues that Said's civilisational dichotomy can scarcely be applicable to Russia's interaction with the Orient since there is

---

[29] See Evgenii Belozerskii, "Pis'ma iz Persii ot Baku do Ispagani, 1885–1886," *Sbornik geograficheskikh, topograficheskikh i statisticheskikh materialov po Azii 25* (1887): 1–108. See also Zhukovskii's criticism of such attitudes (AV, f. 117, op. 1, d. 24, l. 1–19).

[30] See Andreeva, *Russia and Iran*, 78, 86, 92, 104, 109.

[31] See Fedor Dostoevskii, *Dnevnik pisatelia, 1881*, http://az.lib.ru/d/dostoewskij_f_m/text_0530.shtml (accessed on 21 August 2012).

[32] See Andreeva, *Russia and Iran*, xii, 3.

[33] James Brown, "A Stereotype, Wrapped in a Cliché, inside a Caricature: Russian Foreign Policy and Orientalism," *Politics* 30/3 (2010): 155–6. The tendency towards this kind of juxtaposing by the scholars and practitioners of Russian Oriental studies is also mentioned in Tolz, *Russia's Own Orient* (for example, p. 30).

'the awkward triptych in the Russian case: the west, Russia, the east'. He puts forward a thesis about the simultaneous existence of 'Occidentalist and Orientalist tropes' that makes Russia stand out of the row of Western imperialist powers. Drawing on Grigor'ev's example, Knight contrasts his acceptance of the Orientals' ability to develop and progress against Said's Orientalism, which reckons them 'utterly incapable of positive change either as individual or as part of a nation'.[34] This belief in the historic opportunity to transform Orientals and to integrate them into Russian civilisation, *ipso facto* enhancing it and making up for the sense of inferiority and backwardness towards the West, shaped a significant part of internal Russian nationalist discourses of the late nineteenth and the early twentieth century.[35]

Thus, contrary to Said's dichotomy, Knight assumes a much more entangled set of power relations in the Russian case, which is supported by Todorova, emphasising the determinative role of cultural context in the debate on Orientalism.[36] However, Khalid, strongly warning against creating too much sophistication about Russian Orientalism, champions a thesis that such an approach can result in the development of a new variety of Orientalism, aiming at alienating Russia and emphasising its Otherness, like the West alienates the Orient, according to Said. Khalid argues that in imperialist Russia the state of affairs in dealing with the Orient was quite similar to that in the main European powers of the time.[37] Undoubtedly, there are more underlying similarities than differences between Russian Orientalism and that in France and Britain. By and large, the main task of the Orientological apparatus in Russia was to technically facilitate the dealings of its imperialist government with the Orient through their knowledge of its languages and local attitude of mind; however, on an individual level many of them would envisage different and more far-reaching aims and would try to find more space for their operational autonomy, and this will be dealt with further in the following chapters. Therefore, Khalid's simplification seems unjustified in

---

[34] Knight, "Response to Khalid," 708. See also Knight, "Grigor'ev," 77; Appendix (Grigor'ev).
[35] See Knight, "Grigor'ev," 81.
[36] See Todorova, "Russian Soul," 724.
[37] See Khalid, "Russian History," 691–9, 696.

overlooking the influence of various internal Russian discourses on the Russian local Orientalist content.

The journal article format may not have allowed Knight and Todorova to go into much detail in identifying and studying these discourses; however, the influence of various internal Russian discourses has been studied by another researcher in the format of a book. Vera Tolz's *Russia's Own Orient* tackled their impact on one particular group of Russian Orientologists: members of the Academy of Sciences from St Petersburg. One of Tolz's main arguments is the great nationalist impact of the scholars of Baron Rosen's school on late Imperial and early Soviet Orientology; they propagated Russia's better understanding of the East and, hence, its better efficiency – in comparison with West European countries – in the civilising mission, which consisted, according to them, in the Orient's ultimate integration into Russian culture.[38] The same notion allowed Knight to deduce the existence of a contemporary discourse defining Russia as a 'bearer of enlightenment'. He wrote in his response to Khalid: 'Not only would Russia bring order and civilisation to the peoples of the East, nationalists argued, it would do a better job of this than England, France and the other colonial powers.'[39]

The same is evident in the words of the rector of St Petersburg University, who wrote to the Russian Minister of Education on 19 April 1888:

Our enlightenment mission in the Orient, political consolidation of Russian might and influence in all parts of Asia cannot be put into effect unless we actively prepare for it, unless along with military measures we train people, possessing both the knowledge of regions, of the way of life and spirituality of their inhabitants as well as of the language of the latter. Only by means of possessing a cohort of Asian languages experts will we be in position to study and assess Asian affairs with our own eyes, not with those of others, and we will have our own pioneers of the Russian influence in the Orient who, collecting a variety of first-hand intelligence, will provide a solid base for state considerations on where and how to act in future.[40]

---

[38] See Tolz, *Russia's Own Orient*, 3–5.
[39] Knight, "Response to Khalid," 706.
[40] The Letter of the Rector of the St Petersburg University M. Vladislavlev to the Minister of Education in *Materialy dlia istorii Facul'teta Vostochnykh Iazykov*, vol. 2 (St Petersburg: Tipografiia A.A. Stasiulevicha, 1905): 185.

Besides a belief in Russia's superior right to civilise non-European people and the statement of its ongoing competition with European powers in this process, this letter, requiring tangible state support in this respect, also well illustrates the scholars' attempts at promoting their own scholarly institutions while using current discursive developments within the context of the interaction with state power that could be found in Foucault's works.[41]

In the Russian imperialist context, Said's Orientalism applies more straightforwardly to those domains which were directly linked to state power, namely the military, diplomacy and the Orthodox church. Whereas, when it comes to Russian scholars, the question becomes much more entangled and multifaceted because of their greater susceptibility to domestic intellectual discourses on Eurasianism and Slavophilism, as well as the fact that Russian Oriental studies were subject to the profound influence of German Orientology, Germany having only belatedly engaged in colonial adventures overseas.[42] As Tolz fairly mentions, Russian Orientologists even argued that 'the German Orientological scholarship model could serve Russia better' than the British model of practice-led Orientology.[43] Thus, Said's Orientalism seems to be merely a particular, rather limited case of something much vaster which did not necessarily imply the dichotomy of subjugation and submission but rather could be defined as something where the interplay of power relations, knowledge and discourses provides the main inherent components. In this respect, Knight's opinion seems quite justified when he argues: 'One must be careful to distinguish

[41] The Foucauldian capability of "civilian" scholars, using capacities emanating from the state, to benefit from state interests by means of creating discourses, necessary for pursuing their own interests, often aimed at the institutional advancement of their scholarly field, was also studied in Krementsov's work, though mostly for the early Soviet period. See Mills, *Michel Foucault*, 33, 58; Krementsov, *Stalinist Science*, 4–5, 29–30. See also Chapter 1, 'The Foucauldian Discourse' and 'Foucauldian Power/Knowledge' regarding the fact that individuals tend to use the capabilities they are endowed with by power for pursuing their own interests.

[42] See Schimmelpenninck van der Oye, *Russian Orientalism*, 8. During the second half of the nineteenth century, most of Russia's scholars of the field were of German origin and extensively drew on German-language works. Even the first textbook of Persian grammar, *Persische Grammatik mit Literatur, Chrestomathie und Glossar*, was written in German by Karl Salemann and Valentin Zhukovskii in 1889.

[43] Tolz, *Russia's Own Orient*, 84.

Said's model of Orientalism as discourse from the views of Michel Foucault that Said drew upon.'[44]

Russian Oriental Studies Academic Scholarship in the Late Nineteenth and Early Twentieth Century

Throughout the nineteenth century Russian Oriental studies scholarship was greatly influenced by the foreign policies of the Russian Empire, which resulted in gradually developing, self-reliant utilitarian military and diplomatic domains. However, academic Oriental studies kept constituting its basis and simultaneously living on their account[45] to a great extent. Organised teaching of Oriental languages at the higher educational level began in Russia in 1804 when the first joint charter of Russian universities was adopted. Chairs of Oriental languages (mainly Persian, Arabic and Tatar) were established in the universities of Moscow, Kazan' and Kharkov.[46] At the time, the term Tatar designated various Turkish dialects, mainly Azeri, as spoken throughout Northern Persia.[47] In 1816, due to the efforts of the President of the Russian Academy of Sciences, Sergei Uvarov, the teaching of Persian and Arabic was established in St Petersburg. His words illustrate the attitude of the then enlightened circles towards Persian culture, comparing Persian poetry and people to 'the French of Asia',[48] which seems also to be a sign of that very romanticised

---

[44] Knight, "Grigor'ev," 99.

[45] Russian Oriental studies scholars and scholarly institutions greatly benefited from the primary area-study information and manuscripts Russian military officers and diplomats (voluntarily and/or to order) regularly brought from their mission-trips to the Orient. See Schimmelpenninck van der Oye, "Imperial Roots," 37; Denis V. Volkov, "Persian Studies and the Military in Late Imperial Russia: State Power in the Service of Knowledge?" *Iranian Studies* 47/6 (2014): 915–32. See also Chapter 4 on Zhukovskii's scholarly intelligence networks.

[46] See Vasilii Bartol'd, "Obzor deiatel'nosti fakul'teta vostochnykh iazykov," in *Sobranie sochinenii*, vol. 9 (Moscow: Nauka, 1977): 42–3; Richard N. Frye, "Oriental Studies in Russia," in *Russia and Asia: Essays on the Influence of Russia on the Asian Peoples*, ed. Wayne S. Vucinich (Stanford, CA: Hoover Institution Press, 1972): 38–9.

[47] See Vigasin and Khokhlov, *Istoriia*, 126.

[48] Bartol'd, "Obzor," 54. See also Schimmelpenninck van der Oye, *Russian Orientalism*, 168; Liudmila Kulagina, ed., *Iranistika v Rossii i iranisty* (Moscow: Institut vostokovedeniia RAN, 2001): 23.

perception of the Orient inherent to European Orientalism but with a Russian tinge of the then elite's sympathy towards all things French.[49] It also supports Knight's above-mentioned thesis on the existence of the 'Russian triptych'. Needless to say, the first university teachers of Oriental languages in Russia were from France, two disciples of Sylvestre de Sacy, 'the father of all Orientologists',[50] the most famous scholar of Persian studies of the time.

In general, the process of shaping Russian Oriental studies was taking place under the significant influence of European Oriental studies (the French and German schools), which was already rather developed by that time.[51] Moreover, as the existing literature on the issue and the historical context demonstrate, it was initiated and carried out by state power, which was pursuing its own agenda in the practical field of foreign policy and in discursive manifestations concerning catching up with the West. Right in the first half of the nineteenth century Russia witnessed the exhilaration of its foreign policy in the East, especially in the Muslim East. It also had to compete with European powers not only in terms of the organisation of scientific and scholarly knowledge but also in the field of measuring strength of influence in the East.[52]

This situation brought Russia's state closer to further understanding of the practical applicability of Oriental studies for state benefit, which resulted in the full-scale organisational reform of Russian Oriental studies in 1854 that saw the issuance of the decree on the establishment of the Faculty of Oriental Languages at St Petersburg University.[53] The motion also stipulated the closure of Oriental studies chairs in Kazan', Odessa and Kharkov,[54] reportedly because of the poor quality of training they had been offering. Indeed, the development of Russian Oriental studies in the first half of the nineteenth

---

[49] See Edward Said, *Orientalism* (London: Routledge & Kegan Paul, 1978), 1–9, 14–123, 222–3; Bartol'd, "Russkaia nauka," 541.

[50] Schimmelpenninck van der Oye, *Russian Orientalism*, 164. Later Demange and Charmoi were employed by the Russian MID to kick off the Persian courses in the Educational Section just established in 1823 (see Vasilii V. Bartol'd, "Proekty spetsial'nykh shkol: Vostokovedenie v S.-Peterburge," in *Sobranie sochinenii*, vol. 9 (Moscow: Nauka, 1977): 57).

[51] See Tolz, *Russia's Own Orient*, 83, 84; Bartol'd, "Russkaia nauka," 537–40; Vigasin and Khokhlov, *Istoriia*, 4.

[52] See Bartol'd, "Russkaia nauka," 535–40.

[53] AV, f. 17, op. 1, d. 183, l. 11ob.

[54] See Bartol'd, "Obzor," 103.

century could be characterised by an extensive or quantitative mode of development. Notwithstanding the considerable number of Oriental studies chairs in various cities, there was no unified curriculum that would be accepted by all interested state institutions and the crisis in Russian Oriental studies in the second quarter of the nineteenth century was explained, first of all, by the 'implicitness of goals and the trends of the further development of universities' Orientology'.[55]

Within the period 1845–50 this state of affairs was frequently pointed out in his reports to Russia's Minister of Education by the privy councillor Count Mikhail Musin-Pushkin, who was appointed the warden of St Petersburg and Kazan educational districts in 1845. He criticised the then organisation of Oriental studies training in Russian universities and persistently proposed reforms to its organisational set-up, which were to add up mainly to the concentration of the all-Russia higher educational Orientology within only one university, however at a separate faculty with a curriculum that conformed to the needs of state entities engaged in dealing with the Orient.[56]

The above-mentioned goals and awareness of the factors which had caused the crisis in Russian Oriental studies training helped to make crucial emphases while implementing the new project.[57] All financial, administrative and tangible facilities from other cities were handed over to the new faculty. As a result, the best of the Russian Oriental studies community were concentrated in St Petersburg and most of them, in one way or another, dealt with Persian studies which, in turn, occupied if not the main, then at least a very significant space in the curriculum.[58] The first Dean of the newly established Faculty of Oriental Languages of St Petersburg University was Aleksandr Kasimovich Kazem-Bek (1802–70), professor of Persian, who would be at its head during two periods: 1855–8 and 1866–70.

---

[55] Andrei Kononov, *Vostokovedenie v Leningradskom Universitete* (Leningrad: Izdatel'stvo Leningradskogo Universiteta, 1960): 9, 11.

[56] See the reports of Musin-Pushkin to the Minister of Education in *Materialy dlia istorii Facul'teta Vostochnykh Iazykov*, vol. 1 (St Petersburg: Tipografiia A.A. Stasiulevicha, 1905): 5–7. See also Bartol'd, "Obzor," 86; Vigasin and Khokhlov, *Istoriia*, 5.

[57] See Bartol'd, "Obzor," 109–11.

[58] See Schimmelpenninck van der Oye, *Russian Orientalism*, 169; Kononov, *Vostokovedenie*, 11; Kulagina, *Iranistika*, 25–6.

Kazem-Bek was born in Persian Azerbaijan to the family of a Muslim cleric who later moved to Astrakhan' (Southern Russia) to run a mosque. In adolescence, under the influence of Irish missionaries, Aleksandr converted to Christianity and became interested in philosophy and history. In addition to his native Persian and Azeri, he mastered Russian, Arabic and the main European languages. He authored works on the Persian, Arabic and Turkish languages, the history of Persia, Islam and Babism, and was an associated member of the Russian Academy of Sciences and a member of the Royal Asiatic Society of Great Britain. Being an active advocate of the centralisation of Russian Oriental studies and of the practical emphasis in training, from the very establishment of the faculty he announced the strong orientation at practical training of specialists for state entities.[59] In his letter to the rector of the university he wrote: 'the purpose of our Faculty is purely practical, directly applicable to use, namely – the preparation of young people for service in the Ministry for Foreign Affairs, the military and others ... Scholarly purpose should interest our Faculty to the extent it is necessary for the preparation of Asian languages teachers'.[60] However, Kazem-Bek's perception of what should be taught and how encountered strong opposition among the faculty scholarly community, which led to his replacement three years later by an individual orientated towards the enhancement of scholarly components in teaching.[61]

If we compare the curricula of 1854, 1863, 1884 and 1913[62] it is clear that an academic trend steadily increased throughout the period and, by the early twentieth century, the faculty had become a full-scale academic division with an emphasis on ancient and medieval Oriental studies, lacking attention to the present, which in effect corresponded to the perceptions of the main scholars of Oriental studies about the faculty activities (Rosen, Zhukovskii, Barthold, Salemann and others).[63]

---

[59] See Bartol'd, "Istoriia izucheniia Vostoka," 467.

[60] The letter of the Dean of the Faculty of Oriental Languages in *Materialy dlia istorii Facul'teta Vostochnykh Iazykov*, vol. 1 (St Petersburg: Tipografiia A.A. Stasiulevicha, 1905): 392.

[61] See Vigasin and Khokhlov, *Istoriia*, 9–10.

[62] In 1863 and 1884 new University Charters were adopted which introduced changes into the faculty curriculum. In 1913 new 'Rules, programs and examination requirements of the testing commission' were elaborated by the faculty itself.

[63] Tolz, *Russia's Own Orient*, 73–9; Appendix (Zhukovskii). See also Kulagina, *Iranistika*, 45; Kononov, *Vostokovedenie*, 18–22.

However, contrary to Khalid's and in support of Knight's and Tolz's argument on the existence of greater sophistication and diversity in opinions among Russian academic Orientologists, it is pertinent to mention that it was happening during the period when the Educational Section of Oriental Languages and the Officers' Courses of Oriental Languages under the MID had gained enough productive strength and training quality mainly on account of the active efforts of the above-mentioned scholars.[64]

One of the important features of the scholarly orientation of the faculty was its immensely close cooperation with the Asiatic Museum, another crucial scholarly institution in the Russian Oriental studies organisational set-up. Organised on the basis of Peter the Great's *Kunstkamera*, since the early nineteenth century this institution had been the main place for storing, processing, codifying and studying manuscripts, books and other materials written in Oriental languages.[65] Taking into consideration that at its early stages Russian Oriental studies paid most attention to studying written primary sources,[66] it is possible to envisage what enormous importance this institution had for Orientology in the country.

In support of the thesis on the underlying role of Persian studies in Russian Orientology as a whole at the time, it is also noteworthy that the Asiatic Museum was, for the major part of its history, headed by eminent scholars of Persian studies: academicians Boris Dorn (1842–81) and Karl Salemann (1890–1916), who also taught at the Faculty of Oriental Languages.[67] In general, it was typical of the Russian Oriental studies community that the same scholars acted and even headed chairs in various Oriental studies institutions at the same time. The convergence of the faculty and the Asiatic Museum under the auspices of the Academy of Sciences was so organic and productive that it formed an integral centre of Oriental studies, appraised by the Permanent

---

[64] AV, f. 17, op. 1, d. 184, l. 76–77ob.

[65] See Vigasin and Khokhlov, *Istoriia*, 19.

[66] See Kononov, *Vostokovedenie*, 22, 23; Kulagina, *Iranistika*, 30, 31, 45; Ashot Baziiants, "Iz istorii Sovetskogo vostokovedeniia v 1917–1922 gg.," in *Stanovlenie Sovetskogo vostokovedeniia*, ed. Ashot Baziiants (Moscow: Nauka, 1983): 42.

[67] Boris Anreevich (Iogann Albrekht Berngard) Dorn (1805–81), Member of the Russian Academy of Sciences, Orientologist and pioneer of the teaching of Dari in Russia; Karl Germanovich Salemann (1850–1916), Member of the Russian Academy of Sciences, philologist-Iranist.

Secretary of the Academy, Sergei Ol'denburg, as: 'the first place in the history of Russian Oriental studies, beyond debate, belongs to the Faculty along with the Academy of Sciences'.[68]

In addition to that and, presumably, less important in scholarly terms, Moscow's Oriental studies school was represented by Moscow State University and the Lazarev Institute of Oriental Languages, funded by a wealthy Armenian family of Persian origin and preparing practitioners, mainly, for Russian private business in Trans-Caucasia and the Middle East. The activities of these institutions intensified in the late nineteenth and the early twentieth century, even resulting in preparing such scholars of Persian studies as Fedor Korsh (1843–1915), Vsevolod Miller (1848–1913), Agafangel Krymskii (1871–1942), Minorsky and others. Thereby, the main Moscow centre of Oriental, and in particular Persian, studies was the Lazarev Institute.[69] It gradually gained a tinge of a contrast to St Petersburg Faculty – the training emphasis in the institute was on utilitarian aspects in view of the fact that graduates could be used by private entities or by organisations of state power such as the MID or others.[70]

Another form of scholarly contribution to Russian Oriental studies was made by various scholarly public societies. The underlying feature of these scholarly societies consisted in the consolidation of interests, efforts and potentials of people, representing completely different professional domains, in the course of the attainment and development of knowledge, albeit with final outcomes applicable to their own professional needs. All representatives used their membership of these societies for championing and promoting their own professional interests, which would result, mainly, in the production and development of

---

[68] Sergei Ol'denburg, "Pamiati V. P. Vasil'eva i o ego trudakh po buddizmu," *Izvestiia Rossiiskoi Akademii Nauk* (1918): 535.

[69] See Kulagina, *Iranistika*, 28, 29, 45. The Lazarev Institute was established in 1815 with the private financial means of the Armenian family Lazarev (Lazarian), who originated from the area Julfa, the Armenian settlement in Esfahan. Initially an ordinary secondary school for poor Armenian children with training in Persian and Arabic as its minor activities, by the middle of the nineteenth century it turned into a full-scale educational institute and one of the main centres of Russian Oriental studies. In 1892 Moscow University Professor Korsh was appointed Persian Linguistics Chair and in 1897 another Moscow University Professor-Iranist, Miller, was appointed Director of Lazarev Institute (see Vigasin and Khokhlov, *Istoriia*, 27–35).

[70] See Kulagina, *Iranistika*, 104.

scholarly knowledge. However, in the field of foreign policy these groups and their activities were rather homogeneous in the context of being an integral part of discursive manifestations existing at that time in Russia. Their efforts were focused on the promotion of *Russkoe delo* (the Russian Cause), which, in fact, contained two main discursive components: the "civilising influence" exerted on Orientals by Russia as part of European culture, and the protection of all modes of Russian presence in the Orient in the context of Russian competition with the main European powers. This statement of purpose is discernible in almost all programmes of Oriental studies at scholarly institutions and societies, and in the views of diplomats, military officers and other Orientologists-practitioners, and was mentioned in the books and correspondence of the time as well as in the contemporary literature on the issue.[71]

For instance, IRGO, established in 1845, set 'the study of Russia and neighbouring countries for pursuing the interests of Russia' as its main goal and since the middle of the nineteenth century it had concentrated its main attention on Central Asia. The same factor helped its founders to obtain His Majesty's permission for their activities (expeditions, missions, trips, etc.) within the shortest time.[72] Being heavily dependent on the current political agenda, the society organised or participated in the organisation of multiple expeditions to Central Asia, Iran and Afghanistan with the aim of gathering geographic, ethnographic and other country-study material. For example, the society took an active part in organising the expedition of Nikolai Khanykov, who was an employee of the Persian Desk of the Russian MID, to Persia.[73] The society was funded from private sources, as well as through special financial grants from the Asian Department of the MID and the Asian

---

[71] See the correspondence between the Head of the Asian Department of the MID, subsequently the Russian Minister to Persia, Hartwig, and Staff-Captain Smirnov, the tutor of the Persian Crown Prince Ahmad-Mirza (GNCM, f. 39, d. 78, 1–4ob). See also Nugzar Ter-Oganov, "Pis'mo N. G. Gartviga K. N. Smirnovu kak tsennyi istochnik dlia kharakterisiki anglo-russkikh otnoshenii v Irane v nachale XX veka," in *Iran: Istoriia, ekonomika, kul'tura*, ed. Nina Mamedova and Liudmila Kulagina (Moscow: Institut Vostokovedeniia RAN, 2009): 207–16; Andreeva, *Russia and Iran*; Brown, "A Stereotype," 149–59.
[72] See Vigasin and Khokhlov, *Istoriia*, 86, 88.
[73] AVPRI, f. 'Glavnyi arkhiv 1–9, 1858', d. 25, l. 220–5, in N. V. Khanykov, *Ekspeditsiia v Khorasan* (Moscow: Nauka, 1973): 190–3. See also Bartol'd, "Iran," 326.

Department of the War Ministry and, partly, directly from the Imperial
Court. From the outset, Russian senior military officers and diplomats
were among its founding members. In the late nineteenth and early
twentieth century scholars of Oriental studies took an active part in its
activities. Every expedition brought back materials that were valuable
to each interested part of the society.[74]

However, along with Russian scholars' zeal for being useful to their
state, which remained mainly unrequested on behalf of the late Imperial
government,[75] there also was debate on the dissociation of scholarly
knowledge from politics within Russian Orientological scholarship.[76]
In 1887, the Oriental Commission of Moscow's Archaeological Society
was established 'for the purpose of the cultural and historical study of
the ancient and modern Orient'. It was headed by Iranists Korsh, Miller
and Trutovskii until 1917.[77] According to their initial idea, this society
was supposed to host "pure scholars" and to pursue pure scholarly
goals alone.[78] Academician Barthold also advocated pure scholarship;
consequently, the journal *Mir Islama* (World of Islam), established on
his initiative in 1912, had a pure scholarly orientation. However, these
discursive developments at the institutional level had the least impact
on the overall involvement of Oriental studies in state power activities.

For instance, shortly after its establishment, the Commission
developed strong ties with state entities in Central Asia, which were at
the forefront of Russian Imperial policy at the time. The employees of
state institutions engaged in foreign policy, such as Minorsky (when
in Bukhara and after), would take an active part in its activities.
Barthold also participated widely in Russia's activities in the Orient
through his membership of manifold inter-institutional societies with
close links to state power, and contributed to the institutional development of Oriental studies in all domains. On top of that, his pure
scholarly journal *Mir Islama* did not last even a year; it was closed
by its funder – the Interior Ministry – for being useless for promoting
Russia's presence in her own Orient.[79]

---

[74] See Vigasin and Khokhlov, *Istoriia*, 85–90, 117.
[75] See Bartol'd, "Russkaia nauka," 534, 543–45. See also Tolz, *Russia's Own
Orient*, 73. See also Vigasin and Khokhlov, *Istoriia*, 261.
[76] See Tolz, *Russia's Own Orient*, 69–70.
[77] See Appendix (Trutovskii).
[78] See Vigasin and Khokhlov, *Istoriia*, 90–102.
[79] See Tolz, *Russia's Own Orient*, 74. See also Vigasin and Khokhlov,
Istoriia, 261–2.

Drawing on the role of scholarly societies, which, in fact, were the driving forces of practical Orientology, it is worth mentioning RKISVA, whose activities were particularly significant in this context. Its institutional status also indicates the similarity of goals and practices with West-European Orientalist institutions. Established in 1902 at the Thirteenth International Congress of Orientologists in Hamburg as the central organ of the International Association for the Study of Central and Eastern Asia, it unified almost all Russian state and pure scholarly entities and coordinated their work on Asia till 1918. This was a completely new type of institution for Russia in terms of its organisation, scale and the character of goals,[80] which clearly speaks for the presence of the institutional forms of Western Orientalism depicted by Said in the examples of such learned societies as the Royal Asiatic Society, the American Oriental Society and, particularly, La Société Asiatique with its 'embeddedness in the government'.[81]

The importance of this institution for the Russian government can be illustrated by the fact that it was under the direct patronage of Nicholas II himself and was affiliated with the MID. All interested state entities (the MID, the Interior Ministry, the War Ministry, the Ministry of Finance, the Ministry of People's Enlightenment, the Imperial Court) and scholarly institutions (the Academy of Sciences, St Petersburg University's Faculty of Oriental Languages, the Oriental Commission, the Russian Geographical Society, the Russian Archaeological Society) delegated their representatives to become members of the Committee. Among the governing board of the Committee were leading scholars of Persian studies such as Zhukovskii, Barthold and Salemann, and high-ranking military experts on Persia such as General-Major Vasil'ev, Head of the Asian Department of the General Staff.[82] The Charter of the Committee set up the strategic goals of spotting – through establishing necessary contacts and interacting with local institutions and individuals – what cultural heritage, what peoples, what areas were subject to first-hand study 'and, thereby, to be saved for scholarly study'.[83] This wording also provides partial support for Khalid's

---

[80] Vasilii Bartol'd, "Russkii Komitet dlia izucheniia Srednei i Vostochnoi Azii v istoricheskom, arkheologicheskom, lingvisticheskom i etnographicheskom otnosheniiakh, 1903–1909," in *Sobranie sochinenii*, vol. 9 (Moscow: Nauka, 1977): 503–9.

[81] Said, *Orientalism*, 43, 99–100, 165, 220, 275.

[82] See Vigasin and Khokhlov, *Istoriia*, 104.

[83] Izvestiia RKISVA, 1903, No. 1 in Vigasin and Khokhlov, *Istoriia*, 104.

argument on the existence of underlying commonalities between the
European and Russian cases of Orientalism, which could be seen in
the light of Said's depiction of the indisputable sense of superiority and
belief in the right of the European Orientalist scholarship to decide
what was worth being saved, studied, developed, etc.[84]

Another striking example of the political, as well as discursive, involvement in the promotion of *Russkoe delo* was *Obshestvo
Vostokovedeniia* (Society of Oriental Studies), established through
a private initiative in 1900. However, the new entity benefited from
support by the Ministry of Finance, the Ministry of the Interior and
the Ministry of War.[85] The society pursued the goal of providing for
the needs of Russian political, trade and cultural expansion in Oriental
countries. It was the only entity that dealt with preparing specialists
on the economy of Oriental countries (it also organised courses on
Oriental languages).[86] The existence of another discursive component related to catching up with the West, among other features of the
society, is evident in its strong feminist emancipation trends, which
were actively advocated by the first Russian female Orientologist,
Ol'ga Lebedeva.[87] A considerable number of women were among the
students on the society's courses – a phenomenon which has remained
uncommon after 1917 throughout the whole history of the Soviet
Union and modern Russia.

In 1907, the society was placed under the jurisdiction of the Ministry
of Trade and Industry and partly transformed into the Academy of
Practical Orientology. Pursuing the goal of training specialists for its
own bureaucratic entities among the Muslim population of Russia's
own Orient, in 1911 the Interior Ministry organised special courses
within the Academy.[88] However, the efforts aimed at creating a full-scale
Oriental studies centre for training specialists for state organisations
and private companies within this institution did not prove successful,
and the training quality was very low. This is also evident in the fact
that in 1916 the Academy's activities were intensively criticised by

---

[84] See Said, *Orientalism*, 7–8, 42, 249–50.
[85] AV, op. 2, d. 50, l. 1 (Shvedov's letter to Snesarev).
[86] AV, op. 2, d. 27, l. 1–2; d. 50, l-7 (Snesarev correspondence with Shvedov);
op. 1, d. 288 (Photo of the Board of Directors of the Society with Snesarev).
[87] See Appendix (Lebedeva).
[88] See Marshall, *Russian General Staff*, 165.

such leading Orientologists as Barthold, Zhukovskii, Marr, Ol'denburg and Fedor Sherbatskoi.[89] The fact that the further existence of the Academy was selfishly lobbied for by a group of individuals in the Interior Ministry who had close relations with the Royal Court also played a crucially negative role in the development of Zhukovskii's projects for reforming the practical Oriental studies training, which were supported by MID and the War Ministry.[90]

The training quality in the Academy reportedly remained poor until its closure in 1918. The reforms in Russian Oriental studies, initiated by scholars in alliance with the main state entities engaged in foreign policy, and stipulated in "Zapiska gruppy russkikh vostokovedov" (a report authored by leading Orientologists and presented in 1916 to the government and the Russian Parliament, the Duma) were never realised. The case of the Academy of Practical Orientology and the closely intertwined inter-institutional struggle between state power entities, scholarly institutions and individual interests, which are touched upon in more detail in the section 'Russian Diplomatic Service and Oriental Studies before 1917' later in this chapter, became another striking example of power relations interplay in Russia during the second decade of the twentieth century.

In view of the above it is possible to draw intermediate conclusions on the questions stipulated at the beginning of the chapter regarding the scholarly domain of late Imperial Russian Oriental studies. By 1917, academic Oriental studies had succeeded in developing a relatively comprehensive organisational establishment on the initial basis of European (mainly, French and German) Orientological knowledge. Having emerged as scholarly knowledge with mostly utilitarian application, in the second half of the nineteenth century Russian scholarly Oriental studies evolved into a multi-branch organisational set-up, comprising relevant scholarly and academic entities, societies and institutionalised practices.

The emergence and development of this set-up were heavily dependent on Russian state power institutions, which, in their turn, acted according to the imperatives of Russia's Eastern policy context. The thesis of the strong correlation with foreign policy is also

---

[89] See Vigasin and Khokhlov, *Istoriia*, 114.
[90] See the section 'Russian Diplomatic Service and Oriental Studies before 1917' later in the chapter.

supported by the revealed correspondence between the importance of the Persianate world (particularly, Persia, Afghanistan and Central Asia) for late Imperial Russia and the influential place which the relevant scholars and scholarly practices occupied within Russian Oriental studies. In addition to that, the above analysis of the organisational set-up leads us to conclude that there the Russian Oriental studies scholarly community was deeply interconnected with the state power institutions of late Imperial Russia through various joint institutions and the scholars engaged by the state entities of foreign affairs, albeit too early in this monograph to make conclusions about the influence of these scholars on late Imperial Russia's foreign policy.

It is evident that there were certain discursive practices at the institutional level which deeply influenced not just practical, but also academic Oriental studies. The following two discursive practices, which also seem to have informed Russia's Eastern foreign policy, were particularly prominent: the sense of a civilising mission, which for the scholars of Oriental studies consisted in confidence in their better capability for studying and preserving Oriental artefacts; and, second, the promotion of *Russkoe delo* – in other words, Russian interests – which also included the overcoming of general Russian backwardness vis-à-vis the West (in Oriental studies, in particular) and the spreading of Russian influence in alliance with other Imperial forces which, in this case, were represented by the entities of state power.[91] This is evident in the constant comparing of Russian Oriental studies with those in Europe in the scholarly literature of the early twentieth century (Barthold, Zhukovskii) and later on (Miller, Andrei Kononov, Nina Kuznetsova, Liudmila Kulagina).[92]

At this stage in the monograph, as mentioned earlier, it is not possible to draw conclusions on the individual impact of Russian Oriental studies scholars; however, regarding the issue of how efficiently the late Imperial Russian state used scholarly Oriental studies at an institutional level, it is possible to conclude that, in spite of the

---

[91] See Bartol'd, "Russkaia nauka," 534, 543–5; Tolz, *Russia's Own Orient*, 73.

[92] See Bartol'd, "Istoriia izucheniia Vostoka," 418; B. V. Miller, "Trudy russkikh uchionykh v oblasti iranskogo iazykoznaniia," *Uchionye zapiski MGU* 107/3/2 (1946): 71; Kononov, *Vostokovedenie*, 3–22; Vigasin and Khokhlov, *Istoriia*, 210, 261; Kulagina, "Iz istorii rossiiskoi iranistiki," in Liudmila Kulagina, ed., *Iranistika v Rossii i iranisty* (Moskva: Institut vostokovedeniia RAN, 2001): 33.

deep interconnectedness of scholarly institutions with those of state power, the scope of this utilisation was largely in the training of specialists who would directly work for state entities and in the area of the pertinent institutional construction and development. Naturally, influenced by the discourses spread among them, Russian scholars of Oriental studies, on their own behalf, were not content with the status which the state ascribed to them, and longed for a more active and broader involvement, bringing forward the European example.[93] This will be examined in subsequent chapters.

Russian Military Oriental Studies before 1917

The founding of the Nepliuevskii Military College, in 1825 in Orenburg was the first step undertaken by the Russian military in the direction of establishing training in Oriental languages for officers. The languages taught at the college were the same as in Russian universities, namely Tatar, Persian and Arabic. However, the number of graduates was small and the quality of training was reportedly poor. In the middle of the nineteenth century some eminent scholars, such as Professor Kazem-Bek, prepared a series of specified lectures to be read for the military for free. However, this did not improve the whole situation, which was characterised by the later reformist War Minister Miliutin in his memoirs as amateurish, as he recalled that his peer officer-students had been able to dedicate only their spare time to learning Oriental languages.[94]

The Russian General Staff Academy itself was only founded in 1832 and it took a very long time to establish Oriental studies there that would be tailored to military needs. The professionalisation of the army in general only started in the middle of the nineteenth century, and it was the changes in the General Staff services that had an enormous impact on Russian policy and practical activities in Asia in the late nineteenth and early twentieth century.[95] The General Staff officers working in the Asian Department were part of Russian society and

---

[93] See Bartol'd, "Russkaia nauka," 542–5; Tolz, *Russia's Own Orient*, 69–84; Schimmelpenninck van der Oye, *Russian Orientalism*, 174; Schimmelpenninck van der Oye, "Imperial Roots," 31–42.
[94] See Marshall, *Russian General Staff*, 28.
[95] See Baskhanov, *Russkie*, 126–7. See also Marshall, *Russian General Staff*, 5–7.

thus they, of course, were inevitably influenced by relevant discourses which were widespread in educated Russian circles in general, and in Russia's Oriental studies community in particular.[96]

However, the character of Russian involvement in Asia in the nineteenth and early twentieth century predetermined the substantial role which the Russian military played in the accumulation and development of Oriental studies. At the early stages of its development, Russian Oriental studies particularly needed primary material and in this sense the contribution of the military could scarcely be overestimated. Indeed, many primary source materials, such as manuscripts and artefacts, were gathered during expeditions, in military terms reconnaissance operations, which became routine work in the military domain from the 1860s. The tasks of imperialist expansion dictated the necessity of intensive activities in this field, and Oriental studies as a discipline, dealing with any information on the region of study, greatly benefited from the mode of these activities (collecting all available information), which had been stated as part of the Russian military intelligence doctrine since the 1860s.[97] Thus, we witness another component of power/ knowledge relations – the reciprocal, productive interaction between a state, chasing new sources of power and endowing its agents with capabilities, and knowledge itself, represented by its own practices and institutions, using these capabilities for its own benefit.

The multiple expeditions organised by the Asian Department of the General Staff and by the Turkestan Military Region, particularly to Persia and Afghanistan, made an enormous contribution to Oriental studies in addition to considerable numbers of other activities carried out by Russian military officers.[98] In 1901, a Russian officer, Boris Tageev, with an excellent command of Persian, undertook a covert expedition to Kabul and Mazar-e Sharif under the cover of a Tajik pilgrim. The expedition was sponsored by the Russian Imperial Geographical Society and Turkestan Military Region's intelligence

---

[96] See Tolz, *Russia's Own Orient*, 69–79; Marshall, *Russian General Staff*, 9–10.
[97] See David Schimmelpenninck van der Oye, "Reforming Military Intelligence," in *Reforming the Tsar's Army: Military Innovation in Imperial Russia from Peter the Great to the Revolution*, ed. David Schimmelpenninck van der Oye and Bruce W. Menning (Washington: Woodrow Wilson International Center for Scholars, 2004): 141–3.
[98] See Andreeva, *Russia and Iran*, 64–7; Vigasin and Khokhlov, *Istoriia*, 116, 134; Marshall, *Russian General Staff*, 9, 144–6.

bureau due to his previous close ties with both, which were developed during his service in Central Asia in the 1890s. Three years later a book summarising the substantial scholarly outcome of the expedition was published.[99]

It should be mentioned that it was in the 1860s–1870s when, along with considerable changes in the public life of Russia, the approach towards scholarly knowledge within the military began to change. The new approach, propagated by War Minister Miliutin, stipulated the future rapid development of Russian military Oriental studies. Miliutin argued that the study of Russia's Asian neighbours should be comprehensive (not limited to mere technical reconnaissance) with the descriptive component being complemented by analysis.[100] It was in Miliutin's time that a system of writing graduation papers, similar to preparing a thesis and passing a viva, was introduced for the officers of the Russian General Staff Academy, which later evolved also into the preparation of special reports as a result of the officers' one- to two-year fieldwork carried out in the country of study after graduation from the Academy.[101]

Furthermore, the development of Russia's foreign policy in the Middle East and the resulting sharp political confrontation with Great Britain dictated that serious efforts in this direction were made, given the increased need for well-trained officers with comprehensive knowledge of the region. In 1863, after the merging of the Department of the General Staff and the Depot of Military Topography into the Headquarters of the General Staff, the status of the Asian Section within the new structure became permanent.[102] However, the state bureaucratic mechanism of the Russian Empire slowly realised the vital and urgent importance of gaining further expertise on the Orient. Throughout the second half of the nineteenth century, war operations and military reconnaissance expeditions remained the main if not almost the only sources for obtaining information on Oriental countries. Analysing the Oriental studies of that time and acknowledging the direct beneficial correlation of activities, pursuing state interests

---

[99] See Appendix (Tageev).
[100] See Schimmelpenninck van der Oye, "Reforming Military Intelligence," 141–3; Marshall, *Russian General Staff*, 21–30.
[101] See Baskhanov, *Russkie*, 5–7; Marshall, *Russian General Staff*, 48.
[102] See Vigasin and Khokhlov, *Istoriia*, 139–41.

and institutionalised Oriental studies, Barthold wrote that the study of the Middle East had been possible very often only due to colonial wars.[103]

At the same time, these power relations could also be characterised by inter-institutional competition and even strife. The Imperial MID still kept the monopoly on dealing with the Orient on behalf of the state and resisted any suggestions for reform that would involve its own structures or would delegate activities to other state entities.[104] Several projects for the reorganisation of Oriental studies in Russia failed because they included proposals to change the status of the Educational Section within the MID. The War Ministry's suggestions for using diplomatic missions and consulates in Asian countries for enhancing military intelligence work suffered the same fate. Military officers working in Persia and Turkey needed cover and the most ingenuous form of cover was diplomatic status; however, the MID was extremely reluctant to provide posts in its missions and consulates to the military.[105]

However, officers working in Persia were among the first to conclude that for an efficient military intelligence and for later tactical work it was necessary to deploy military agents to the Russian consulates in border and coastal regions of Persia. The Chief-Commander of the Persian Cossack Brigade (1894–1902), Colonel Kosagovskii, during his tenure in Persia, repeatedly applied to his top brass in St Petersburg to obtain the replacement of at least one purely diplomatic employee per consulate with a dedicated military agent on the payroll of the War Ministry, a quest in which he was later also supported by some of his colleagues working on Mesopotamia and Turkey, but which evoked an abrupt and negative response from the MID and resulted in a bitter exchange between the two ministries.[106]

[103] See ibid., 152; Bartol'd, "Istoriia izucheniia Vostoka," 467; Marshall, *Russian General Staff*, 26.
[104] See Marshall, *Russian General Staff*, 16; Vigasin and Khokhlov, *Istoriia*, 146; Bartol'd, "Istoriia izucheniia Vostoka," 470–80.
[105] See Andrei Kononov, "Introduction," in Vasilii V. Bartol'd, *Sobranie sochinenii*, vol. 9 (Moscow: Nauka, 1977): 9; Marshall, *Russian General Staff*, 16, 124.
[106] RGVIA, f. 446, d. 45 (regarding the appointment of military agents). See Baskhanov, *Russkie*, 126–27; Marshall, *Russian General Staff*, 124.

2.1 Staff Captain Andrei Snesarev, at the graduation ceremony at the Officers' Courses of Oriental Languages, fourth from the left, behind the rest (1899).
Source: www.snesarev.ru

Throughout the nineteenth century the War Ministry was also completely dependent on the MID for the Oriental studies training of its officers. It was only in 1883 that the War Ministry succeeded in accomplishing what had been demanded by Miliutin: a dedicated course in Oriental languages aimed at officers only was inaugurated under the auspices of the Educational Section at the MID. The curriculum comprised the three main Oriental languages of the time: Persian, Turkish and Arabic. That was also characteristic of the section itself and the priorities that were being pursued by the Faculty of Oriental Languages of the University of St Petersburg and Lazarev's Institute of Oriental Languages in Moscow. It reflected the main trends within Russia's foreign policy of the second half of the nineteenth century: military confrontation with the Ottoman Empire and colonial competition with Britain in Asia.[107]

---

[107] Frye, "Oriental Studies in Russia," 43–4. See also Marshall, *Russian General Staff*, 30, 43–5; Vigasin and Khokhlov, *Istoriia*, 137–41.

Besides Oriental languages, students were taught Muslim and International Law, French and, after 1907, also English. In general, there was little difference in terms of the academic content of the dedicated officers' course in comparison with the curriculum of the civilian students because the officers' course had been designed by the same academics who taught Oriental studies at universities and academic institutes – which says much about the influence of scholarly institutions and practices, if not of scholars themselves, yet, on state power. In fact, the courses were even run by them. For instance, Zhukovskii, one of the main scholars in the field of Persian studies of the time and the Dean of the Faculty of Oriental Languages in St Petersburg, was also the director and lecturer of these courses.[108]

An illustrative example of the contribution of Russian military Oriental studies could be also found in the activities of another military scholar who was among the first graduates of the courses – Aleksandr Tumanskii (1861–1920), Rosen's disciple, a later General-Major and a prominent scholar in Persian, Turkish and Arabic studies and the main expert of his time on Babism. The future coryphaeus of Soviet Orientology Ignatii Krachkovskii mentioned him as 'an Orientologist by vocation, not by profession'.[109] In 1894 Tumanskii was sent on a reconnaissance mission from the southern Caspian coast through the entire Persian territory right up to the Persian Gulf. Besides the accomplishment of his main professional duties and gathering the necessary material, he obtained a number of precious documents and manuscripts on the Babi sect, copies of which he made available to his teachers – a contribution that was separately pointed out by Rosen.[110]

In 1908 and 1909 Tumanskii regularly visited Persia on missions, also using these trips for his scholarly activities. The fact that he actively participated in the activities of the Eastern section of the Russian Imperial Archaeological Society supports the thesis about the deep interconnectedness of all Russian Oriental studies institutions. Significantly contributing to the relevant knowledge production, he left multiple works on the history and economy of Persia and a series of works on Babism and translations of key Babi texts, including

---

[108] AV, op. 2, d. 22, l. 34–5 (Zhukovskii's correspondence with von Klemm on curriculum). See Bartol'd, "Istoriia izucheniia Vostoka," 472.

[109] See Appendix (Krachkovskii).

[110] ARAN(St.P.), f. 208, op. 3, d. 496, l. 62ob (Rosen's letter to Ol'denburg, 7 October 1893).

2.2 The twenty-fifth anniversary of the establishment of the Officers' Courses of Oriental Languages. Andrei Snesarev is third from the left in the second row from the back. His teacher, Professor Valentin Zhukovskii, is sitting in front of him (1908).
Source: www.snesarev.ru

"Ketab-e Aghdas". He also discovered and translated a tenth-century manuscript of the "Hodud-ol'-Alam", which, however, was only published as a result of Barthold's efforts in 1930 and in 1937 translated into English by Minorsky, then Professor of Persian studies at the University of London (SOAS) and Tumanskii's former colleague in the Russian diplomatic service (at one point Tumanskii served under diplomatic cover in Persia).[111] In 1911 Tumanskii was appointed head of the Tiflis Regional Training School of Oriental Languages.[112]

---

[111] RGVIA, f. 409, op. 1, d. 172812, Service Record 148–610, l. 1–23.
[112] Ibid., l. 20ob.

The Tiflis Regional Training School of Oriental Languages, in fact, personified the crucial changes in the system of military officers' Oriental studies training that took place in 1910–11 because of a last-minute rush for training military interpreters at a time of serious financial constraints. The debate on the preference for an academic or sheer utilitarian emphasis in Oriental studies within the War Ministry ended up in favour of the latter and resulted in the dismantling of the dedicated officers' course at the Educational Section of the MID in 1910.[113] The War Ministry established its own regional training schools affiliated with the Headquarters Staff of the Turkestan and Caucasus Military Regions, with centres of deployment in Tashkent and Tiflis. The training was changed to eight months of language training followed by two years of fieldwork.[114]

The Turkestan Military Region School, based in Tashkent, was much better prepared to cope with the new situation because its Oriental studies were established on the basis of Urdu courses in 1897, owing its existence to the personal efforts of Staff-Captain Ivan Iagello (1865–1942), who had graduated from the above-mentioned MID dedicated officers' courses three years after Tumanskii, in 1895. Having learned Persian and Arabic, Iagello was assigned to the Staff of the Turkestan Military Region, which sent him to France where he studied at Paris' renowned School of Living Oriental Languages, the famous *Langues O'*, learning Urdu. On his return to Turkestan, Iagello initiated the establishment of Urdu courses, which was followed by courses teaching Persian and Arabic, thus laying the ground for the setting up, in 1908, of a full-scale Officers' School of Oriental Languages in Tashkent where history, geography and Islamic law were also taught.[115]

It is worth mentioning that the nascent Oriental studies activities in Tashkent – and Iagello's scholarly work in particular[116] – were widely

---

[113] AV, f. 17, op. 1, d. 168, l. 1–3ob. (War Ministry correspondence with Zhukovskii).
[114] Ibid., 3ob. See also Z. P. Vashurina and A. I. Shishkanov, "Rodoslovmaia voennykh perevodchikov," *Voennoe Obozrenie Nezavisimoi Gazety*, 19 May 2000, http://nvo.ng.ru/notes/2000-05-19/8_interpreters.html (accessed 15 November 2011); Klub Voennogo Instituta Inostrannykh Iazykov www .clubvi.ru/news/2011/05/20/vash/ (accessed 15 November 2011).
[115] RGVIA, f. 400, op. 1 (Asian Section), d. 3522, l. 38–52 (Iagello's activities); op. 2, d. 23872, Service Record 313–964a, l. 3ob.–6.
[116] See Marshall, *Russian General Staff*, 169.

criticised by the St Petersburg scholarly community (of Persian studies) at the turn of the century. The scholars in the capital questioned the idea of establishing a military Oriental studies institution of higher education, as propagated in 1902 by Russian Academy of Sciences member Ol'denburg.[117] In contrast to him, some representatives of Persian and Central Asia studies, such as Barthold, were convinced that the establishment of an institution such as this, far from Russia's main academic centres and libraries, would not be efficient and could even harm Russian Oriental studies, wasting efforts and funds which could have been used more efficiently elsewhere. Speaking strongly for the thesis on institutional interplay, this also indicates further support for direct and strong dependency of all Russian Oriental studies on state power. The leading scholars' opinions and activities played their significant, albeit not decisive, role and deferred the implementation of the project. Finally, the issue was given up because of the lack of state funds – until the state bureaucrats learnt a lesson from the Russo-Japanese War and began gradually comprehending the harm of the dearth of Orientologists to *Russkoe delo*.[118]

After the Russo-Japanese War of 1904–5 military Oriental studies became part of the debate within the scholarly community and Russian society on the further development of Oriental studies, which took place on the pages of various periodicals affiliated with ministries, military regions, institutes and societies. So, the enhancement of the role of military Oriental studies in the discourse of *Russkoe delo* resulted in the desperate attempt to re-examine and re-structure its institutional set-up after the 1904–5 war.[119] Under the conditions of financial constraint and lack of time the choice was made in favour of waiving a rather wide and strong theoretical education for the sake of practical efficiency and an increase in the quantity of graduates. However, as history shows, this motion had advantages, as well. It laid the foundations of a new institutional form of Russian Oriental studies that was taken up and successfully developed later by the Bolsheviks,

---

[117] See Baskhanov, *Russkie*, 278. See also Marshall, *Russian General Staff*, 169–70.

[118] See Vasilii Bartol'd, "Po povodu proekta S. F. Ol'denburga," in *Sobranie sochinenii*, vol. 9 (Moscow: Nauka, 1977), 492.

[119] See Bartol'd, "Russkaia nauka," 543. See also Vigasin and Khokhlov, *Istoriia*, 73–4.

namely regional, or peripheral Orientology with specialised scholarly centres in the main cities of the Soviet republics.[120]

As mentioned above, having emerged in the first half of the nineteenth century as a narrowly profiled domain of utilitarian knowledge, by World War I Russian military Oriental studies had evolved into an organisationally structured, self-contained branch of scholarly and practical knowledge, making contributions to the development of adjacent fields of general scholarly knowledge. One of its underlying features was that military Oriental studies, being an intrinsic part of Russia's general Orientological knowledge, were developing hand in hand with the Asian policies of the Russian Empire.[121] This immense interconnection with the state's foreign policy preconditioned the fact that Persian studies occupied a prevailing position within Russian military Oriental studies in the late nineteenth and early twentieth century.

It is also clear that close institutional interconnectedness between the military, diplomatic and scholarly domains resulted in a very dynamic, interrelated development of both utilitarian and scholarly knowledge. As is clear from the above, senior military officers were members of various Orientological societies, using their activities and effecting scholarly outcomes, as well as prominent Russian scholars of Persian studies; for instance, Kazem-Bek, Rosen, Barthold, Zhukovskii and others had strong ties with the military and played major roles in the Oriental training of officers.[122] However, this close organisational interconnectedness also had its disadvantages because if there were disagreements in one area, they would then immediately affect others. The common cause would also considerably suffer from inter-organisational feuding and factions, as was shown above.[123]

At the same time, there were obvious, strong discursive components in the activities of institutions and individuals, which consisted of the dichotomy of promoting *Russkoe delo*, which implied protecting the expansionist goals of the Imperial state in the Orient against Western powers, concurrently with the civilising role of Russia in the Orient which was stipulated by the affiliation of Russia with the European

---

[120] See Chapter 3.

[121] See Andreeva, *Russia and Iran*, 67; Vigasin and Khokhlov, *Istoriia*, 136, 141; Baskhanov, *Russkie*, 5; Marshall, *Russian General Staff*, 2–4.

[122] See Bartol'd, "Istoriia izucheniia Vostoka," 446; Marshall, *Russian General Staff*, 24, 164–5, 168; Vigasin and Khokhlov, *Istoriia*, 128–9.

[123] See Marshall, *Russian General Staff*, 166.

civilisation.[124] However, when it comes to the entities of state power, particularly in the Russian military domain, whose vocation was to protect and promote Russia's state interests, manifestations of this kind should be regarded as naturally inherent and were much more pronounced than, for example, in the civil scholarly domain.

Thereupon, a lot of supporting evidence can be found in Kosagovskii's Persian diaries, where he presented as his task the need to make the indigenous 'semi-wild population' familiar with the Russian way of life or, upon the withholding of Russian officers and their units from taking part in the punitive actions of the "Asiatic" Persian government towards its people during bread riots, ipso facto stressing the "humane" and "truly civilised" character of the Russian mission.[125] Something similar could be also found in Staff-Captain Smirnov's reports on his activities in the Shah's Court and in his correspondence with the Russian Minister to Persia, Nikolai Hartwig.[126] The two above-mentioned discursive components also appear distinctly in the reports and travelogues of other Russian military officers, which were studied scrupulously in *Russia and Iran in the Great Game: Travelogues and Orientalism* by Elena Andreeva. Given the above in application particularly to the military domain, Khalid's argument on the universality of Said's model seems to be quite fair in the Russian case; however, Knight's warning against simplifications and his assumption of the existence of more sophistication turns out to also be justified since the Russian picture, in addition to the traits of Said's Orientalism, was diversified by Russia's own discourses on its place between the West and the Orient.

Considering the efficiency of the state's use of military Oriental studies, it is obvious from the above that, in general, at the turn of the century, lack of funding was one of the main constraints. Even the previously mentioned officers' courses under the auspices of the Foreign Ministry's Educational Section would not have been established if

---

[124] See Khalid, "Russian History," 691–9. See also Knight, "Response to Khalid," 701–15.

[125] RGVIA, f. 400, op. 4, d. 279, l. 9–10.

[126] GNCM, f. 39 (Smirnov's Private Collection), d. 11 (Diaries, 1907), l. 18, 21; d. 12 (Diaries, 1909), l. 43ob.-46; d. 13 (Diaries, 1910), l. 26ob.–27, 95–6, 142. GNCM, f. 39 'Smirnov', d. 78 (Hartwig's letter to Smirnov, dated 2 August 1909, with Smirnov's later remarks, dated 1933). See Appendix (Smirnov); also Ter-Oganov, "Pis'mo N. G. Gartviga," 207–16.

Russian academics had not offered to teach for free.[127] In spite of the understanding which resulted in the aftermath of the Russo-Japanese war and which can be formulated in the words of Count Vladimir Kokovtsov, the Russian Finance Minister of the time (1904–14), regarding the imbalance between the far-reaching foreign policy aims and the scant assets in hand, no efficient measures were taken.[128]

Thus, as Alex Marshall notices in his work *The Russian General Staff*: 'It was this sense of drift and Imperial overstretch which was to become the dominant concern during the final period of tsarist military involvement in Asia between 1895 and 1917, and which was to be the predominant theme and topic of criticism for [...] military orientalists.'[129] The Russian Empire simply set up goals in its foreign policies that greatly exceeded its abilities and, in spite of all enormous efforts undertaken by some bright minds, they were doomed to failure – mainly due to Russia's own economic backwardness. Furthermore, in spite of the fact that by the start of World War I Persia had already become one of the most heated areas of Russian confrontation with future war enemies, Russia did not succeed in properly arranging and using military Oriental studies in that period, and the institutional activities of this domain were significantly disorganised and had almost run dry by 1917.

Russian Diplomatic Service and Oriental Studies before 1917

The second half of the nineteenth century is the period which saw a significant build-up in Russia's foreign policy activities in Asia. After Prince Aleksandr Gorchakov's appointment to the post of Minister for Foreign Affairs (1856–82), the Ministry, like the whole of Russian society in the 1860s and 1870s, underwent a series of reforms. While Gorchakov was totally concentrated on Western affairs, Russian foreign policy in Asia was mainly determined by General Egor Kovalevskii, Head of the Asian Department of the Ministry, as well

---

[127] See Marshall, *Russian General Staff*, 29.

[128] AVPRI, f. 144 'Persidskii stol', f. 4028, l. 42. See also Aleksandr Popov, "Stranitsa iz istorii Russkoi politiki v Persii," *Mezhdunarodnaia zhizn'* 4–5 (1924): 154, as quoted in Ter-Oganov, "Zhizn'," 7.

[129] Marshall, *Russian General Staff*, 167.

as Deputy Head of the Imperial Geographical Society, and also an academician and a famous expert on the Orient.[130] Diplomatic rivalry with Great Britain became one of the central issues of Russian foreign policy. Due to its strategic location Persia played a key role in this rivalry. From the Russian perspective there was a risk of Britain being able to gain a dominant position in Persia and use this as a staging post for securing an exclusive position of power in Central Asia and in the Persian Gulf region.[131] For this reason Russia could not allow Britain to bring Persia under her full control. In addition, Persia was also vulnerable to potential political and military penetration on the part of the Ottomans, while Russian commercial interests were also on the rise in Persia.[132]

Given this, and having comprehended the importance of the power/ knowledge liaison, the MID took active measures aimed at gaining comprehensive knowledge about the region. The employed practices were similar to those used in two other domains – scholarly and military – that were enhanced by strong interconnectedness at institutional and individual levels. So, the second half of the nineteenth century witnessed multiple expeditions to Persia, which were organised by the Ministry in alliance with scholarly and military entities. Here, Khanykov's expedition, undertaken in 1858–9, is a particularly illustrative case in point.[133] Between 1854 and 1857, Khanykov served as Consul General in Tabriz before, in 1858, the Ministry charged him with heading an expedition that included several scholars and scientists. Having arrived at Mazandaran Province via the Caspian Sea, the party made its way to Tehran before heading eastward again to explore Khorasan, as well as Herat and Kandahar in Afghanistan, and then Tabas, Yazd, Kerman, Esfahan and finally returning home via Tehran. Besides achieving remarkable results in terms of military reconnaissance and the establishment of politically crucial contacts, Khanykov, who was also a full member of the Russian Imperial Geographical Society, with the help of the other scholars, brought

---

[130] See Vigasin and Khokhlov, *Istoriia*, 116, 136, 140. See also Kulagina, *Rossiia i Iran*, 128.

[131] See Kulagina, *Rossiia i Iran*, 129. See also Vigasin and Khokhlov, *Istoriia*, 140.

[132] See Kulagina, *Rossiia i Iran*, 130.

[133] See Kulagina, "Iz istorii," 31. See also Vigasin and Khokhlov, *Istoriia*, 117.

2.3 The Russian Legation in Tehran (1907).
Source: Korneli Kekelidze Georgian National Centre of Manuscripts

home unprecedentedly rich materials on the geography, ethnography, economy, history and culture of the visited regions.[134]

The Ministry succeeded in considerably increasing Russian influence by extending its institutional presence in Persia through opening new consulates. This went hand in hand with rapidly increasing trade and, as an effect of the latter, a significant growth of the Russian community in Persia. In addition to the Russian Legation in Tehran and the Consulate-General in Tabriz, in the 1880s and 1890s consulates were established in Esfahan, Mashhad, Ahvaz, Anzali and many other Persian cities and towns.[135]

---

[134] AVPRI, f. 'Glavnyi arkhiv', 1–9, 1858, d. 25, l. 220–5, in N. V. Khanykov, *Ekspeditsiia v Khorasan* (Moscow: Nauka, 1973): 190–3. See also Vigasin and Khokhlov, *Istoriia*, 116–18.

[135] See Father Superior Aleksandr Zarkeshev, *Russkaia Pravoslavnaia Tserkov' v Persii-Irane (1597–2001)* [The Russian Orthodox Church in Persia-Iran (1597–2001)] (St Petersburg: Satis, 2002): 76. See also Vigasin and Khokhlov, *Istoriia*, 120.

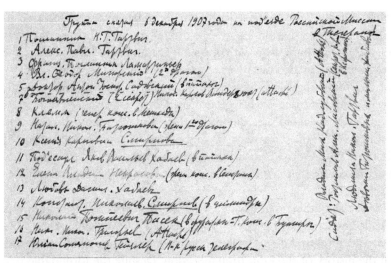

2.4 The Russian Legation in Tehran: (1) Russian Minister Nikolai Hartwig; (3) French Minister Maximilien de la Martinière; (4) Vladimir Minorsky; (10) Kseniia Smirnova; (14) Konstantin Smirnov.
Source: Korneli Kekelidze Georgian National Centre of Manuscripts

This intensified policy towards Persia implied the availability of sufficient well-trained staff within the Ministry. In the period between 1883 and 1891, the Head of the Asian Department of the Ministry was Ivan Zinov'ev (1835–1917), who had for many years worked in the Russian Legation in Tehran and the Russian Consulate in Rasht, before becoming Consul General in Tabriz and, finally, Russian Envoy Extraordinary to Persia. It is fair to assume that Zinov'ev's long-term experience in Persia contributed to the considerable intensification in the activities of the Ministry's Educational Section of Oriental Languages, particularly in the field of Persian studies, after his return to the Imperial MID in the 1880s.[136]

According to the charter of the Educational Section, initially the emphasis was on training in Persian, Arabic and Turkish. In 1888, the Tatar language was added to the curriculum. As was mentioned earlier, at the time Turkish dialects, mainly Azeri as spoken throughout Northern Persia, were subsumed under the category of Tatar languages.

---

[136] See Vigasin and Khokhlov, *Istoriia*, 123.

The students were supposed to learn three languages in addition to Muslim and International Law. The training quality of the section was high even in comparison with academic training, not least because the teaching was carried out by academics from the St Petersburg Faculty of Oriental Languages. Moreover, the activities of the academic staff were complemented by teaching provided by experienced diplomats and native speakers. The quality of the training in the section is also witnessed by the fact that, in the run-up to the establishment of London's SOAS, the British Foreign Office asked its Russian counterpart to kindly share its experience and the details of its curriculum as early as 1907.[137]

It is also notable that during two prolonged periods the section was headed by scholars of Persian studies, namely Matvei Gamazov (1872–93) and Zhukovskii.[138] The latter played a particularly important role in the history of the Educational Section. Despite the formidable role which it played in the training of Russian diplomats (by 1914, in Persia all diplomatic posts were occupied by graduates of the section (31 out of 31), in Turkey the proportion was 38 to 31, in Bukhara, 5 to 4),[139] financial constraints caused by the increasing distance between far-reaching Imperial ambitions and the economic development of Russia would soon tell. At various moments in the early twentieth century, for instance, in 1907 and again in 1912, some high-ranking bureaucrats in the Ministry called for the section to be closed down because of a shortage of funds.[140]

Yet again, the interplay of power relations, expressed herein in institutional interconnectedness and discursive manifestations in the context of *Russkoe delo*, played their productive role. In many respects, the section survived due to Zhukovskii's vigorous efforts. It was him who, citing the historical significance of the period for Russian national interests and the crucial necessity of the diversified development of Russian Oriental studies, persistently tried to prove the vital importance of the section to the public and the people of the Duma, and put forward various projects for its improvement. In 1907 he wrote that universities were not able and must not replace the section because of

---

[137] AV, f. 17, op. 1, d. 183, l. 4–5.
[138] See Appendix (Gamazov).
[139] See Vigasin and Khokhlov, *Istoriia*, 131.
[140] *Rossiia* (Protokoly zasedanii Dumy), 15 April 1912, no. 1969, 3450–3 in ibid., 129.

the difference in goals and because, given the tasks assigned to Russia at that time, there was no other alternative.[141]

Mainly due to Zhukovskii's efforts, channelled through the MID and the War Ministry, in 1912 the Duma was approached with a project prepared by him and the Asian Department that implied a considerable multi-branch enhancement of the section: increase in the quantity of students, intensification of training, annual fieldwork missions, adding civil and criminal law of relevant countries to the curriculum, etc. If the Duma had adopted the project, the section would have been transformed into a powerful centre of Oriental studies for diplomatic and military services.[142] However, this time the inter-institutional feud represented by the lobbying on behalf of the Ministry of the Interior and, particularly, Lieutenant-General Nikolay Shvedov, hampered the project. Shvedov was Head of the Imperial Society of Oriental Studies and the President of the Practical Oriental Academy, in addition to his post of Deputy Minister. Moreover, he was close to the court through his devotion to Rasputin and, therefore, much appreciated by Nicholas II's wife. So, it did not take him much to impede the adoption of the project – it did not even pass through the relevant committee in the Duma.[143] That speaks for the absence of any well-structured consistent state policy towards Oriental studies in Russia.

Studying the impact of this domain, it is worth mentioning that Russian diplomats themselves made a significant contribution to the production of Orientological knowledge. Along with carrying out their official duties, they would spend their spare time conducting scholarly research or would even spend their own money on artefacts and ancient manuscripts in order to later donate them to Russian museums and universities. Among them the works by the following authors were most notable in terms of their scholarly value: the travel notes by the First Secretary to the Russian diplomatic mission in Tehran, Baron K. Bode; *Ot Bosfora do Persidskogo zaliva* by Gamazov, who later became Head of the Educational Section (1873–92); the book *Rossiia, Angliia i Persiia (1912)* by the earlier-mentioned Zinov'ev, Head of the Asian Department.[144] The works of Minorsky – who from the

---

[141] AV, f. 17, op. 1, d. 183, l. 5–23ob.
[142] AV, f. 17, op. 1, d. 185, l. 1-6ob.
[143] V. I. Fedorchenko, *Imperatorskii Dom. Vydaiushiesia sanovniki*, vol. 2 (Moscow: OLMA Press, 2003): 544.
[144] See Vigasin and Khokhlov, *Istoriia*, 123.

very outset of his diplomatic career was interested in Persian history, ethnography and literature and who ended up as a Corresponding Member of the British Academy of Sciences and SOAS Professor of Persian studies – are worth mentioning separately. His works written before 1917 on Babism, Sufism and the Kurds greatly contributed to late Imperial Russian Orientology.[145]

It is also noteworthy that the practice of providing their scholarly teachers with primary sources was rather common and widespread among Russian diplomats. In this respect, the reciprocal institutional interconnectedness was fruitful. Kazem-Bek, Rosen, Zhukovskii and other Persian studies scholars would often receive primary materials from their former students who worked in consulates in Tehran, Tabriz, Rasht and other Persian cities, on demand or on a quite voluntary basis.[146]

In sum, there was a significant departmental contribution of the Russian diplomatic service to Oriental studies. Problems caused by a lack of funding and by inter-agency feuding should not be underestimated and affected Oriental studies activities to a certain extent; however, taking into account the prevailing role of the MID and its monopoly on dealing with foreign countries, it is possible to state that, in terms of organising Oriental studies training, its outcomes and the overall contribution to Russian scholarly knowledge, the Russian diplomatic service was much more successful than the War Ministry. The considerable volume of works on Persia and the scholarly effectiveness of the Ministry's activities in this field are explained by its important place in the Russian foreign policies of the late nineteenth and the early twentieth century.[147]

In addition to that, from reading the memoirs of Kalmykow, who had been taught by Rosen, Salemann and young Zhukovskii,[148] and later became a prominent Russian diplomat, it becomes clear that the Ministry's strength in this sphere can also be accounted for by a focus on the individuals involved: Persia was considered a difficult posting and serving there initially was not meant to particularly help with rapid career progression within the diplomatic service. Thus

[145] See Bartol'd, "Iran," 326.
[146] See Vigasin and Khokhlov, *Istoriia*, 133.
[147] See Kulagina, *Iranistika*, 31–3; Vigasin and Khokhlov, *Istoriia*, 124.
[148] ARAN(St.P.), f. 208, op. 3, d. 496, l. 30 (Rosen's letter to Ol'denburg).

most of those who took up Persian studies within this domain were the individuals who tended to regard this subject as a veritable vocation or indeed as their life cause, which implied the strong presence of romantic perceptions, inherent to Said's Orientalism,[149] or, in broader Foucauldian terms, of discursive components, manifested in the sense of a personal mission for "civilising the Orient" and promoting Russian national interests, as well as expressed simply in a personal drive for the study of the Orient, which had been significantly stimulated by their teachers.[150]

Russia's Missionary Activities in the Late Nineteenth and Early Twentieth Century

The activities undertaken within this domain seem to be of particular interest since, despite its stated peaceful mission, it was, in alliance with all the above-mentioned domains, at the front line of the Imperial turf war between Russia and the European powers. The Russian Empire would broadly employ clerical scholarly institutions for the purpose of gaining influence among the peoples of other beliefs, particularly among the Muslims in the inner and neighbouring areas. The Russian missionary Oriental studies in both fields, scholarly and practical, could be a perfect illustration of the thesis on the interconnectedness of state power and knowledge, inter-institutional mutual penetration and the role of discourse.

In spite of the closure of the Faculty of Oriental Languages at Kazan University in 1854, the Russian Imperial state kept local Oriental studies within the walls of the Kazan Ecclesiastical Academy in the form of teaching Persian, Arabic and the Tatar languages as well as Muslim Law and anti-Islamic polemics. The direct engagement of this institution with state policies and the relevant discourse on the superiority of Russian culture, in particular the superiority of the Orthodox Christianity, is bluntly supported by an organisational feature of this Academy that speaks for itself, namely the establishment and

---

[149] See Said, *Orientalism*, 224.
[150] See Andrew D. Kalmykow, *Memoirs of a Russian Diplomat: Outposts of the Empire, 1893–1917* (New Haven, CT: Yale University Press, 1971): 13–17. See also AV, f. 17, op. 2, d. 9 (Zhukovskii's correspondence with Bravin, twenty-three letters).

functioning of the chair of Anti-Islamic Subjects. It implied research and training activities aiming at countering Islam from the standpoint of the Russian Orthodoxy.[151]

Kazem-Bek's disciple – Professor of Islamic studies Il'minsky – initiated the establishment of this chair and was the first to head it, as well as being the person who significantly accelerated and promoted the establishing of relevant institutional structures on behalf of the Russian state and the Orthodox clergy for the training of ministers in Oriental studies for missionary activities among Muslims.[152] Special courses on anti-Islamic polemics were developed and taught by Nikolai Il'minsky (1822–91), Evfimii Malov (1835–1918), Mikhail Mashanov (1852–1924) and Nikolai Ostroumov (1846–1930)– all these scholars of Kazan's Islamic studies literarily fought Islam, heavily relying on their personal beliefs in the superiority of the Orthodox Christianity and sincerely trusting in their beneficial scholarly impact on state policies towards Muslim peoples. Their scholarly and practical activities were conscientiously adjusted to the Russian state interests which, for them, were inseparable from the Orthodox Christianity.

In this sense, the examples of Mashanov and Ostroumov – who, being committed Orthodox believers and closely engaged in scholarly activities, who worked in various state power capacities and actively consulted Russian high-ranking military and diplomatic functionaries – were very indicative within the discourse of promoting Russian interests abroad.[153] These activities also included conventional practices, adopted in three other domains of Russian Oriental studies, namely multi-task mission trips. The instructions composed by Malov by order of the Kazan Ecclesiastical Academy Council for Mashanov's two-year mission trip to Middle Eastern countries, besides the scholarly component, contained substantial missionary tasks.[154] The

[151] See Schimmelpenninck van der Oye, *Russian Orientalism*, 131, 134–6, 138; Vigasin and Khokhlov, *Istoriia*, 38, 39, 41–3.

[152] See Schimmelpenninck van der Oye, *Russian Orientalism*, 129–31, 134; Paul Werth, *At the Margins of Orthodoxy: Mission, Governance, and Confessional Politics in Russia's Volga-Kama Region, 1827–1905* (Ithaca, NY: Cornell University Press, 2002): 177–99.

[153] See Khalid, "Russian History," 691–9; Schimmelpenninck van der Oye, *Russian Orientalism*, 138; Robert Geraci, *Window on the East: National and Imperial Identities in Late Tsarist Russia* (New York: Cornell University Press, 2001): 91–2.

[154] See Geraci, *Window on the East*, 91–2; Vigasin and Khokhlov, *Istoriia*, 41–2.

above-mentioned scholars trained future Orientologists not only for missionary purposes, but also for state power entities. For example, the Interior Ministry was invariably interested in the graduates of the Academy.[155] This Academy also produced some ministers for the Orthodox missionary cause in Persia.[156]

In 1998–2001, noteworthy research was conducted by the Father Superior of St Nicholas Church in Tehran Aleksandr (Zarkeshev) which resulted in the publication of a book *Russkaia Pravoslavnaia Tserkov' v Persii-Irane (1597–2001)* (The Russian Orthodox Church in Persia-Iran (1597–2001)). Although the published monograph, as such, is of extremely limited academic value because of the absence of references and bibliography as well as the journalistic style it is written in, the author – in the cause of research – made significant efforts in order to reconstruct the history of Russian religious missions to Persia from the reign of Shah Abbas I (1587–99) to 2001 with the help of AVPRI, fragments of documents related to missionary activities and the reminiscences of elderly Russian residents in Iran. Though the work does not lack in self-serving discursive connotation concerning the superiority of Orthodox Christianity towards Islam and of all things Russian towards all things Persian and, in this sense, could be well placed in a row with the works of the above-mentioned clerical scholars, it still remains the only relatively comprehensive, albeit rather brief, research on the history of the Russian Orthodox Church in Persia/Iran.

In support of the similarity of the institutional practices of various domains of Russian Oriental studies, the above-mentioned research includes the study of multiple expeditions and mission trips undertaken by Russian clergymen to Persia which resulted in gathering valuable ethnographic and historical material, in particular on the history, traditions, modes of life and cult of the Nestorians in Persia. Based on this information and in line with the foreign policy tasks of Imperial Russia in terms of the peaceful comprehensive penetration into Persia proclaimed by Witte and Kuropatkin, the St Petersburg Sacred Governing Synod took the decision on the reunification of the

---

[155] See Schimmelpenninck van der Oye, *Russian Orientalism*, 93–121; Vigasin and Khokhlov, *Istoriia*, 35–43, 210.
[156] See Zarkeshev, *Tserkov'*, 85; Schimmelpenninck van der Oye, *Russian Orientalism*, 122.

Assyrian population of Persia with the Russian Orthodox Church and on the establishment of the Orumiye Russian Orthodox Permanent Mission.[157]

By the beginning of World War I there were ten Russian Orthodox parishes mainly under Russian diplomatic missions and consulates, and almost forty Orthodox churches under the jurisdiction of the Orumiye Mission.[158] In view of such a broad presence in Persia, on the one hand, and given the inertness and even backwardness of the Russian Orthodox Church of that time – which was slightly touched upon by Schimmelpenninck van der Oye in his book *Russian Orientalism*[159] – on the other, Russian clerical institutions in Persia generally lacked their own experts on Persian studies, which itself does not say much for the efficiency of the organisational activities of this domain and of the relevant state participation. However, taking into consideration the underlying factual proximity to and the dependence of the Russian Orthodox Church institutions on Russian state entities in Persia – diplomatic and military – the necessary linguistic and expert assistance was usually provided by them.

Being part of the foreign expansion of late Imperial Russia, Orthodox missionary activities also implied intensive translation work into Persian and Assyrian, aimed at disseminating religious literature and converting new followers to the Orthodox doctrine, and, in this context, were assisted by Russian-speaking Persian Assyrians.[160] That constituted another feature of this domain that was common to the rest: the accumulating and processing of Orientological knowledge and the sequential exerting of influence, which ultimately results in the production of more power. The activities undertaken by the Russian Orthodox Church in alliance with other Russian Orientological domains on the gathering and studying of local historical, ethnographic and religious data secured its subsequent actions in the precise application of institutional influence to certain areas and peoples of Persia which were the most susceptible to it, and on the production of power in the context of the conjoint national discourse on the promotion of *Russkoe delo*.[161]

---

[157] See Zarkeshev, *Tserkov'*, 68–9, 82, 91.
[158] Ibid., 109.
[159] See Schimmelpenninck van der Oye, *Russian Orientalism*, 122.
[160] See Zarkeshev, *Tserkov'*, 86–7, 109.
[161] See Tolz, *Russia's Own Orient*, 31–46.

Conclusion

The above analysis, made partly on the basis of the most recent secondary sources and the relevant primary sources, allows us to ascertain
the presence of four main domains in late Imperial Russia's Oriental
studies, namely academic scholarship, the military, the diplomatic service and missionary activities. This set-up becomes particularly clear
when drawing on the example of Persian studies. The trade domain
could not play any considerable role in Oriental knowledge production in the context of Russia's activities in the East because of the nascent condition of capitalism inside Russia itself. The above-mentioned
four domains were strongly represented within late Imperial Russia's
foreign policy towards Persia. As it appears from the above study,
all four domains had been quite well institutionalised by the turn of the
twentieth century. However, along with their professional self-
consistency, they were closely intertwined. In addition to the close
connections between academic training institutions and the entities
for the practical application of Orientological knowledge within each
professionally defined domain, all these four domains were deeply
interconnected at both institutional and individual levels – a fact
which has been left in the cold by the above-mentioned participants in
the debate on Russian Orientalism but which has crucial importance
for the study of power/knowledge relations.

Indeed, the emergence of academic scholarship in Oriental studies
was initially instigated by the demands of Russia's Eastern policy as
well as the fact that the sequential development of Oriental studies,
in general, went hand in hand with these demands. Russia's foreign
policy emphasis on the East and, within that, on the neighbouring
Persianate world predetermined the role occupied by Persianate studies
within Russia's Orientology. As Tolz points out: 'Oriental studies was
one of the strongest areas of the [Russian] academy's research. In the
period between 1846 and 1924, there were fifteen full members of the
academy who were specialists in Oriental studies. The only other field
to which more academicians belonged in the same period, was Russian
language and literature.'[162] The research shows that all key members
of the main scholarly, training and practical institutions within the
four domains were individuals who had majored mainly or partly in

---

[162] Tolz, *Russian Academicians*, 7,192.

Persian studies. Persian, Arabic and the Tatar languages (later Turkic languages), which included mainly those spoken in the northern areas of Persia under the classification of the time, invariably were the initial curriculum nucleus of almost all training institutions set up throughout the nineteenth and early twentieth century. The character of the massive Russian presence in Persia and the development of its modality were reflected at an institutional level in all domains.

The study also demonstrates a significant contribution to Orientological knowledge made by all four domains in Persian studies, particularly by the military, which used the practices of mission trips (reconnaissance) more intensively, considerably contributing to general area-study knowledge at the stage of its primary accumulation. Given the initial connection of military and diplomatic domains to the state power decision-making area, the impact of Oriental studies within these domains on state policies was more palpable. In terms of solving state power tasks, their significant role could be identified more straightforwardly in comparison with the activities of those individuals who were, first of all, scholars and were only in addition to their "genuine status", one way or another, engaged in state politics. Overlooking this nuance in scholar Grigor'ev's activities, Knight tries to identify an unequivocal and straightforward impact on state power and, certainly, does not find it. Khalid critically points this out, saying that 'Knight demands proof of the connection between knowledge and power at such a crudely instrumental level that nothing short of Orientalists issuing marching orders to troops conquering regions of their expertise would satisfy him';[163] whereas I would argue that in the Russian case the impact of "pure" scholarly institutions and relevant scholars should be mainly sought in their indirect influence on state power.

Although Rosen's disciples tried to position themselves as impartial and independent from politics (the most sound example was Barthold, who tended to call himself and his colleagues 'closet scholars'[164]), as well as to distance themselves from the Imperial and colonial context of the time, nonetheless they were keen on preserving and expanding the nexus between scholarship and state power, in order to be able to hand down their "correct" beliefs and perceptions of the East to that

163 Khalid, "Russian History," 696.
164 Bartol'd, "Russkaia nauka," 534.

very state power and, as was more important for them, underscore the discursive importance of Oriental studies for the state, to be able to better promote their scholarly institutions. Therefore, the undertaken study demonstrates that they were much more successful in their latter enterprise. With the exception of inter-domain scholarly societies, which connected the activities of the representatives of all domains, our research did not reveal any effective, direct scholarly Oriental studies involvement at an institutional level in late Imperial Russia's foreign policy towards Persia. However, at an individual level the impact of scholars on the emergence and development of institutions for training practical experts in the three other domains was enormous.

In spite of the vast diversity of discourses among Russian scholars, which was noticed by Knight and scrupulously studied by Tolz,[165] all four domains were relatively coherent in the advancement of *Russkoe delo* and the comprehension of "the civilising mission" when it came to foreign policy activities in the East. The spirit of patriotism – boiled down to the promotion of Imperial Russia's state interests and Russian culture in Persia, which was mixed with the sense of "civilising mission" and took place against the backdrop of concomitant turf war with European powers – was generally inherent to the activities of all domains. At the same time, in the development of Knight's argument and contrary to Khalid's belief in the universality of Said's model, it is possible to mention separately Russian Oriental studies scholars who were less united in their comprehension of the Russian mission in the Orient. For instance, within the discourse of separating scholarly knowledge from politics there were also various efforts to dissociate Oriental studies from state power at the institutional level. But these efforts could not change the pattern of the deep involvement of scholarly institutions in training practical specialists and their intense production of country-study knowledge at least potentially for sequential state utilisation – the thesis that was, actually, glossed over by Knight in his *Grigor'ev in Orenburg*.

At the same time, the study could not retrieve any evidence that in late Imperial Russia the state had fully apprehended the direct link between power and knowledge (knowledge is power), which, on the other hand, was 'the main slogan of scholarship in the nineteenth

---

[165] See Knight, "Grigor'ev," 81. See also Tolz, *Russia's Own Orient*.

century', as Tolz and Knight argue, referring to Grigor'ev's words.[166] There was no well-thought-out and structured policy towards Oriental studies on behalf of the state. It would happen that their very existence in some domains was in question, let alone the lack of proper funding throughout all domains. The state kept using scholars as a source of primary country-study knowledge and constrained their role mainly within the area of training experts necessary for the state. Using this state interest in them, some scholars played on it to attain the goals of promoting their scholarly institutions under the condition of lack of funds and the ensuing choice of priorities by the state.

It consequently appears that the state generally preferred to foster Oriental studies experts within each domain, directly engaging them in state power activities, including the Church, and to resort to their competence rather than to grant academic scholars access to the political decision-making arena. In contrast to the scholarly domain, Orientological institutions, and even individuals of the three other domains to a significantly greater extent, were capable of directly influencing Imperial Russia's foreign policy activities towards Persia – a fact which was ignored by the participants in the debate on Russian Orientalism. Neither Knight, referring to Grigor'ev's tenure with the Ministry of the Interior, nor Khalid, using the contrasting example of Ostroumov's service with the War Ministry, paid attention to the fact that their characters could no longer be scrutinised as academics during their tenures but only as the employees of state power institutions, with all-ensuing consequences which implied much less intellectual autonomy in their activities but endowed them with far more capability to influence state power.

In general, all participants in the above-mentioned debate agree that Said's concept of 'Orientalism is definitely relevant for Russia insofar as it describes the power relations in a concrete Imperial/colonial context'.[167] However, it is clear that the whole debate whirls mainly around Said's eponymous model and the two-vector relations between knowledge and state power, whereas the gist, I would argue, is in the manifold multi-vector relations of the power/knowledge nexus where power is exerted by all agents of this interplay towards each other: scholars,

---

[166] Tolz, *Russia's Own Orient*, 70. See also Knight, "Grigor'ev," 74–100; Knight, "Response to Khalid," 701–15.

[167] Todorova, "Russian Soul," 720.

experts, institutions, discourses, state, etc. Unfortunately, Knight's attempt to break away from this narrow circle of Said's model and to return to the origins of the Foucauldian remained mostly unnoticed by the others.[168]

In addition to the distinctions between the domains it is also possible to point out that from the outset the Russian MID played the prevailing role in foreign policy activities in terms of the subordination of other state entities, in particular the military. A similar situation was found in terms of the institutional organisation of military Oriental studies, which, in fact, were hosted by the MID. However, throughout the period, especially after the turn of the century, military Oriental studies began to gain more self-consistency, exactly as was the case in the relationship between the MID and the War Ministry in Russia's foreign policy activities, in particular in Persia. It resulted in the establishment of specialised military Orientological institutions in Tashkent, Ashkhabad and Tiflis, in the dismantling of the officers' courses under the Educational Section in 1910 and in the establishment of courses in Oriental languages under the staffs of Central Asian military districts by World War I. After 1917 this motion was developed by the Bolsheviks and spread to all Soviet Oriental studies, which led to the creation of a vast and rather efficient institutional set-up of Oriental studies with centres of specialisation in all Eastern republics of the Soviet Union, which will be studied in the following chapter.

Similarities between the domains were presented by their scholarly and practical Oriental studies' deep institutional interconnectedness both within each domain and between them, as well as by similar practices in Orientological knowledge production and by significant contribution to general scholarly knowledge. This modality was intrinsic to all three "practical" domains. Their entities would turn into powerful Oriental studies institutions, partly due to the new approaches adopted by the government, partly due to the efforts of separate individuals personally interested in Oriental (Persianate) studies.

This phenomenon can be particularly well illustrated by the example of the military domain. Suffice it to remember the Persian Cossack Brigade which, in addition to its important political and military role,

---

[168] See Knight, "Grigor'ev," 100.

had become a seminal source of country-study information since Kosagovskii's tenure. Staff Captain Smirnov's posting with the Shah's court (1907–14), which was to become, first of all, the conductor of Russian cultural influence in Persia and the source of valuable first-hand intelligence on the country, additionally resulted in the production of a series of unique scholarly works in various fields of Persian studies. The above cases will be studied in detail later in this monograph. So the development of Russian Oriental studies went hand in hand with foreign policy and, within the context of late Imperial Russia's foreign policy in the East, the Oriental studies of all domains were subject to the main discourses of "civilising mission" and promoting *Russkoe delo*, which, by and large, were directly associated with the core of the foreign activities of the Russian Empire by the representatives of all domains.

3 | *Organisational Set-Up of Early Soviet Oriental Studies (1917–41)*

Introduction

This chapter draws on Soviet and post-Soviet literature on Iran, as well as on recent Western scholarship studying the developments of Soviet foreign policy towards Persia during the period from 1917 to 1941. The analysis presented in the chapter also includes the data retrieved from archival documents, which helps fill in the gaps in the literature, mentioned previously, and allows researchers to look at the relevant historical events from a different perspective. The underlying aim of the chapter is to present a comprehensive analysis, at the institutional level, of the emergence and activities of the scholarly, military and diplomatic structures which dealt with Persia during more than two decades after the collapse of the tsarist power. Naturally, this comprises the study of institutional practices within three early Soviet Orientological domains. I also touch upon the relevant discourses which influenced the establishment and development of these institutions and secured their tight nexus with Soviet state policy towards Persia. Therefore, the chapter mainly answers the questions relating to the organisation of early Soviet institutions for the study of Persia/Iran and on the technicalities of the involvement of academic scholars and practical experts in Soviet Persian foreign policy, as well as giving a partial answer to the question of the efficiency of the the early Soviet state in bringing into play Orientological scholarship, which will be supplemented by the case studies in Chapter 5.

In order to better situate the organisational activities in question within the field of foreign policy the chapter is divided into two chronological periods, embracing two different courses of early Soviet policy towards Persia, namely 1917–21 and 1921–41. The former period saw the attempted forced sovietisation of Persia, whereas the latter covers the gradual cultivation of Persian society for social conversion via the support of the bourgeois national government. For both periods, the

academic domain is studied after the other two (military and diplomatic) because of its total marginalisation from the decision-making
and operational fields of Soviet Persian policy, which happened after
1917. For the second period, the study of the military and diplomatic
domains is merged into one section because of the absence of Oriental
studies training institutions within the latter until the early 1930s and
the immense overlapping, at the institutional and individual levels,
of the two in the operational field.

Political Context of Russo-Persian Relationships in 1917–21

As in the preceding period, the Russo-Persian relationships after
1917 remained deeply affected by the factors of international politics. Persia, as before, was the arena of a close fight between the main
European powers. This time, the political games were complicated by
military operations which had been held on Persian territory.[1] With
the outbreak of World War I, considerable changes took place in
British policy towards Persia in terms of strategic goals. Great Britain
no longer intended to keep Persia as a buffer zone between Russia and
British colonial possessions in India and embarked upon the road of
separating the southern part of Persia to secure its access to Persian
Gulf oil.[2] In 1914–15, the British policy aim of decentralising Persia
was repeatedly reported to St Petersburg by the Russian Minister in
Persia, Ivan Korostovets. In 1915, the British Foreign Office officially
proposed revising the Convention of 1907 in part to assign a neutral
stripe to the British zone.[3] It should be mentioned that similar ideas
were wandering in the Russian MID regarding the northern parts
of Persia. They were even aired by Minorsky and Smirnov as early
as 1909.[4]

---

[1] See Kulagina, *Rossiia i Iran*, 149; M. S. Ivanov and V. N. Zaitsev, *Novaia istoriia Irana* (Moscow: Nauka, 1988): 292, 296, 297; Aliev, *Istoriia Irana*, 76, 77. Zarkeshev, *Tserkov'*, 111.

[2] See Captain Noel's letter to Sir Percy Sykes which was intercepted by the Germans, later handed over to the Russians, and is still kept in AVPRF (f. 028, op. 10, d. 11, papka 31, l. 8–9). See also AV, f. 134, op. 1, d. 502, l. 1 (Minorsky on Captain Noel's report, 1918).

[3] See Kulagina, *Rossiia i Iran*, 192; Aliev, *Istoriia Irana*, 78, 79.

[4] GNCM, f. 39, d. 12, 73ob–75; d. 11, l. 3, 16ob. On Minorsky's Azerbaijan Project of 1909 and his efforts to revive it in 1917, see Aliev, *Istoriia Irana*, 90–1.

The Soviet and post-Soviet scholarship on Iran is unanimous in believing that such political rapprochement between Russia and Britain on the eve of World War I caused the relevant counteraction on behalf of Germany and Turkey which skilfully took advantage of the increased inner dissatisfaction of all strata of Persian society with these intensified Anglo-Russian policies. The increased nationalist-patriotic spirit of the Iranians was also encouraged by German–Turkish pan-Islamism and anti British–Russian propaganda. All these factors led to the weakening of Russian political influence and to the growth of antipathy towards Russians.[5] They also created fertile soil for the German–Turkish politico-economic penetration on the eve of the war and for the rapid and successful military occupation of the western and southern parts of Persia by 1915.[6]

Therefore, the forecast held in the Russian military intelligence reports of 1889 and 1899 on the peril of 'drawing Persia into war by other hostile states' came true.[7] Though Russian troops prevented the coup prepared by Germans and Turks and, by early 1916, they had recaptured Qom, Karaj, Hamadan and Kermanshah, it took considerable military efforts and the bringing of new troops into Persia. It also left Russian troops in solitude in the hostile environment of the Kurds and other nomadic tribes. The events that followed in 1917 in Russia resulted, generally, in the massive desertion of Russian troops in Persia and, by the summer of 1917, in the total collapse of the Persian front.[8]

After the February Revolution, the previous Imperial foreign policy towards Persia was reconsidered from a new angle. Though in her book on Russia and Iran in the nineteenth and early twentieth century, Kulagina argues that 'the Provisional Government made no changes in Russo-Iranian relationships' and this corresponds to Lenin's characterisation of the Provisional Government policies towards Persia,[9]

---

[5] See Ivanov and Zaitsev, *Novaia istoriia*, 292–4; Kulagina, *Rossiia i Iran*, 189, 190; Aliev, *Istoriia Irana*, 80.
[6] See Zarkeshev, *Tserkov'*, 110–11.
[7] Marshall, *Russian General Staff*, 108.
[8] See Aliev, *Istoriia Irana*, 87; Zarkeshev, *Tserkov'*, 112; Kulagina, *Rossiia i Iran*, 193.
[9] Kulagina, *Rossiia i Iran*, 194; V. I. Lenin, "Rech ob otnoshenii k Vremennomu pravitel'stvu na Pervom Vserossiiskii s'ezde Sovetov rabochikh i soldatskikh deputatov, 3–24 iiunia 1917 g.," in *Sobranie sochinenii*, vol. 32 (Moscow: Progress, 1970): 268.

works by other scholars such as Saleh Aliev and Vladimir Genis present evidence of intensive exchange of correspondence on the issue between Minorsky, the acting Head of the Russian diplomatic mission in Persia, and two ministers for foreign affairs of the Provisional Government, Pavel Miliukov (1859–1943) and Mikhail Tereshenko (1886–1956). Indeed, judging by the documents in Minorsky's private collection, all participants confirmed Russia's adherence to all previous agreements with Britain;[10] however, they acknowledged the underlying need to conduct Russia's foreign policy towards Persia based on new democratic principles that corresponded to the new republican status of Russia. Finally, Minorsky received direct instructions not to counteract any democratic manifestations, to support liberal nationalist movements and to sever all kinds of overt support for "reactionary" elements. Minorsky also tried to resume his project of creating Persian Azerbaijan and Kurdistan autonomous democratic republics and transforming the negative Persian perception of Russia.[11] However, the Bolshevik coup brought a halt to all these plans.

On 3 December 1917, the Bolshevik government published an appeal 'To all labouring Muslims of Russia and the Orient' – a crucial document that laid down the official principles of the new foreign policy towards Persia. The Soviet government announced the abolition of all agreements and conventions infringing on the rights and interests of Persia as well as the repudiation of all Imperial Russian property and financial assets in Persia.[12] However, this motion gained the sympathy of nationalist and liberal groups of the Persian society and did not secure the immediate establishment of diplomatic relations between Persia and the Bolshevik government.[13] Using that as a pretext, and following their own political expediency,[14] in 1918,

---

[10] AV, f. 134, op. 2, d. 197 (Minorsky's correspondence with the Ministry, 1916–17), l. 1–50; d. 211(April 1917–June 1917), l. 1–14.

[11] Ibid., d. 197 (Minorsky's correspondence with Miliukov), l. 1–3, 6, 23, 24ob, 43–4.

[12] See Nina Mamedova, "Istoriia Sovetsko-Iranskikh otnoshenii (1917–1991)," in *Iran: Istoriia, ekonomika, kul'tura*, ed. Nina Mamedova and Liudmila Kulagina (Moscow: Institut Vostokovedeniia RAN, 2009): 157. See also Aliev, *Istoriia Irana*, 93; Kulagina, *Rossiia i Iran*, 194–5.

[13] See Kulagina, *Rossiia i Iran*, 195, 200.

[14] The Bolshevik leaders reckoned that their young socialist state could not survive in the hostile environment of capitalist countries. On the other hand, in 1918–19 it became clear that the many socialist revolutions anticipated

the Soviet government launched a rapidly intensifying campaign to support the armed nationalist movements in Persia, aiming to stir up socialist revolution.[15]

Relatedly, a noteworthy piece of research by Oliver Bast was published in 2006. Bast scrupulously traced the twists and turns of the organisation of the abortive Persian Socialist Revolution during 1919–20 and the significant contribution made to this process by local Bolsheviks from Turkestan, Azerbaijan and Persia itself.[16] The relevant inspiration for such activities was overtly derived from Stalin's inaugural speech at the First Congress of Communists-Muslims in November 1918 and from Lenin's inaugural speech at the Second All-Russia Congress of the Communist Organisations of the Peoples of the Orient.[17] Although nothing was said about military intervention, the debate on this issue and, finally, the working design was circulated in secret between Trotsky, Lenin, Zinov'ev and other leaders, in their relevant correspondence, reports and the protocols of special sessions.[18]

By the early 1920s, the main 'strike directions' about which Trotsky had been speaking were chosen, namely India and Persia.[19] Shortly before, in August 1919, the Soviet government had issued an appeal 'To the workers and peasants of Persia', which debunked the just-signed British–Persian Agreement and announced its refutation of it.[20] Under these circumstances, following Lenin's and Trotsky's orders, in late 1919–early 1920 the Soviet government organised a special centre in Turkestan which was supposed to become the military, industrial, financial and scholarly base for the forthcoming socialist revolution in Persia. Lenin particularly emphasised the necessity of organising a

---

in the main European states were far from realisation. Having realised this, they sought an alternative in the Orient (see Moisei Persits, *Zastenchivaia interventsiia: O sovetskom vtorzhenii v Iran i Bukharu v 1920–1921* (Moscow: Izdatel'skii Dom 'Muravei-Gaid', 1999): 11–15).

[15] AVPRF, f. 04, op. 18, d. 50638, papka 109, l. 1ob.

[16] Oliver Bast, "The Council for International Propaganda and the Establishment of the Iranian Communist Party," in *Iran and the First World War*, ed. Touraj Atabaki (London: I. B. Tauris, 2006): 163–76.

[17] See Persits, *Zastenchivaia interventsiia*, 12, 17, 18.

[18] Ibid., 19–20, 23, 33.

[19] Ibid., 22, 27.

[20] See Mamedova, "Istoriia Sovetsko-Iranskikh otnoshenii," 158–9; Aliev, *Istoriia Irana*, 98.

centre for propaganda in Tashkent among the neighbouring countries' Muslims.[21]

However, in their studies both Bast and Moisei Persits overlook the crucial roles played in these activities by former tsarist Orientologists Nikolai Bravin and Ivan Iagello, discussed in Chapters 2, 4 and 5 of this monograph. Without them, the Bolsheviks would have been unable to so rapidly and qualitatively unfold Oriental studies training of their agents on such a scale. In this sense, the report from the then commander of the Persian Cossacks in Khorasan, Colonel Starosel'skii, to the Russian Minister in Persia, Nikolai von Etter (1865–1935), about Bolshevik activities in the region is noteworthy. In the end, he emphasises: 'The Persian Iomuds have been totally converted by Bolsheviks … The Bolsheviks' propaganda is carried out by them on a grand scale for which they spend huge resources. In Tashkent, a special school has been established for propaganda in all local dialects. The Propaganda Section is headed by Bravin, who is famous in Persia'.[22] The example of Bravin's and Iagello's activities and of their results clearly supports postulations on the productivity of power relations that were intensified by the interplay of expert knowledge and the enhanced capabilities vested in these individuals.

Unfortunately, the role of the former tsarist experts is not even touched upon in another fundamental work either, namely *Red Persia* by Genis; however, the work presents a valuable, detailed account of the attempted military sovietisation of Persia. Genis' emphasis is on Bolshevik military activities in Persia that followed the intensified combat actions undertaken in Gilan by armed insurgents with Mirza Kuchek-Khan as head of the nationalist movement. They were holding active combat operations against the corps of General Dunsterville, who were on their way to Baku. The British troops, supported by the Shah's forces – consisting, in fact, of Russian Cossacks, headed by Colonel Starosel'skii – succeeded in cracking down on the *jangalis* who, in January 1920, had to sign a peace agreement.[23] However, during the next months the representatives of Persian insurgents took

[21] See Persits, *Zastenchivaia interventsiia*, 20–3, 25; Mamedova, "Istoriia Sovetsko-Iranskikh otnoshenii," 158–9.

[22] AV, f. 134, op. 1, d. 212 (Starosel'skii's report to von Etter), l. 13–19ob.

[23] See Vladimir Genis, *Krasnaia Persiia: Bol'sheviki v Giliane, 1920–1921* (Moscow: MNPI, 2000): 51–8.

part in meetings among the Bolshevik leaders regarding the military sovietisation of Persia.[24]

On 18 May 1920, the Soviet troops, headed by Fedor Raskol'nikov,[25] with the help of the Volga-Caspian fleet, captured Anzali and the neighbouring areas. Shortly after, on capturing Rasht on 4 June, the establishment of the Soviet Socialist Republic of Persia was declared. The Vice People's Commissar for Foreign Affairs, Lev Karakhan (1889–1937), following Trotsky's orders, gave instructions for the organisation of state administrative and military apparatus consisting of undercover Soviet citizens but financed from local funds. Traces of the official Soviet presence were not supposed to be seen and even the troops who had come from Russia were instructed to act under the colours of the local communist party – at worst, of the Azerbaijan Autonomous Republic.

In this respect, Trotsky's wording, which was in full conformity with the discourse on the forced sovietisation of the Orient, is rather illustrative: 'Fourth – to secretly create and to leave a vast Soviet organisation in Persia. *To force* them to understand that we have nothing against the people of Persia and we are not going to seize anything in the Orient.'[26] Raskol'nikov was also ordered to organise a powerful propaganda establishment in Persia.[27] All this demanded a significant quantity of Persian studies specialists.

Bolshevik Military Oriental Studies, 1917–21

As a result of Russia's extensive involvement in World War I and the concentration of its military activities in the western direction, Russia was unable to pay as much attention to its activities in the Orient. Even troops for the Persian front, which was, in fact, the south-eastern flank of the war theatre, were allocated with significant difficulties.[28] In support of this, Marshall writes: 'Over the course of the

---

[24] See Mamedova, "Istoriia Sovetsko-Iranskikh otnoshenii," 159; Genis, *Krasnaia Persiia*, 62–3.

[25] See Appendix (Raskol'nikov).

[26] RGVA, f. 157 (The Revolutionary Military Council of the First Army), op. 8, d. 7, l. 11 (Trotsky's cable), (emphasis added).

[27] Ibid., 3, 3ob, 11.

[28] See Aleksandr Shishov, *Persidskii front (1909–1918)* (Moscow: Izdatel'skii dom Veche, 2010): 175.

subsequent World War the establishment of the Asiatic Department of the General Staff itself withered on the vine as a natural consequence of the concentration of all material and human resources upon the western frontier.'[29] After 1915, there were only two officers left in the Asian Department, processing both routine work and country-study material.

In 1917, a certain Colonel Smirnov was offered to the department as a desk-head by the Headquarters of the Caucasus Military Region. It was that very Konstantin Nikolaevich Smirnov who had served at the Qajar Court as a tutor of Heir to the throne Ahmad-Mirza (1907–14), and then served in the Headquarters of the Caucasus Army in the intelligence and counter-intelligence sections.[30] Ter-Oganov separately points out that, having written a considerable number of works on Persian history, ethnography and economy, Smirnov – a high-ranking military officer – was also known as a scholar of Persian studies by that time.[31] However, Ter-Oganov does not go further than enumerating Smirnov's merits and does not study their implications, whereas I would argue that, according to conventional institutional practices of the time, Smirnov's scholarly record turned out to be a decisive factor in his nomination for the post, and resulted in him significantly contributing to the production of Orientological knowledge within the domain.

Marshall also notices the potential operational significance of this nomination, writing that Smirnov's forthcoming appointment was meant to rescue the department from reassignment to the Ministry of the Interior and, thus, its virtual dismantling; however, the October coup contributed the demise of the department, bringing a palpable rupture.[32] As we can see, similarly to Minorsky's case in the diplomatic domain, scholarly expertise really was an added value not only for the personal interests of individuals but also for the production of knowledge itself, and the state had learnt to value its ad hoc scholars within each practical domain by the end of the late Imperial period.[33]

---

[29] Marshall, *Russian General Staff*, 174.
[30] GNCM, f. 39, d. 3–3ob.
[31] Ter-Oganov, "Zhizn'," 12–13.
[32] See Marshall, *General Staff*, 174.
[33] See Minorsky's case in Chapter 4.

Having in mind the forthcoming military activities in the southern direction, in particular in Persia, the Bolshevik government realised that the planned sovietisation of Persia would be impossible without relevant experts or, at least, people speaking Persian. Following Lenin's and Trotsky's orders regarding the organisation of a 'military-industrial base in Turkestan', the Chief Commander of the *Turkfront*, M. V. Frunze, invited the former Head of the Tashkent Officers' School, Colonel Iagello, to organise and head the training in Oriental languages in Tashkent.[34] Thus, in 1919, the Turkestan Oriental Institute began its work.[35]

Furthermore, three months before Raskol'nikov's landing in Anzali, on 16 February 1920, the *Revvoensovet* of the RSFSR ordered the *Razvedupr* 'to organise agent reconnaissance on large scales' in, first of all, those countries with which the possibility of a military clash was most likely. Among those countries were Persia, Afghanistan and the Democratic Republic of Azerbaijan.[36] Based on the experience of Soviet activities in the north of Persia during spring/summer 1920, which further revealed the extreme dearth of specialists on Persia, in October the *Revvoensovet* of the Turkestan Front introduced a separate military curriculum within the institute which in 1922 resulted in the establishment of the Tashkent Higher Military School of Oriental Studies.[37]

In the same year, a successor to the former Asian Department – the Oriental Section of the General Staff of the Red Army – was established. According to Order 137, signed on 20 January 1920 by Head of *Revvoensovet* Trotsky, its educational part, called the Oriental Section, was organised and subordinated to the Academy of the General Staff. In addition to Persian, Arabic, Turkish and other Oriental languages, the curriculum consisted of such subjects as Muslim law, country-study, military geography, history and practice of diplomacy, trade law and others.[38] The section trained specialists

---

[34] Persits, *Zastenchivaia interventsiia*, 26; RGVA, f. 400, op. 1 (Asian section), d. 3522, l. 38–52. See Marshall, *Russian General Staff*, 189–90; see Appendix (Frunze).

[35] See Nina Kuznetsova and Liudmila Kulagina, *Iz istorii sovetskogo vostokovedeniia, 1917–1967* (Moscow: Nauka, 1970): 11.

[36] See A. I. Kolpakidi and D. P. Prokhorov, *Imperiia GRU. Ocherki istorii Rossiiskoi voennoi razvedki* (Moscow: Olma Press, 1999): 47.

[37] See Vucinich, "Structure," 56–7.

[38] RGVA, f. 11, op. 1, d. 186, l. 15–20ob. (Vostochnoe otdelenie).

in Oriental studies for both the military and the Soviet diplomatic service.[39] In the period 1919–21, the Academy was headed by the former tsarist General, Andrey Snesarev.[40] As is clear from the above, and supported by Stephan Conermann, Said's Orientalist nexus is most evident in early Soviet Oriental studies, where the Soviet military domain, I would argue, became its supreme manifestation during the period 1917–21.[41]

As remarkably noticed by Marshall, 'in the immediate course and aftermath of the Civil War, Russia's new rulers found themselves in a terrifying state of strategic and scientific ignorance'.[42] The Bolshevik government realised that it simply could not do without the former Imperial military and scholarly experts. Having forgotten its distrust towards them, the government decided to use them for solving practical tasks and bringing on a new generation of Soviet scholars and experts. Following this principle, it employed experienced military experts who were also eminent scholars of Persian studies, such as General Snesarev, Colonel Iagello, Colonel Smirnov and others.

General Snesarev[43] was an expert on a broad spectrum of studies, including Persia and Afghanistan, and by right received fame as the founder of the Soviet military Oriental studies.[44] Due to the administrative efforts and scholarly contribution of Snesarev, the Oriental Faculty of the Military Academy, in addition to training military and diplomatic Orientologists, was also extremely efficient in training scholars of Oriental studies in various other fields: linguistics, history, economics and others.[45] Throughout a period of five years this military scholarly institution provided three-quarters of the whole Soviet diplomatic and military staff in the Near and Middle East,[46] among whom were Sergei Pastukhov, a future Ambassador to Persia (1933–5) and Soviet scholar on Persia, and Iakov Bliumkin (1900–29), a notorious

---

[39] See Vucinich, "Structure," 56. See also Kuznetsova and Kulagina, *Iz istorii*, 12.
[40] AV, op. 1, d. 202 and d. 204.
[41] Stephan Conermann, "Foreword," in *The Heritage of Soviet Oriental Studies*, ed. Michael Kemper and Stephan Conermann (Abingdon: Routledge, 2011): xiii.
[42] Marshall, *Russian General Staff*, 189.
[43] See Baskhanov, *Russkie*, 217–20.
[44] See Baziiants, "Iz istorii," 56. See also Marshall, *Russian General Staff*, 190–1.
[45] RGVA, f. 11, op. 1, d. 186, l. 18. See also Kuznetsova and Kulagina, *Iz istorii*, 12.
[46] See Marshall, *Russian General Staff*, 191.

revolutionary terrorist who was head of Trotsky's personal security guard and one of the founders of the Communist Party of Persia, as well as a member of its Central Committee, a military Commissar of the Red Army of Persia and unaccomplished Head of *Cheka* of the Soviet Socialist Republic of Persia.[47]

Taking the above into consideration, it is possible to conclude that, although World War I and the subsequent events of the immediate post-1917 years had an enormous adverse impact on the organisational structure of the military domain and its ability to contribute to scholarly knowledge, the Bolsheviks' readiness to incorporate inherited expertise into the process of exerting new foreign policy and to overwhelmingly invest in the direct "state power/knowledge nexus" resulted in a quick overcoming of ruptures and in reviving continuities from Imperial institutional practices, albeit with considerable qualitative transformations. In other words, one of the main features of the period was that the new government had to employ Imperial experts and scholars in order to reach out with its political agenda, and these people tried to extract lessons from their past experience and to reform military Oriental studies in the way they reckoned expedient before 1917, when it lacked state support. They also secured the transfer of the Imperial institutional practice of bringing in scholarly active officers-*vostochniki* for training new specialists, which would be implemented later in the 1930s as new Soviet Iranists with practical knowledge returned from abroad.[48]

Another underlying feature was the scale of activities undertaken by the state in this field. Following its ambitious and sometimes hectic political agenda, the Bolshevik government spared no moral or practical efforts to, in the shortest possible period, fulfil its need for Oriental studies knowledge and, more importantly, for trained

---

[47] RGASPI, f. 85'Secret Persia', d. 26, l. 1. See also Igor Simbirtsev, *Spetssluzhby pervykh let SSSR, 1923–1939* (Moscow: Tsentrpoligraf, 2008): 95–6; Marshall, *Russian General Staff*, 191.

[48] See Vashurina and Sishkanov, "Rodoslovnaia voennykh perevodchikov". The term *vostochniki* derives from *Vostok* ('the East' or 'the Orient' in Russian) and was used officially in late Imperial Russia for differentiating the military officers and the employees of the Ministry for Foreign Affairs from their colleagues who had not received the appropriate Oriental studies training. It can be translated as 'orientalist'. Since the early 1920s the term *vostokoved* ('orientologist') has officially been used for everyone professionally trained in Oriental studies. The latter sounds more scholarly in Russian.

military Orientologists. It would adversely tell upon the quality of training but had positive organisational outcomes in terms of the institutional extension of Oriental studies from a long-term perspective.

Bolshevik Diplomatic Service and Oriental Studies, 1917–21

There is neither English- nor Russian-language scholarship specifically dedicated to the institutional activities of the Oriental Section of the Bolshevik successor to the Russian Ministry of Foreign Affairs. Moreover, there is little profound ad hoc literature studying its institutional activities in general because of the regime of secrecy and the impeded access to its post-1917 archive –old-fashioned Soviet practices which are still unjustifiably maintained by Russia's current political establishment. However, there are recent noteworthy works such as, for example, *Russian and Soviet Diplomacy, 1900–1939* by Alastair Kocho-Williams, who tries to emphasise continuities rather than stunning differences in the activities of the new institution, whereas I would argue that its nature was based much more on a rupture than continuities – at least, for its Oriental Section.[49]

In view of the fact that after the October coup the staff of the MID refused to fulfil the orders of the Bolsheviks, on 13 November 1917 all operating employees of the Ministry were fired. The day after, the process of creating its successor – the People's Commissariat for Foreign Affairs – began from scratch. By the end of November, the new structure had a modest but quite workable organisational set-up: the Commissar for Foreign Affairs had two assistants, supervising two main sections – Western and Oriental. The operating personnel counted less than twenty people.[50] So it is not surprising that, during the first years after the revolution, the organisation of any training in Oriental studies within the diplomatic domain was out of the question.

---

[49] Alastair Kocho-Williams, *Russian and Soviet Diplomacy, 1900–1939* (Basingstoke: Palgrave Macmillan, 2012). For detailed information regarding the difficulties in accessing Russian archives or particular files see my article on archival work: Denis V. Volkov, "Fearing the Ghosts of State Officialdom Past? Russia's Archives As a Tool For Constructing Historical Memories on its Persia Policy Practices," *Middle Eastern Studies* 51/6 (2015): 901–21.

[50] See S. V. Zarnitsky and L. I. Trofimova, *Tak nachinalsia Narkomindel* (Moscow: Politizdat, 1984): 13–14.

Similarly to the military domain, at the start, the Bolshevik government decided to draw to its side former Imperial experts. In November 1917, the then Commissar for Foreign Affairs, Trotsky, sent a cable to all Russian consulates in Persia containing the demand that they accept the new Soviet power. Bravin, Head of the Vice-Consulate in Khoi, was the only one who took up the call of the new power – the only one out of the several dozen Russian diplomatic staff working in Persia at that moment.[51] Under Trotsky's orders he was immediately appointed the Soviet diplomatic representative in Persia.

However, Bravin's credentials were not accepted by the Persian Court.[52] As Minorsky pointed out later, this failure and the fact that Bravin had to experience public loathing from the Russian colony, in general, and from all his former colleagues, in particular, during several consecutive months, eventually made him give up his mission and return to Russia in summer 1918, without authorisation from Moscow.[53] This situation testifies to significant ruptures at the institutional and individual levels within the diplomatic domain over the 1917 watershed – staff of the former power were reluctant to associate themselves with the new power, arguably because of a huge difference in social status between them and the image of the new polity.

The following developments prove that nobody in Petrograd (formerly St Petersburg) or Moscow was ready to cooperate, either. In the summer of 1918, Vice-Commissar Karakhan, supervisor for the Oriental countries, entrusted the Head of the People's Commissars Council in Baku, Stepan Shaumian (1878–1918), with choosing another candidature. Thus Ivan Kolomiitsev, aged twenty-one, became a Soviet diplomatic representative in Persia.[54] Shaumian chose him because of his alleged knowledge of Persia and because he was known among the Azeri Bolsheviks for his revolutionary activities while he served with Russian troops in the north of Persia. As Kolomiitsev wrote himself, he spoke fluent Persian and French and had worked for

[51] AVPRF, f. 94, op. 2, d. 2, papka 1, l. 1 (Bravin's appointment, 22 November 1917). See Pezhmann Dailami, "Bravin in Tehran and the Origins of Soviet Policy in Iran," *Revolutionary Russia* 12/2 (1999): 67.

[52] AVPRF, f. 94, op. 2, d. 1, papka 1, l. 4 (Chicherin's diplomatic notes to the Persian Government).

[53] AV, f. 134, op. 1, d. 224, l. 1–3ob.

[54] AVPRF, f. 04, op. 18, d. 50638, papka 109, l. 5.

more than a year in Persia. The situation being what it was, that was more than enough for the new state.[55]

It is worth mentioning, based on biographical information found in a few works on the issue, including the work *Tak nachinalsia Narkomindel*, that before the war Kolomiitsev studied at certain commercial courses and in 1916 was sent, at the rank of warrant officer, to Russian troops in Persia with the assignment of identifying Bolshevik agents in the army, albeit that he ultimately joined them himself, having become a member of the Party in 1917. This information leads to the assumption that he was one of the graduates of those courses under the Practical Oriental Academy that had been organised by the Interior Ministry's General Shvedov and Colonel Snesarev in 1911 and went to Persia as the agent of *Okhranka* (*Okhrannoe otdelenie* – the tsarist secret police).[56] The long and short of it is that Kolomiitsev's first mission in Tehran was smashed by the Cossacks and the British, and when in 1919 he was again sent to Tehran with a special appeal from the Soviet government he was intercepted by the Cossacks and arbitrarily executed on the island Ashuradeh in the Caspian Sea.[57]

Given the importance which the Bolsheviks assigned to their revolutionary activities in the Persianate world, by late 1920 – the time when Persian policy started to switch from the aim of organising an immediate revolution to cultivating the national bourgeoisie – in addition to the Oriental Faculty of the Military Academy, which was the main scholarly training institution covering the needs of NKID, a number of others had already been established.[58] In 1918, the Institute of Oriental Languages was established in Kiev and shortly after transformed into the Institute of Foreign Relations.[59] Under the decree of the People's Commissars Council, on 7 September 1920, the Central Institute of Living Oriental Languages was set up. It was immediately assigned the status of a military entity and graduates were supposed to work either for the military or the Soviet diplomatic service.[60] This is another

---

[55] See Zarnitsky, *Tak nachinalsia Narkomindel*, 225–6.
[56] AV, f. 115, op. 2, d. 50 (Snesarev's correspondence with Shvedov), l. 1, 3 and 6. See also Chapter 2.
[57] AVPRF, f. 94, op. 4, d. 4, papka 2, l. 5–5ob. (Chicherin to Raskol'nikov, 20 May 1920); see Appendix (Kolomiitsev).
[58] See Kononov, *Vostokovedenie*, 24–5.
[59] See Vucinich, "Structure," 53, 378.
[60] See Kuznetsova and Kulagina, *Iz istorii*, 12–13.

testimony to the fact that, in contrast with the preceding period, after 1917 the military domain prevailed over the diplomatic one both at organisational level and in Orientological training.

In general, this period brought much more disruption to diplomatic Oriental studies than to the military and academic domains. Old, experienced specialists were discursively excluded from the field but new ones had not been nurtured yet.[61] During this time, the Bolsheviks realised their inability to successfully tackle such a subtle issue as diplomacy in the Orient and took up the policy of accelerating the training of new experts on the basis of the other two domains, mainly the military one. Simultaneously, significant efforts were undertaken for creating a preliminary organisational basis for the future Marxist diplomatic Oriental studies, which later transformed into a substantial contribution to the new Marxist Orientological knowledge.[62]

Bolshevik Oriental Studies Scholarship Set-Up, 1917–21

The disruption caused by the events of the revolutions also told upon the Oriental studies scholarly community which, instead of carrying out its scholarly activities, had to get down to arranging its relationships with the new state power. After long and multiple discussions within the walls of the Academy of Sciences, academicians embarked upon the road of cautious cooperation with the Bolshevik state.[63] However, in addition to political contradictions of a new everyday social life, the main difficulty which Russian academic Oriental studies encountered after the Bolshevik coup was the imposed necessity of changing methodology. 'It was the so-called new Soviet Orientology the major task of which was defined as the study of nationalist-liberation movements and the problems of socio-political and economic life of the countries and peoples of the Orient mainly during the modern history and based on the Marxist methodology.'[64] Such an attitude posed the question of the usability of Orientological knowledge and became the foundation

---

[61] Ibid., 11.
[62] See Kemper, "Soviet Discourse," 2; Kemper, "Red Orientalism," 452–8.
[63] See Baziiants, "Iz istorii," 18–19.
[64] Aleksandr Tamazishvili, "Vladimir Aleksandrovich Gurko-Kriazhin: sud'ba boitsa 'vostokovednogo fronta'," in *Neizvestnye stranitsy otechestvennogo vostokovedeniia*, ed. Vladimir Naumkin (Moscow: Vostochnaia literatura, 2008): 44.

for the emergence and rapid development of the discourse on the expedient utilitarianism of Oriental studies for state interests.

The new polity needed Orientological knowledge, first of all, for assisting in the organisation of revolution in the oppressed Orient.[65] Consequentially, the former Imperial Oriental studies which had allegedly paid too much attention to ancient and medieval history and "abstract" linguistics needed to be changed from within and organisationally restructured in order to serve the goals of the world revolution. Simultaneously, in view of the politically vital importance of the issue, the new state urgently needed the expansion of this scholarly field both in terms of increased output and the adaptation of the new methodology, the combination of which was to result in producing a great number of specialists, trained in full conformity with this new methodology.[66]

The organisational changes in Soviet academic Oriental studies started with the unsuccessful attempt to reorganise and then to close down the Lazarev Institute of Oriental Languages in Moscow.[67] The problem was that the elaboration of the project of reorganisation was entrusted to academician Nikolai Marr, who, realising the uniqueness of such a scholarly educational institution (secondary and higher schools together), engaged other academicians (Bartold, Ol'denburg, Orbelli) in the work, trying to enhance its positive unique features for the sake of a better scholarly outcome.[68] However, his final project drastically diverged from the demands of the Bolsheviks. He did not succeed in, as Pavlovich put it, 'bringing scholarly knowledge closer to the political struggle of the Soviet country and of the peoples of the Orient'.[69]

Therefore, the Institute was doomed to closure. Only one of the symbolic figures of revolutionary arts, the writer Maksim Gorkii, could save the Institute by writing a letter to Lenin and proposing the establishment of the Institute of Oriental Studies. Lenin supported

---

[65] GARF, P-1335, op. 1, d. 5 (constitutive documents of Oriental studies institutes), l. 41–9, 52–4ob.
[66] See Tamazishvili, "Gurko-Kriazhin," 44; Kononov, *Vostokovedenie*, 22–3; Kuznetsova and Kulagina, *Iz istorii*, 5.
[67] See Baziiants, "Iz istorii," 50.
[68] See Appendix (Marr); Baziiants, "Iz istorii," 51.
[69] Baziiants, "Iz istorii," 52.

the idea and authorised the *Narkomnats* to organise the Institute of Oriental Studies in Moscow and the Petrograd Institute of Living Oriental Languages. Pavlovich, who at that time lived in Moscow, was appointed the first director of the Institute.[70] So the precious staff of Persian, Arabic and Turkish studies (by 1917 there were only these three fields left at the Lazarev Institute) were transferred to the Institute of Oriental Studies; and, on 4 March 1919, a new Armenian Institute was created, on the basis of the Lazarev Institute, which dealt only with Armenian studies.[71] However, the demand for new Marxist scholars and experts of Oriental studies was far from being met and, on 7 September 1920, Lenin signed the decree on the establishment of the Central Institute of Living Oriental Languages in Moscow, too.[72]

In general, Gorkii played a very important role in securing the institutional interests of Soviet Oriental studies.[73] The above-mentioned developments clearly show that, in contrast with the late Imperial period, after 1917 academic scholars began to lose their relative institutional autonomy in resolving organisational affairs within their domain. State interference in the *pure* scholarly domain produced indirect counteraction within the Foucauldian grid of power relations, which resulted in the emergence of the phenomenon, pointed out by Krementsov, of 'spokesmen' and 'patrons'.[74] Given his acquaintance with Lenin and his ability to play politics, Ol'denburg became the 'spokesman', first of all, for his own institution. He negotiated deals with the state, trying to secure and promote the interests of the scholarly community of the Academy of Sciences, whereas Gorkii was the 'patron' of scientific and scholarly activities – a person outside the scholarly community but at the level of a statesman who, being close to the highest government circles, was able to lobby for the interests of various groups of scientists and scholars. In the context of the new polity one of these groups became Orientologists.

[70] Georgii Ezhov, "Polveka tomu nazad v Tegerane (Otryvki iz vospominanii sovremennika)," in *Iran: Istoriia, ekonomika, kul'tura*, ed. Nina Mamedova and Liudmila Kulagina (Moscow: Institut vostokovedeniia RAN, 2009): 79.
[71] See Baziiants, "Iz istorii," 52–3. See also Kuznetsova and Kulagina, *Iz istorii*, 9.
[72] See Baziiants, "Iz istorii," 54.
[73] See Chapter 1. See also Baziiants, "Iz istorii," 48.
[74] See Chapter 1.

The last bastion of the *ancien régime* – the St Petersburg Faculty of Oriental Languages – did not lack the Bolsheviks' attention either and in September 1919 it was merged with the Historico-Philological and Judicial Faculties into the Faculty of Social Sciences. This motion also resulted in a manifestation of resistance on behalf of the intellectual: in 1920, Barthold established *Kollegiia Vostokovedov* (the Collegium of Orientologists), which united the *ancien régime* scholars of the former faculty. They adhered to their traditional methodology in teaching and scholarly work on the premises of the newly established Faculty of Social Sciences, although the curriculum was enriched by politico-economic subjects. However, Persian studies were taught by former Imperial professors (Barthold, Freiman, Inostrantsev, Romaskevich).[75]

One of the main features of this period is that, within the context of the overwhelming discourse on the proliferation of revolution in the Orient, there were laid the foundations for another discourse which would determine the development of Soviet Oriental studies throughout the 1920s and until the late 1930s, namely the necessity of practical applicability of Orientological knowledge solely for state interests. This discursive utilitarianism resulted in the palpable marginalisation of the classical Iranists, who were reluctant to meet the demands of the new state as they applied to the Persianate world, which was situated at the spearhead of the Eastern foreign policy of the early Soviet state. The same utilitarianism explains the fact that the Bolsheviks were eager to so urgently establish that significant number of training institutions in Oriental studies – another distinctive feature of that period.[76] Under the harsh conditions of the Civil War and with a lack of resources, the Bolshevik government succeeded in launching the reorganisation and enormous expansion of the inherited scholarly institutions of Oriental studies and, more importantly, laid a solid foundation for the creation of similar institutions in remote regions of Russia – the vital need of Russian pre-Revolution Oriental studies scholarship which Grigor'ev and Rosen had often pointed at.

---

[75] See Baziiants, "Iz istorii," 58–9.

[76] Another remarkable organisational feature of the new Soviet Oriental studies scholarship was the development of peripheral centres. Besides Tashkent, in 1918 Oriental studies educational and scholarly institutions were opened in Rostov-on-Don, and in 1919, in Kazan and Baku.

Political Context of Soviet–Iranian Relationships in 1921–41

During the second half of 1920, along with the gradual realisation of the fact that the sovietisation of Persia had proved a failure[77] and the simultaneous change of political priorities, deeply influenced by developments in the western direction, the trend within the Bolshevik government towards normalising relationships with Persia as an independent state significantly intensified.[78] In 1920, Fiodor Rotshtein, an experienced Bolshevik who had an excellent knowledge of British politics but had had very little to do with Persia, was appointed the Soviet diplomatic representative to Persia (the mission was based in Baku until February 1921).[79] It is unlikely that Lenin and the members of the *Politbiuro* were familiar with the institutional practices of the military and diplomatic domains of Imperial Russia which had embraced the successful employment of specialists on Persia also in the area of British affairs;[80] in any case, this, almost similar, choice seems to have been dictated by the expedient necessity determined by the preserved continuities within the triangle-shaped Russo-Brito-Persian complex relations of both the pre-1917 and post-1917 periods.

Rotshtein became the conductor of Moscow's strengthening guideline of curtailing Soviet armed interference and championed the urgent establishment of conventional diplomatic and trade ties with Persia.[81] He had to act against the backdrop of local authorities' opposition in Baku and Tashkent; they were vigorously inclined to build up armed assistance to the Persian revolutionaries, ultimately aiming to forcefully

---

[77] As early as 10 November 1920 the Commander-in-Chief of the [Soviet] Persian Army, Gikalo, newly appointed by Ordjonikidze, wanted from him a warrant for the liquidation of Kuchek-Khan, referring to him as conducting negotiations with the Shah's government and the British, and, in general, pointed out that the revolutionary movement in Persia had collapsed. Not having authorised the liquidation, Ordjonikidze later instructed on the necessity of striking a peace deal with the Shah's government (RGASPI, f. 85 'Secret Persia', d. 27, l. 5, 12; d. 47, l. 2).

[78] RGASPI, f. 85, d. 47, l. 2 (Chicherin to Ordjonikidze); d. 38, l. 1.

[79] See Appendix (Rotshtein).

[80] See Denis V. Volkov, "Vladimir Minorsky (1877–1966) and the Iran–Iraq War (1980–1988), or The Centenary of 'Minorsky's Frontier'," in *Russians in Iran: Diplomacy and Power in Iran in the Qajar Era and Beyond,* ed. Rudolph Matthee and Elena Andreeva (London: I. B. Tauris, 2018): 188–216.

[81] AVPRF, f. 028, op. 10, d. 11, papka 31, l. 6,7, 39, 63 (Chicherin to Rotshtein).

oust the British from Persia and topple the Persian government.[82] The counter-stance even led to Stalin's coming to Baku, Tashkent and Poltoratsk (Eshgabad) with Lenin's assignment to 'adjust our Oriental policy'.[83] Sultanzadeh, Head of the Persian Communist Party at that time and a future scholar of Persian studies, was dismissed and the policy of peaceful assistance to the Persian bourgeois revolution was confirmed.[84] The same Georgy Chicherin (1872–1936), who a year before had sent a letter to Lenin with congratulations on the forthcoming Bolshevik military sovietisation of Persia,[85] cabled to Rotshtein in summer 1920: 'Our activities in Persia aim at [...] opening the way for the Persian bourgeoisie to consolidate its dominancy.'[86]

In February 1921, the Bolshevik government signed the Treaty of Friendship between Soviet Russia and Persia, officially confirming the abrogation of all Imperial Russia's agreements and handing over Russian buildings, land and financial assets to Persia, provided they were not subject to be used by third countries.[87] After the multiple political debacles in Europe the Orient was regarded by the Bolsheviks as the area with great revolutionary potential. Due to its strategic position and profound cultural, economic and political ties with neighbouring regions, the Persianate world was to become the springboard for cultivating the necessary social conversion in the whole East, where Persia was to become the main point of application for these efforts. On 5 October 1920, Chicherin wrote to Rotshtein: 'the road to the liberation of the whole East, most likely, runs through Persia [...] our policy in Persia is an initial-experimental part of the general, immensely complex, liberating policy in the whole East'.[88] As General Edmund Ironside wrote about that time in his diaries, later published under the name *High Road to Command*: 'Soviet Russia had plenty of trouble on her hands in Europe. The Russians might confine their efforts to

---

[82] RGASPI, f. 85, d. 14, l. 3 (Rotshtein to Chicherin, 26 December 1921); d. 38, l. 1 (Chicherin to Ordjonikidze, 13 March 1921).

[83] See Aliev, *Istoriia Irana*, 125.

[84] AVPRF, f. 028, op. 10, d. 11, papka 31, l. 65 (Protocol of *Politbiuro*). See also Persits, *Zastenchivaia interventsiia*, 150–1.

[85] RGASPI, f. 159, op. 2, d. 49, l. 122 (Chicherin to Lenin, 7 June 1920).

[86] AVPRF, f. 028, op. 10, d. 11, papka 31, l. 7.

[87] The Persia and the Russian Socialist Federal Soviet Republic Treaty of Friendship, 1921, http://en.vionto.com/show/me/Russo-Persian+Treaty+of+Friendship+(1921) (accessed 12 March 2013).

[88] AVPRF, f. 028, op. 10, d. 11, papka 31, l. 63.

peaceful infiltration of their ideas amongst the Persian politicians.'[89] This confirms the previously mentioned changes in Soviet foreign policy towards Persia.

Having come to power, Reza Khan (1878–1944) became that political figure who succeeded in preventing the disintegration of the country through using force and also took advantage of the nationalist slogans so topical for Persia then.[90] Both countries, Persia and Soviet Russia, during the period 1923–5 almost solved the problems in the field of state construction, put an end to various counter-regime and separatist manifestations and centralised state power by using mainly military force. There were corresponding trends in the economic policies of both countries: the Bolshevik government declared the NEP[91] and the Persian government undertook efforts aimed at the encouragement of civilised private business in the form of *sherkat* (company). This backdrop positively influenced Soviet–Persian relations. The two countries established official trade representations not only in the capitals but also in other important cities. A considerable number of joint Soviet–Persian export-import companies were established during the 1920s. For instance, in 1923 two joint companies, *Perskhlopok* and *Persshelk*, were set up which, in fact, revived the Persian cotton and silk industries. A joint Soviet–Persian bank, *Ruspersbank*, was also established for servicing entities engaged in the bilateral trade.[92]

In the first half of the 1930s, the USSR was the main trade market for Iran in the field of export-import activities. In terms of Iran's export, the Soviet Union was a consumer of 100 per cent of fish production, almost 100 per cent of rice and cattle, 90 per cent of cotton, more than 80 per cent of wool, almost 70 per cent of silk and half of

---

[89] *High Road to Command. The Diaries of Major-General Sir Edmund Ironside, 1920–1922*, ed. Lord Ironside (London: Leo Cooper, 1972): 177. William Edmund Ironside (1880–1959) was a Chief-Commander of the British forces in Persia in 1921. According to his memoirs, he initiated using Reza Pahlavi by the British as a promising political figure in Persia.

[90] Ibid., 177.

[91] The New Economic Policy (NEP) was proposed by Lenin; it started being implemented in 1921 and lasted until 1927–8, when it was replaced by Stalin's industrialisation and collectivisation. The NEP implied a kind of mixed economy with the state sector in the main areas and the private sector in less important areas, with legislative liberalisations in the approach to private owners. The NEP was aimed at the exhilaration of the economy after the Civil War and the policy of War Communism.

[92] See Mamedova, "Istoriia Sovetsko-Iranskikh otnoshenii," 161–2.

the total export of Iranian leather.[93] However, with the changes in the countries' domestic policies (the enhancement of dictatorship trends and the dismantling of the NEP in the USSR) after the early 1930s, the character of the Soviet–Iranian[94] trade relations started to change, too. Trade operations between the countries were later carried out only by official state organisations. Cultural ties became restricted.

Simultaneously with the changes in the geopolitics of the 1930s and the rise of Nazi Germany, Reza Shah gradually embarked on the road of making use of a third political power. He had always tried to draw on nationalism-tinged motions in his policies and a third force had been always considered as a promising factor in political games with Great Britain and Soviet Russia. In the 1930s, the German political and trade stands in Iran enhanced year by year. In the second half of the 1930s, the Soviet Union's share of Iranian trade drastically diminished, so that in 1939 it constituted only 0.5 per cent of the whole trade turnover of Iran.[95] The increase in German political and trade influence was widely pointed out in Western and Soviet post-war historiography. However, such allegedly common knowledge was questioned by some post-Soviet researchers, in particular by Aliev, who in 2004 argued that the extent of this influence had been exaggerated and that there was no evidence behind the multiple references to the massive presence of fascist intelligence in Iran and its plans to organise a pro-fascist coup in Tehran, and that the figures for Germans residing in Iran were also significantly exaggerated.[96] One can only assume that this exaggeration was for the sake of more solid substantiation of the Allies' occupation of Iran. Aliev's arguments, of course, are potentially harmful to and inconsistent with the official discourse of Putin's regime underpinning the current political and military rapprochement between Russia and the Islamic Republic of Iran, which maintains that

[93] See ibid., 163.

[94] The term *Persia/Persian* (distorted *Fars/Pars*) entered European languages through Hellenistic historians and initially implied subjugating motives on behalf of European civilisation. *Iran* is the only word available in Farsi for referring to the country. Following the nationalist trend undertaken in his policies, in 1935 Reza Shah ordered the Ministry for Foreign Affairs to announce to all countries that the only word that could be used to refer to the country in diplomatic correspondence was *Iran*.

[95] See A. B. Orishev, *Iranskii uzel: Skhvatka razvedok. 1936–1945 gg.* (Moscow: Izdatel'skii dom Veche, 2009): 13.

[96] See Aliev, *Istoriia Irana*, 195–201.

there are no unanswered questions in the history of Russo–Iranian relations.

Therefore, another researcher whose writings are in full conformity with official patriotic discourses and Putin's foreign policies, Aleksandr Orishev, has recently been granted access to the archives of SVR[97] and the restricted files of AVPRF.[98] Drawing on the documents originating from these archives only and dispensing with the other archives crucial for this topic, including German and Iranian ones, he offered his own narrative in defence of the Soviet post-World War II historiography and tried to prove not only the enormous rapprochement of Iran and Nazi Germany on the eve of World War II but also the existence of a Nazi coup plot in Iran and plans to turn the country into a spring-board for attacking British India and Soviet Central Asia.[99] Therefore, allegedly there was an imminent military threat emanating from Iran's territory, hence the 1941 Soviet invasion of Iran was totally legitimate, according to the 1921 Soviet–Iranian Treaty of Friendship, in contrast with the illegitimacy of the British occupation of Iran. In any case, regardless of state-sponsored manipulations of historical evidence, it appears a commonly acknowledged fact that by the late 1930s the volume of Soviet–Iranian relations had reached its historical minimum at all levels. According to the Iranian customs registration, in 1937 the German share of Iranian imports was 50 per cent more than that of the Soviet Union, and in export – twice as much.[100] Unlike the dimmed trade ties, Soviet political and intelligence activities highly intensi-fied, which entailed the further impetuous development of Soviet Iranology.[101]

Soviet Diplomatic and Military Oriental Studies, 1921–41

In January 1919, one of the founders of Soviet Oriental studies, Gurko-Kriazhin, wrote that the course of events clearly proved 'the truth of comrade Lenin's assertions that the world war could not

---

[97] *Sluzhba Vneshnei Razvedki*, since 1991 the post-Perestroika successor to PGU (*Pervoe Glavnoe Upravlenie KGB*) – the directorate within the former KGB responsible for intelligence activities abroad; now independently subordinated to the President of the Russian Federation.

[98] See Orishev, *Iranskii uzel*, 4–6.

[99] Ibid., 16–28, 53–7, 77–85.

[100] Ibid., 29.

[101] See Appendix (Teimurtash).

finish without the world revolution [which in its turn] could not be over barely within Europe. Beyond doubts, the mortal strike to Imperialism will be inflicted only after the flames of the revolution also envelope the Orient which is the main source of strength and wealth for Imperialism'.[102] So, the first years after the establishment of the Oriental Section in the Military Academy and of the Special Courses in Tashkent passed under the aegis of the training of specialists for future revolutionary battles in the Oriental countries.

However, the early 1920s made their amendments in Soviet foreign policy towards the Orient and in the modality of military Oriental studies training. In the 1920s, the heroes of the unsuccessful sovietisation of Persia (such as Sultanzadeh (Avetis Mikaelian), Rudol'f Abikh, Ehsanulla) were back in Soviet Russia and had started working both in Soviet state bureaucracy and scholarly institutions, making a feasible contribution to the new Soviet Oriental studies, particularly Persian studies.[103] Others, such as Osetrov (Irandust), Pastukhov (Iranskii), Il'in (Raskol'nikov) and Vladimir Tardov, continued to work in Afghanistan and Persia, contributing by writing articles and supplying valuable, first-hand country-study materials.[104]

As a result of the organisational volatility of the first post-Revolution decades and the dearth of Oriental studies specialists, the Soviet military and diplomatic services were significantly more intertwined in comparison with the late Imperial period. For instance, Raskol'nikov, after commanding the Bolsheviks' expedition corps in Persia and then the Soviet fleet on the Baltic Sea, was appointed the Soviet diplomatic representative to Afghanistan (July 1921–December 1923).[105] Abikh was the Secretary of the Political Section of the Persian Red Army and

---

[102] Vladimir Kriazhin, "Retsenziia na Troianovskii K. Vostok pri svete revolutsii," *Sovetskaia strana* 1 (27 January 1919).

[103] See Appendix (Mikaelian, Abikh and Ehsanulla). See also Liudmila Kulagina, "Moskovskaia shkola iranistiki: Izuchenie istoricheskikh problem," in Kulagina, *Iranistika*, 47. See also Vladimir Genis, "Rudol'f Abikh – istorik Gilianskoi revoliutsii," in Kulagina, *Iranistikai*, 151.

[104] See Appendix (Osetrov, Pastukhov and Tardov); Nina Kuznetsova and Liudmila Kulagina, "Vsesoiuznaia Nauchnaia Assotsiatsiia vostokovedeniia, 1921–1930," in *Stanovlenie Sovetskogo vostokovedeniia*, ed. Ashot Baziiants (Moscow: Nauka, 1983): 151. See also Genis, "Rudol'f Abikh," 145, 147, 152–3.

[105] RGASPI, f. 159, op. 2, d. 49, l. 51–63 (Raskol'nikov's correspondence with Chicherin). See also Iaroslav Vasil'kov and Marina Sorokina, eds, *Liudi i sud'by: Bibliograficheskii slovar' vostokovedov-zhertv politicheskogo*

a member of the Military Committee for the Liberation of Persia. On returning to Moscow, he entered the Oriental Section of the Military Academy and simultaneously was a research officer at the All-Russia Scholarly Association of Oriental studies (VNAV).[106] After his graduation from the Military Academy he became Head of the information subsection of the Press Department of *Narkomindel* and after that, in 1926, he was appointed the TASS (the Telegraph Agency of the Soviet Union) representative under the Soviet diplomatic mission in Tehran.[107] In 1918–19, Tardov worked in the Supreme Military Inspection and the *Narkomvoendel* of the USSR (Ukraine). After graduating from the Persian courses of the Military Academy, he was appointed the NKID representative to the short-lived Soviet Socialist Republic of Persia and then Head of the Soviet General Consulate in Esfahan (1921–8).[108] As demonstrated in Chapter 2, such a situation would have been impossible during the late Imperial period.

Naturally, in view of the extraordinary conditions of the new polity and the dearth of qualified staff, the Soviet entities dealing with Oriental countries would also accept employees with any kind of training or simply people who spoke the necessary languages, having been born and lived in the relevant regions. The most important criterion was ideological fidelity to the polity, not professionalism.[109] This quite often led to productive manifestations. An interesting example was Khaji-Murat Muguev (1893–1968), whose Oriental background and experience of serving at the Persian front in 1914–17 were used by the Bolsheviks, who appointed him Head of the Intelligence of the Persian Red Army. After leaving Persia in 1920, he went on working in the military intelligence structures of the Soviet Army on Iran in the 1920s and 1930s. His contribution to Oriental studies was realised through literature, as he became a famous Soviet writer. His novels, shedding light on the nineteenth and twentieth centuries' historical

terror v sovetskii period, 1917–1991 (St Petersburg: Peterburgskoe vostokovedenie, 2003).

[106] GARF, f. P-1335, op. 1, d. 6, l. 55.

[107] See Genis, "Rudol'f Abikh," 146–7, 151–2.

[108] GARF, f. 7668, op. 1, d. 2883 (Tardov's personal file), l. 1–3ob. RGASPI, f. 85, d. 96, l. 1–4 (Tardov's cooperation with Rotshtein). RGALI, f. 626, op. 1, d. 2, l. 344.

[109] See M. Kullanda and N. Sazonova, "Zabytoe imia (V. G. Tardov)," in Kulagina, *Iranistika*, 132. See also Tamazishvili, "Gurko-Kriazhin," 52, 64, 69.

events in Persia, and his poems about Persia were among his multiple literary works.[110]

However, Orientologists-practitioners, in particular Iranists, were trained mainly at the Oriental Faculty of the Military Academy. It should not be omitted that Persian courses were established in the NKID on 15 November 1919; however, they ceased to function shortly after, with Konstantin Chaikin's departure for his posting as an interpreter of the Soviet plenipotentiary mission in Turkey and Persia (based in Baku in 1920).[111] Training in Oriental languages was finally launched on the premises of NKID in the early 1930s. For the NKID staff dealing with Oriental countries, learning Oriental languages became obligatory and study hours were considered as working hours which, in actual fact, revived the traditions of the Educational Section of the late Imperial period.[112]

In 1924, the Oriental Section of the Military Academy was transformed into the Oriental Faculty of the Military Academy. In view of its purposes and its academic composition (the organisational and scholarly set-up was drawn up by Snesarev, which beneficially influenced the teaching process and the quality of training), the faculty succeeded in developing the scholarly training of the "old" scholarship against the backdrop of its practical orientation.[113] It hence occupied, in this sense, a place between the *ancien régime*, academic Leningrad Institute of Living Oriental Languages and the MIV, which was organised to meet the state organs' demands for Orientologists.[114]

In the 1920s and 1930s, Persian studies at the Military Academy were also taught by Chaikin, who was a talented young scholar of pre-Revolution Persian philology. He also worked as an interpreter in the Soviet Embassy in Tehran in 1921–6. Having returned to the Soviet Union, Chaikin occupied himself mainly with scholarly activities: he went on teaching in the Military Academy, became an associate

---

[110] See "Voennaia literatura," http://militera.lib.ru/memo/russian/muguev_hm/index.htm. See also "Osetiia i osetiny," http://osetins.com/2007/10/26/muguev-khadzhi-murat-18931968.html; www.livelib.ru/author/24014.

[111] GARF, f. 7668, op. 1, d. 2889 (Chaikin's personal file), l. 1–5ob.

[112] See Volkov, "Persian Studies," 915–32. See also the site of the MID of the Russian Federation (www.mid.ru/nsite-sv.nsf/mnsdoc/03.15.03.01).

[113] AV, f. 115, op. 2, d. 63 (Snesarev's correspondence with the Oriental Section of the General Staff about the curriculum of the Academy), l. 1.

[114] See Tamazishvili, "Gurko-Kriazhin," 69–71. See also Baziiants, "Iz istorii," 56.

professor in the MIV and prepared a number of works on Persian literature and language,[115] including linguistic works in co-authorship with the Academician Marr. By the late 1920s, the NKID had employed a sufficient number of Persian language specialists and throughout the 1930s Chaikin was engaged by the NKID for interpreting and translating only from time to time, on very important occasions, such as interpreting for high-ranking Iranian delegations or double-checking the translation of Soviet–Iranian trade treaties.[116]

In the late 1920s, Chaikin also taught at the KUTV, another scholarly and educational institution of Oriental studies, founded in 1921 and responsible for training political activists in Soviet and foreign Asia. Being affiliated with the Central Committee of the USSR Communist Party, in the context of the foreign Orient this institution played the role of training activists for the organisation of communist parties in neighbouring Oriental countries. The main feature of this university was that its students mainly originated from the places at which they were later expected to work.[117] The first Persian group, consisting of twenty-four students, was formed on 2 August 1921. Judging by their curriculum, comprising the study of Turkestan, Bukhara, Khiva, Persia and Afghanistan, they would later have been assigned to become operatives throughout the Persianate world.[118] The potential of the periphery, never previously used in Imperial Russia, became immensely useful under the conditions of the dearth of practical Orientologists, and also because it eliminated the necessity for cultural and ethnographic induction of students. One of the noteworthy organisational features of this institution was that it almost did not accept students who spoke Russian, believing that they either had been connected to the *ancien régime* state organs (the Imperial Ministry of the Interior) or originated from wealthy families – in both cases they were 'class-alienated elements'.[119]

This trend in Soviet Oriental studies for the establishment and rapid development of new institutions on the periphery continued in the 1920s and 1930s. In 1922, in Tashkent, the Military Courses of

---

[115] See Appendix (Chaikin).
[116] AVPRF, f. 08, op. 10, d. 190, papka 33, l. 22.
[117] GARF, f. p-1335, op. 1, d. 5, l. 55.
[118] Ibid., l. 61, 80–1.
[119] Ibid., l. 52ob.

Oriental Studies were transformed into the Higher Military School of Oriental Studies with the Iranist Ivan Iagello as its head. The main goal of the school was stipulated as the preparation of 'military and political-military specialists with special Orientological training sufficient for independent scholarly activities, connected with the knowledge of Oriental languages'.[120] The period of training was three years, during which students would study at least two Oriental languages from Persian, Urdu, Uzbek and Kazakh.

Following the call of the times, as early as the late 1920s such subjects as Muslim Law and History of the Muslim Orient were removed from the curriculum and replaced by Leninism, Modern History, Soviet Development, Economy and mode of life of the Muslim countries, Historical Materialism and other signs of the new humanities. In the field of Persian studies, during the 1920s and 1930s Iagello went on with his own unique pre-1917 system of teaching Persian and Arabic through pictures. He also authored a number of works on Persian linguistics. In 1928, due to his contribution to Soviet Orientological knowledge, Iagello was awarded the Honourable Letter of Commendation of the Revolutionary Military Council of the USSR. In 1930–2, he also taught at the Oriental Faculty of the Military Academy in Moscow.[121]

The susceptibility of Iagello, Snesarev and Chaikin to the pre-1917 discourse of *Russkoe delo*,[122] which metamorphosed after 1917 into the discourse of "service to their nation who had chosen the Bolsheviks", prevented them from withdrawing from scholarly and administrative activities, which, in actual fact, resulted in them becoming Foucauldian vehicles of power, manifested in the preservation of Imperial institutional practices in Oriental studies within, mainly, the military domain. In contrast with the military domain, which in this sense, as Hirsch maintains, turns out quite similar to the academic domain,[123] this phenomenon is not seen in the diplomatic domain, whose scholarly active *vostochniki* all preferred the preservation of, mostly, personal interests in this interplay of power/knowledge relations, hence opting for emigration. This leads us to the

[120] B. V. Lunin, "Vostokovedenie v respublikakh Srednei Azii posle Velikoi Oktiabr'skoi Sotsialisticheskoi revoliutsii," in *Stanovlenie sovetskogo vostokovedeniia*, ed. Ashot Baziiants (Moscow: Nauka, 1983): 111.

[121] Ibid., 111–13.

[122] See Chapter 2. See also Volkov, "Persian Studies," 917, 927–8, 930–1.

[123] See Hirsch, *Empire of Nations*, 22, 48.

assumption that the susceptibility to the discourse of *Russkoe delo* which had been identifiable in the activities of Russian diplomats-*vostochniki* and particularly glaring in their utterances (for example, the correspondence between Minorsky and Vvedenskii, Minorsky's private diaries and Bravin's letters to Zhukovskii and to the Imperial MID)[124] was of a more outward nature and was perceived by them, consciously or unwittingly, as an intrinsic part of their beliefs simply because those practices and utterances, arguably, coincided with their personal interests, such as tangible remuneration, career promotion and prestige. This, of course, will be dealt with in more detail in Chapters 4 and 5.

Notwithstanding the dominancy of military structures in Persian studies until the late 1930s, there was one institution that at least nominally can be subsumed under the jurisdiction of the diplomatic domain. Based on the initiative of the Soviet diplomat Iakov Surits (1882–1952)[125] in 1922, the Tashkent Special Scholarly Oriental Commission was established under the representative offices of the NKID and *Narkomvneshtorg*.[126] The main goal of the Commission was the comprehensive study of the countries 'adjacent to Turkestan, namely Khiva, Bukhara, Persia, Afghanistan, West-China and India' with the emphasis on the study of contemporary issues.[127] The Commission also assisted in establishing the Newsletter of the Central Asia Media, publishing materials from foreign newspapers of the region.[128]

Thus, the study of the military and diplomatic domains of Soviet Oriental studies during the 1920s and 1930s makes it possible to state a deep, even hectic interconnectedness, which also engulfed civil scholarly institutions, and is rather easily understood in the circumstances post-1917. During the 1930s, the situation, to an extent, improved and the organisational overlapping of the domains significantly diminished; however, the military component continued to dominate. Even Soviet ambassadors were ultimately subordinated to GRU and INO OGPU station-chiefs, in full contrast to the Imperial period

---

[124] AV, f. 134, op. 2, d. 525, l. 1–4; op. 1, d. 803, Two notebooks. AV, f. 17, op. 2, d. 9. AVPRI, f. 144, op. 489, d. 1022b, l. 106.

[125] See Appendix (Surits).

[126] The People's Commissariat of Foreign Trade; also NKVT.

[127] GARF, f. P-1335, op. 1, d. 5, l. 1, 5.

[128] Ibid., l. 1–7.

when the diplomatic domain totally dominated the operational field abroad.[129]

The change in scholarly methodology and the trend towards immediate practical application of Oriental studies knowledge predetermined the relevant organisational structures and the modality of the participation of individuals within them during the period, as long as almost all activities were subjugated to the interests of state power and its political agenda.[130] Due to the change in the character and goals of Oriental studies scholarly activities, the individuals engaged in Soviet military and diplomatic services perceived themselves at the forefront of producing and developing new scholarly knowledge, laying the foundation for the rest of the age of Soviet Oriental studies. It is the discursive endeavour of those experts, who had worked in the Soviet military and diplomacy and then went into academia, that constituted the background of Soviet–Iranian contemporary studies during the 1920s–1950s, even if most were to perish in the purges of the late 1930s. It is also notable that during the 1920s and 1930s in this context Iranology occupied the central place within these two domains in question, being immensely important both in political and military fields.[131]

Organisational Set-Up of Academic Oriental Studies, 1921–41

The field of early Soviet Oriental studies was insufficiently studied in Western scholarship in the twentieth century. Those few works by Richard Frye, Wayne S. Vucinich and Muriel Atkin substantially drew on the works of the Soviet scholars of the mature and late periods of the USSR, who themselves had been subject to various kinds of discourses, inculcated by the Soviet state, and whose research had been

[129] See Chapter 2.
[130] See Chapter 1. See S. M. Ravandi-Fadai, "Vneshnepoliticheskie problemy Irana v rabotakh rossiiskikh uchenykh," in Kulagina, *Iranistika*, 62. See also A. Z. Arabajan, "O nachal'nykh etapakh izucheniia ekonomiki Irana v Sovetskoi Rossi ii SSSR (1920–1956)," in Kulagina, *Iranistika*, 74–5.
[131] See Nina Mamedova, "Issledovanie sotsial'no-politicheskikh problem Irana i iranskogo obshestva," in Kulagina, *Iranistika*, 53–4. See also Kulagina, "Moskovskaia shkola iranistiki," 45–8; Semen Agaev, *Sovetskoe iranovedenie 20-kh godov* (Moscow: Nauka, 1977): 3–4, 7–9; Kononov, *Vostokovedenie*, 117; Baziiants, "Iz istorii," 41.

restricted by the straightforward ideological censorship of the time.[132] Notwithstanding the profound changes in the political and public life of Russia of the 1980s and 1990s which led to significant epistemological shifts in the activities of the Russian scholarly community, mainstream post-Soviet Iranology, in general, and the researchers engaged in the study of Soviet Iranology, in particular, have, surprisingly, preserved many of the scholarly approaches of the Soviet period.[133]

On the other hand, the scarce Western scholarship of the recent period, albeit implementing new historiographic and theoretical approaches, continues to heavily draw on Soviet and post-Soviet works on the organisational set-up of Soviet Oriental studies.[134] While actively engaging with Soviet and recent Russian scholarship, as well as with the available English-language literature on the issue, this chapter still tries to employ as much archival material as necessary for constructing a separate historical narrative on the organisational set-up of early Soviet Iranology. In doing so, it will become a prologue for a more detailed study of the field in the following chapters.

In the era of the NEP – between War Communism (1918–21) and the Great Break (1928–41) – scholarly activities still remained relatively free. Along with the "old" Oriental studies scholarly community, now there was another community consisting of people, standing on strictly ideological positions and conducting research mainly on contemporary aspects of the Orient. Their scholarly activities mostly included writing articles for newspapers and journals on issues related to the study of economic, political, cultural and ideological developments in Oriental countries. Persian studies were no exception to that. The aggressive Soviet foreign policy of 1919–21 towards Persia generated such new Soviet scholars as Pastukhov, Sultanzadeh, Rotshtein, Osetrov, Pavlovich and others who combined work in new Soviet ministries, now called commissariats (NKID and NKVT), with

---

[132] See Frye, "Oriental Studies in Russia"; Vucinich, "Structure"; Muriel Atkin, "Soviet and Russian Scholarship on Iran," *Iranian Studies* 2/4 (1987): 223–71; Kuznetsova and Kulagina, *Iz istorii*; Kuznetsova and Kulagina, "Vsesoiuznaia"; Agaev, *Sovetskoe iranovedenie*.

[133] See Sergey Sukhorukov, *Iran mezhdu Britaniei i Rossiei: Ot politiki do ekonomiki* (St Petersburg: Aleteia, 2009); Kulagina, *Rossiia i Iran*; Kulagina, *Iranistika*; Mamedova, "Istoriia Sovetsko-Iranskikh otnoshenii"; Liudmila Kulagina and Elena Dunaeva, *Granitsa Rossii s Iranom: Istoriia formirovaniia* (Moscow: Institut Vostokovedeniia RAN, 1998).

[134] See Kemper, "Red Orientalism," 435–76; Kemper, "Soviet Discourse."

work in other state and scholarly institutions, public organisations, newspapers and journals. They were real experts on the very recent and current life of Persia and would subjugate the analysis of their subject of study to their personal political and ideological agenda.[135]

The new Soviet Oriental studies were criticised by the "old" school because of the mainly superficial character of their works, their narrow orientation to the present and their utilitarian application.[136] Their scholarly training and quality of professional knowledge were also questioned by classic scholars. For instance, Pavlovich was reprimanded for not speaking any Oriental language and for his lack of Oriental studies education, while he considered himself entitled to express his opinion on all issues of Orientology, particularly on Persia. There also was a sort of confrontation between the Petrograd and Moscow academic Oriental studies' communities in view of the fact that Moscow had become the capital of Soviet Russia and the majority of new scholars were concentrated around the main state organisations, situated in Moscow, while Petrograd stayed the main centre of "old" scholarship.[137] This situation was also pointed out by Ol'denburg, who said in 1927 that for a long period there had been no good relationships between "old" and "new" scholarly communities.[138]

On the other hand, there was even more sharp criticism on the part of Marxist scholars which targeted the "old" school. In 1921, in his note to Stalin, Pavlovich wrote that "old" Orientologists were incapable of creating the work necessary for revealing the true essence of Imperialism and for studying national liberating movements in the Oriental countries. He stressed that these kinds of activities should have been entrusted 'not to our Orientologists but rather to our comrades-communists, familiar with the Oriental issue'.[139] As we see, Pavlovich accentuated ideological fidelity rather than scholarly quality of the individuals in question. Thus these people 'familiar with the

---

[135] M. V. Ivanova, *Vvedenie v regionovedenie: Iz istorii sovetskogo vostokovedeniia* (Tomsk: Izdatel'stvo TPU, 2006): 10–11. See also Kulagina, "Moskovskaia shkola iranistiki," 46–7.

[136] See Vasilii Bartol'd, "Iran," 333–4. See also Kulagina, "Moskovskaia shkola iranistiki," 47.

[137] See Ivanova, *Vvedenie v regionovedenie*, 13. See also Tamazishvili, "Gurko-Kriazhin," 56.

[138] See Sergei Ol'denburg, "Pamiati M. P. Pavlovicha," *Novyi Vostok* 18 (1927): 33.

[139] GARF, f. 5402, op. 1, d. 57, l. 1–2 (Pavlovich to Stalin).

Oriental issue' were the former head of the Persian Communist Party Central Committee, Sultanzadeh, and Tardov who, in 1909–11, had worked in Persia as a journalist and overtly criticised Imperial Russia's policy in Persia and then that of the Provisional Government, and who had actively cooperated with the Bolsheviks since 1918.[140]

Pavlovich also used Barthold's criticism of the pre-1917 Oriental studies and the state approach towards it, but transformed it in such a way that Imperial Oriental studies were criticised for lack of attention to social-economic aspects. He stated that Russia previously had 'no literature about the Orient' and 'there was no correct study of the Orient before 1917'.[141] The scholars of the "old" school were criticised for their sheer theoretical approach, for paying too much attention to philological issues and for underestimating the study of modernity.[142]

In order to improve this situation and 'to disseminate correct information about the Orient among the masses',[143] and hence to surmount the difficulty of that antagonism between the *ancien régime* Oriental studies and the new Soviet Orientology, the VNAV was designed by Pavlovich. In so doing, he was actively assisted by Snesarev, who became a member of the 'organisational fiver'.[144] In general, the Association, established at the very end of 1921, was to draw the "old" scholars over to the new Soviet Orientological scholarship and to become an organisational and governing centre for the country in the field of Oriental studies.

The VNAV was set up under a decree issued on 13 December 1921 by the All-Russia Central Executive Committee of *Narkomnats*. Its charter mentioned that the main aim of its activities was the comprehensive study of both the foreign and the Soviet Orient as well as the dissemination of Orientological knowledge. The Association consolidated all Oriental studies societies and organisations on Russian territory (the Soviet Union, from the beginning of 1922). It was authorised to use all available relevant forces and materials and had the right to contact foreign entities and organise international events and activities. It was also expected to render consultations to

---

[140] GARF, f. 7668, op. 1, d. 2883, l. 3ob.
[141] Mikhail Pavlovich, "Zadachi Vserossiiskoi nauchnoi assotsiatsii vostokovedeniia," *Novyi Vostok* 1 (1922): 9.
[142] GARF, P-1335, op. 1, d. 23, l. 1–6.
[143] GARF, P-1335, op. 1, d. 17 (Charter of VNAV, Pavlovich's manuscript), l. 18.
[144] AV, f. 115, op. 1, d. 222, l. 2–5. GARF, f. P-1335, op. 1, d. 5, l. 10; d. 17, 24.

state entities and to be the source of necessary information and man-power for them.[145]

Pavlovich was appointed Head of the Association. However, he had posts in many other state and public organisations such as *Narkomnats*, the Military Academy, the Oriental Trade Chamber, the Union for Actions and Propaganda of the Peoples of the Orient and other organisations.[146] In spite of his great energy and revolutionary passion, and, in fact, overloaded with his duties, he was unable to lead administrative-organisational work with the same success, and the Association began to function properly only after the appointment of Gurko-Kriazhin as a scholarly secretary in February 1922.[147] By the end of 1922, the first edition of *Novyi Vostok* (The New Orient) journal, the main print media organ of the Association, was published. It contained a programme article by Pavlovich which in addition to scholarly activities proclaimed 'the economic and spiritual liberation of the Orient' among its main tasks. It also mentioned that the Association was going to closely cooperate with the KUTV, MIV and other educational and scholarly institutions in the field of Oriental studies.[148] Throughout the subsequent years, the journal printed articles mainly written by such scholars of new Soviet Oriental studies as Pavlovich, Gurko-Kriazhin, Osetrov, Pastukhov and Shitov, and by those "old" academics who had either accepted the new polity, such as Marr, or decided to at least officially cooperate with it for the sake of knowledge itself, such as Krymskii, Romaskevich and Ol'denburg.[149]

The leading centre of the Association was the Political-Economic Section, headed in 1923 by Gurko-Kriazhin. The period between 1923 and 1927 was considered to be the most successful in the history of the Association activities. Gurko-Kriazhin designed a special programme which, in view of the lack of data on Persia, Turkey and Afghanistan, initially stipulated the development of theoretical studies and the application of Marxist methodology.[150] As the influence of the

---

[145] GARF, P-1335, op. 1, d. 17, l. 2–24.
[146] See Ivanova, *Vvedenie v regionovedenie*, 14.
[147] See Tamazishvili, "Gurko-Kriazhin," 58.
[148] See Baziiants, "Iz istorii," 64–5.
[149] See Tolz, *Russia's Own Orient*, 96–101; A. N. Kheifets and P. M. Shastiko, "V. I. Lenin i stanovlenie sovetskogo vostokovedeniia," in *Stanovlenie Sovetskogo vostokovedeniia*, ed. Ashot Baziiants (Moscow: Nauka, 1983): 18.
[150] See Tamazishvili, "Gurko-Kriazhin," 63.

Association grew the quantity of its members also increased among people who were mainly engaged in practical work and who ultimately helped to gain access to the most information on the Oriental countries. Rotshtein, Osetrov, Pastukhov, Tardov and Raskol'nikov were among the most active members of the Association. Tardov even organised a branch of the Association in Tehran. Other branches of VNAV were also established in other republics of the USSR. The VNAV branches mainly dealing with the study of Persia operated in Tashkent, Baku and Tiflis.[151] The Tashkent Society for the study of Tajikestan and Iranian nationalities, established in 1925, was particularly active in this field.[152]

Kemper and Tamazishvili conclude that by the time VNAV was dismissed in 1930 it had failed to reach the goals stipulated in its charter.[153] This is only partly fair. Indeed, the Association did not succeed in becoming a truly all-Union and central organ, uniting and managing all the Orientological activities in the USSR. However, it did succeed in achieving its other priority, namely the construction of a solid direct, reciprocal nexus between state power and scholarly knowledge, particularly in the field of Persianate studies. Its activities involved the active cooperation of those people who determined early Soviet foreign policy in this region, for example, Pastukhov and Osetrov (their impact will be studied in Chapter 5). Their scholarship, accumulated and processed at VNAV, would directly reach the highest government structures and Orientological training centres. It is noteworthy that the same practical Orientologists designed and took their actions in the field of foreign policy based on their own scholarship as reflected through the VNAV, namely its publishing organ *Novyi Vostok*, organised scholarly debates and other institutional activities.

At the same time, the "old" academic scholarship who, after a series of reorganisations of Oriental studies, mainly concentrated in the Leningrad Institute of Living Oriental Languages, were almost totally marginalised from exerting any influence on early Soviet foreign policy, but were still actively being engaged in the state-run, domestic nationalities project throughout the 1920s, as Hirsch argues in her

---

[151] See Kuznetsova and Kulagina, "Vsesoiuznaia," 151–2.
[152] See also Kuznetsova and Kulagina, *Iz istorii*, 30.
[153] See Kemper, "Red Orientalism," 471–6. See Tamazishvili, "Gurko-Kriazhin," 97.

profound *Empire of Nations*. The *Kollegiia Vostokovedov*, established
in 1921 on Barthold's initiative, regularly printed its *Zapiski Kollegii
Vostokovedov*, reflecting its academic continuities even in the title,
which was a direct reminder of Imperial *ZVORAO*. The above-
mentioned journal and the journal *Vostok* (The Orient), affiliated
with the Asiatic Museum, published scholarly articles on ancient and
medieval history, literature, arts and the general spiritual heritage of
the Orient, hence explicitly stipulating their contributors' reluctance
to engage with *politicised* Orientology.[154] During the NEP's relative
pluralism within academic activities, Barthold, Freiman, Krachkovskii,
Ol'denburg and others mostly pursued the pre-1917 mode of research
and teaching traditions, with the emphasis on ancient and medieval
Oriental history and literature.[155]

The Moscow Oriental studies scholarly community was represented
mainly by the MIV which was formed from the merging of the Central
Institute of Living Oriental Languages and the Oriental Faculty of
Moscow University. The curriculum of the Institute was approxi-
mately the same as the one at the Petrograd Institute of Living Oriental
Languages, but with lower quality philological training, especially in
Persian studies.[156] Kuznetsova and Kulagina, in their work *Iz istorii
sovetskogo vostokovedeniia, 1917–1967*, characterised the MIV as
being much weaker in scholarly terms than that in Petrograd,[157] while
other researchers, such as Kemper and Baziiants, write that it was the
Soviet leading centre for training specialists on the Orient throughout
the 1920s.[158] There is no contradiction. The point is that the teaching
staff of the Moscow Institute mainly consisted either of scholars who
had accepted the new ideology or young tutors, and also it was later
managed by Pavlovich. So, one of the main requirements of that time
was the partial replacement of theoretical studies by practical and
ideological training. Besides that, the Institute was situated in the capital and was orientated, first of all, towards the training of specialists
for state power entities. The main "consumers" were *Narkomindel,
Narkomvneshtorg, Narkomvoendel* and NKVD.[159] This trend was

---

154 See Tamazishvili, "Gurko-Kriazhin," 67.
155 See Kuznetsova and Kulagina, *Iz istorii*, 14–15.
156 GARF, P-1335, op. 1, d. 5, l. 41.
157 See Kuznetsova and Kulagina, *Iz istorii*, 15.
158 See Kemper, "Integrating," 3.
159 GARF, P-1335, op. 1, d. 5, l. 41–49ob.

preserved until 1938 when the Leningrad Oriental Institute (the former Leningrad Institute of Living Oriental Languages since 1928) was merged with the MIV. Thus, by the late 1930s, Oriental studies in Leningrad remained only in the walls of Leningrad University and by that time it had suffered multiple reorganisations into various faculties and institutes and, finally, had been returned under the university auspices.[160]

In 1930, the Asiatic Museum and *Kollegiia Vostokovedov* ceased to exist as independent organisational structures and were transformed into the Institute of Oriental Studies of the Academy of Sciences of the USSR. In general, the years between 1927 and 1934 were a period of crucial restructuring of the Soviet Academia, which began with the adoption of a new charter for the Academy of Sciences in 1927 and the gradual taking over of the Academy by the Bolsheviks. The quality criterion gave its place to quantity. Also, the Oriental studies education of the 1930s could be characterised by the narrow specialisation trend and insufficient linguistic training. Educational institutions confined the subject to learning contemporary newspaper language, which decreased the training level of Soviet Orientologists.[161]

It should also be noted that during the 1920s and 1930s scholarly and educational Oriental studies institutions kept rapidly developing in other cities of the USSR, especially in Asian republics. Among them Tashkent, Baku, Tiflis (Tbilisi from 1936) and Yerevan should be mentioned separately. The Turkestan Oriental Institute and the Philological Faculty of the Turkestan People's University were also established in Tashkent. Barthold cooperated with both institutions and took part in the activities of a special commission on the selection of teachers for the Philological Faculty. In 1922 and 1923, classes were launched at the Oriental Faculties of the Baku and Yerevan universities.[162]

Conclusion

It is possible to conclude that the trend aiming at the complete change of methodology in Oriental studies research that started in the first

---

[160] See Kononov, *Vostokovedenie*, 25.
[161] See Kuznetsova and Kulagina, *Iz istorii*, 70–2, 77.
[162] See Baziiants, "Iz istorii," 66–7.

post-1917 years kept ramping up throughout the 1920s against the backdrop of the fading influence of the "old" scholarship and became totally consolidated in the 1930s. The contemporary issues of the Orient, reviewed from the angle of Marxist ideology, occupied the central place in Soviet Orientological research and training. The demands of state power organisations dealing with the Orient totally defined organisational and training policy in the field of Oriental studies.[163] By the mid-1930s, academic Orientological training had become much more narrowly specialised, which speaks in favour of its rigorous orientation to state power needs. In 1939, the chair of Iranian Philology of the Oriental Faculty of Leningrad University comprised the Persian, Tajik, Ancient Iranian, Kurdish, Osetian and Dari languages sections – a number of Iranian languages that had never been taught before in Russia.[164] Therefore, the emphasis on Iranian studies, which had been characteristic of the late Imperial period due to its scholarly and political importance, continued with further drastic increase during the two decades post-1917 and can be explained mainly by foreign policy institutions' demands. The additional importance gained by Iranian studies in the post-1917 period was also pointed out by Barthold, who in 1926 even proposed the establishment of a special publishing organ on Iranian studies, the journal *Iran* – which did not exist for any other field of Oriental studies.[165]

The instrumental and ideologically driven approach of the new Soviet state towards Oriental studies, in general, resulted in the graduate demise of the classical school of Persian studies by the early 1930s, as also supported by Rodionov.[166] The involvement of "old" Orientologists, including Iranists, with the state-run inner nationalities project, which, according to Hirsch,[167] brought about significant, new capabilities and operational autonomy which those scholars had not had during the Imperial period, did not have a palpable positive impact on Persian studies, except for facilitating the physical survival of those scholars through the 1920s. In the 1930s, their place

[163] See Kemper, "Integrating," 2–3.
[164] See Kononov, *Vostokovedenie*, 116–17.
[165] See Bartol'd, "Iran," 334.
[166] See Rodionov, "Profiles under Pressure," 47–8, 55–6.
[167] See Hirsch, *Empire of Nations*, 7, 140.

was occupied by a new academic generation of ideologically driven Iranists who were carrying out research of rather low quality and were restricted by the postulations of the Marxist methodology. However, in quantitative evaluation, throughout the whole early Soviet period, academic Oriental studies, and Iranology therein experienced enormous institutional expansion in training and later in research fields, due to the state-heightened attention of which late Imperial Oriental studies could have only dreamt.

The same factor resulted in the impetuous quantitative development of Oriental studies within practical domains, particularly of Iranology, due to the fact that the Persianate world occupied an even more important and discursive position in the early Soviet policy than Persian studies had had during the late Imperial period. The continuities which persisted from the Imperial period and were preserved in both the military and diplomatic domains during the early Soviet period, namely the employment of professional postings for gathering multifaceted primary material for sequential scholarly processing, secured the enhanced productivity of power/knowledge relations during the period in question. The lacuna which indeed had existed in the study of the contemporary Orient had become almost replenished by the late 1930s, albeit with knowledge of arguably rather questionable or biased character.

The impetuous expansion of institutional structures within each domain confirms the proposed overall threefold organisational set-up of early Soviet Oriental studies. At the same time, based on the analysis of the Soviet–Persian relationships of the 1920s and, particularly, of the 1930s, and given the presence of multiple Soviet trade and economic representations in Persia, which gathered and produced lots of area-study information on the relevant issues, a presumption of the emergence of a new domain – trade – in early Soviet Iranology would inevitably come to mind. However, taking into account that these activities were carried out under the aegis of NKID and the entities involved were staffed mainly with experts – Iranists from NKID, the military and INO OGPU[168] – the trade activities cannot organisationally be defined as a self-contained domain of Orientological

---

[168] AVPRF, f. 08 *'Karakhan's office'*, op. 10, papka 33, d. 190, l. 5–6 (Karakhan's correspondence with Davtian).

knowledge production. Thus, early Soviet Iranology possessed only a threefold structure: academic scholarship, diplomatic service and the military, whose activities were significantly more intertwined at the institutional and individual levels than of those during the late Imperial period.

4 | Between Cultures and States: Russian Orientologists and Russia's Eastern Policy

Introduction

The involvement of Russia's Orientologists in the intense, manifold interaction between the Russian Empire and Persia during the period from the late nineteenth century to 1917 predominantly took place within the four main professional domains, discussed in Chapter 2 of the manuscript, namely academic scholarship, the military, the diplomatic service and the Orthodox Church's missionary activities. Given the nature and the historical developments of this interaction, the extent of the involvement of each domain was different, as was their impact on Russo-Persian relations of the period. However, as the undertaken research has shown, there were clearly discernible continuities and commonalities in the organisational set-up and practices of these domains as well as in the roles of the individuals – namely academic scholars and practical experts of Persian studies – involved.

This chapter is dedicated to the study of the above-mentioned individuals and their impact within the operational field of Russia's Eastern policy from the late nineteenth century to 1917. Tackling narrowly framed research questions (specified in Chapter 1), concerning their lives, activities and written works, will enable us to ascertain and analyse the presence and interplay of power/knowledge relations at an individual level, as was done in Chapters 2 and 3 at the institutional level. In order to identify the "physical" proximity of these individuals to state power, first it is necessary to examine the modality of their involvement in state activities: their posts, institutional subordination, reports and other writings they produced. This will help identify their basic or "nominal" capacity to influence events and, eventually, state policy.

After that, it is possible to switch to studying their personal contribution to the interaction between Russia and Persia, which will include their personal reasons for being involved in the operational

field of a particular domain, the personal factors (for example, susceptibility to discourses) that influenced the (non-)execution of their
duties, their personal stance and the eventual impact on concrete historical events. The question of the efficiency of the state's employment
of their expertise will be tackled in the conclusion to the chapter. The
initial data for the above analysis have been retrieved from archival
materials which document the activities of the individuals in question,
and from their published and unpublished private and scholarly
writings as well as from the writings of their contemporaries and the
existing literature about them.

The analysis of the political background of Russo-Persian relations
given in the previous two chapters shows that the diplomatic and
military domains were the main spheres of the countries' interaction
and, consequently, the individuals involved in the activities of these
domains were doomed to play if not the main then underlying roles
in the designing and the realisation of late Imperial Russia's foreign
policy towards Persia. However, in addition to the deep interconnectedness of all domains that was discussed in Chapter 2, analysis of the
organisational set-up of Russian Oriental studies of the time shows
the primary influence of academic scholars on their disciples from
both "civilian" and "practical" institutions. The scholars 'exercised
intellectual and political influence beyond their scholarly fields' and
transferred to their disciples 'a number of common perceptions ...
about how to understand the peoples and societies that they studied'.[1]
With this in mind, this chapter starts with the study of the key civilian
academics of Russia's Persian studies of the period[2] and continues with
consecutive studies of the experts involved in the other three practical
domains of Persian studies who, along with their outstanding practical
record, made a significant contribution to Orientological knowledge.[3]

---

[1] Tolz, *Russia's Own Orient*, 3.

[2] The term "civilian" is used throughout this chapter in order to differentiate
scholars who were mostly engaged in teaching conventional students and
who had no diplomatic or military rank, such as Rosen, Barthold, Zhukovskii
and Salemann, from those who genuinely were in diplomatic or military
services and then became scholars, teaching mostly in diplomatic or military
institutions, such as Miluitin, Kuropatkin, Tumanskii, Iagello, Zinov'ev,
Minorsky and Smirnov.

[3] In order to secure the epistemological congruency of my research methodology,
the criterion of "being scholarly active" was applied at the stage of selecting
individuals as subjects for my research within the "practical" domains. Taking

Civilian Academic Scholars

Valentin Alekseevich Zhukovskii – who can rightly be regarded as the token figure of the nexus of state power and scholarly knowledge in late Imperial Russia – has been studied surprisingly little even in Russia itself.[4] For more than fifty years there has been no comprehensive research into the scholarly and administrative activities of this individual whatsoever. Yet, in addition to his scholarly contribution, which laid the foundations of Russia's Persian studies of the twentieth century, he played the key role in the development of Russia's practical Oriental studies. Being the main connecting link between civilian scholarship and the state in the Russian Empire of the late nineteenth and the early twentieth century, he became the most perfect illustration of scholars taking advantage of the state in their own interests, most of all for the benefit of scholarship itself.[5]

Zhukovskii graduated from the St Petersburg Faculty of Oriental Languages in 1880; in 1883, because of the excellence of his Master of Arts thesis, he was retained at the university to prepare for professorship as chair of Persian philology. Following the institutional practice inherent in all domains of Russia's Oriental studies (which was

into account that the notion of "scholarly active" implies a rather broad set of activities – looking for artefacts when in Persia; collecting scholarly observations and processing and sending them to civilian academic scholars and scholarly societies as well as composing and publishing scholarly writings – and a great number of "practical" experts, in one way or another, were engaged in this kind of activity in Russia (see Chapters 2 and 3), another criterion was chosen in order to narrow the focus, namely "being prominent enough" within their own professional domain.

[4] There are three brief works on Zhukovskii that were authored by his colleagues Barthold and Ol'denburg and his disciple Romaskevich shortly after his death in 1918, namely Vasili Bartol'd, "Pamiati V. A. Zhukovskogo," in *Sobranie sochinenii*, vol. 9 (Moscow: Nauka, 1977): 689–703; Sergei Ol'denburg, "Valentin Alekseevich Zhukovskii, 1858–1918," *Izvestiia Rossiiskoi Akademii nauk* 2 (1919): 2039–68; Aleksandr Romaskevich, "V. A. Zhukovskii i persidskaia narodnaia poeziia," in *ZVORAO* 25 (1921). There is also another brief article, published later in the Soviet Union: Petr Bushev, "Zhizn' i deiatel'nost' V. A. Zhukovskogo," in *Ocherki po istorii russkogo vostokovedeniia*, ed. V. Avdiev (Moscow, 1959): 116–36.

[5] In this respect, many noteworthy documents are kept in AV (*Fond* 17 'V. A. Zhukovskii', *dela* 4, 22, 37, 184, 188, 193, 195) that demonstrate how Zhukovskii actively used his connections in the MID and the War Ministry of Russia for the development of Orientological academic knowledge and for the institutional promotion of Oriental studies, first of all, Persian studies.

owing to the earlier activities of Professor Kazem-Bek and Professor Miliutin), Zhukovskii was immediately sent to do fieldwork in Persia, where he spent three years.[6] Living together with Persians and extensively travelling around the country, Zhukovskii realised how deeply Persian culture and Persians themselves were dependent on religion, and this personal finding formed the main field of his future scholarly interests.

His close relative (his sister's husband) and colleague, Vasilii Barthold, wrote: 'Russia's leading expert on the study of Islamic Persia, Zhukovskii was not so much a historian in this field but rather a researcher of the language and literature. Among the spheres of people's life he was particularly interested in religious beliefs.'[7] His first trip to Persia resulted in his gathering a great amount of scholarly material, mainly on Persian dialects, folkloric literature and beliefs. On his return, he authored a number of groundbreaking works, including the first textbook in Russia on the grammar of Persian. The materials gathered by Zhukovskii were supposed to be published in five volumes, the first of which gained him the professorship in Persian studies in 1889. Having institutionalised Persian literature as one of the main fields of Russia's Persian studies, he taught Persian language and literature at the St Petersburg Faculty of Oriental studies throughout the 1890s and 1900s and remained Russia's main scholarly authority on them till his death.[8]

However, besides the abundant scholarly harvest of that fieldwork, there was another component of no lesser importance. During his stay in Persia, Zhukovskii developed relations with high-ranking state functionaries in the main cities of Persia, such as Tehran, Esfahan and Shiraz,[9] and actively cooperated with Russian diplomats, which, most

---

[6] David Schimmelpenninck van der Oye, "Mirza Kazem-Bek and the Kazan School of Russian Orientology," *Comparative Studies of South Asia, Africa and the Middle East* 28/3 (2008): 456–8. See also A. K. Rzaev, *Muhammed Ali M. Kazem-Bek* (Moscow: Nauka, 1989): 75–6; Marshall, *Russian General Staff*, 24–8, 48–9.

[7] Bartol'd, "Iran," 332.

[8] See Bartol'd, "Pamiati V. A. Zhukovskogo," 694, 700–2. See also Vigasin and Khokhlov, *Istoriia*, 197–8.

[9] Zhukovskii so valued his connections within the Persian highest state establishment that many scholarly materials, received from Persia, and works on the issues of contemporary life in Persia remained unpublished (see Bartol'd, "Pamiati V. A. Zhukovskogo," 699; Iurii Borshevskii, "K kharakteristike rukopisnogo naslediia V. A. Zhukovskogo," in *Ocherki po istorii russkogo vostokovedeniia*, ed. Iosif Orbeli (Moscow: Nauka, 1960): 8).

likely, was part of his assignment when he was sent to Persia.[10] This behaviour, though, fully complied with the conventional institutional practices of Russian Orientology at the time, which are also touched upon in *Russia's Own Orient*.[11] In fact, this three-year trip laid the foundations for Zhukovskii's close and intensive cooperation with the Ministry of Foreign Affairs and the War Ministry of Russia until November 1917 – the year when he, along with all other Imperial Foreign Affairs employees, simply did not turn up at the Ministry on the day after Leo Trotsky took it over.[12] During the 1890s, Zhukovskii, alongside his academic activities at the faculty and in the Educational Section of the MID, undertook other scholarly expeditions to Persia and the Trans-Caspian region that were organised with the assistance of the two above-mentioned ministries.[13] Having become an associate fellow at the St Petersburg Academy of Sciences in 1899, three years later he was appointed the Dean of the Faculty (1902–11) and in 1905 Head of the Educational Section of the MID.[14]

As a 'closet scholar', as Barthold used to call himself, and a staunch promoter of the dissociation of scholarship from state, Barthold could not help implicitly disapproving of Zhukovskii's preoccupation with state activities, which eventually, indeed, turned out to be to the detriment of Zhukovskii's scholarly output.[15] The rest of the five volumes remained unpublished until after Zhukovskii's death since he had not

[10] AV, f. 17 (Zhukovskii), op. 1, d. 24; see also Zhukovskii's correspondence with Bravin (ibid., f. 17, op. 2, d. 9). From the materials, kept in the above-mentioned archive, it is also clear that on his return to Russia Zhukovskii had access to the secret documents of the War Ministry. In 1887 Zhulovskii heavily criticised both the report of Staff-Captain Evgenii Belozerskii, who had been sent to Persia on a reconnaissance mission under the cover of a journalist, and the mode of the activities practised by this officer in Persia in 1885. See also, on Zhukovskii's letter to Baron Rosen about his acquaintance with Naser al-Din Shah, Firuza Abdullaeva, "Zhukovskii Valentin Alekseevich," *Encyclopaedia Iranica* (15 August 2009), www.iranicaonline.org/articles/zhukovskii-valentin-alekseevich.

[11] Tolz, *Russia's Own Orient*, 73.

[12] See Zarnitsky and Trofimova, *Tak nachinalsia Narkomindel*, 7–9.

[13] See Valentin Zhukovskii, *Drevnosti zakaspiiskogo kraia: Razvaliny Starogo Merva* (St Petersburg: Ministry of the Imperial Court, 1894): 1.

[14] See Vigasin and Khokhlov, *Istoriia*, 128. In 1915 he was also appointed the Head of Translation Section of Political Departments of MID. See also Bartol'd, "Pamiati V. A. Zhukovskogo," 696–5.

[15] Bartol'd, "Russkaia nauka," 534. See also Bartol'd, "Pamiati V. A. Zhukovskogo," 699–701.

had enough time to finalise the materials. His contemporaries usually saw piles of manuscripts in his office that were half-ready for publication but never published.[16] Instead, albeit at the expense of his own scholarly output, Zhukovskii created a whole system of relations which resulted, in particular, in the promotion of the scholarly institutions in which he was engaged, and the advancement of all Oriental studies of late Imperial Russia in general. This crucial component of Zhukovskii's activities has not properly been studied yet.

Having begun with his own scholarly field, he developed and industrialised what had been initiated by Baron Rosen, namely making use of his former students as a source of raw materials on the country.[17] Almost all former students of Zhukovskii who worked in Persia provided him with artefacts, manuscripts and scholarly reports on various aspects of Persian history and culture on a grand scale. He would openly state it as the direct duty of those Russians with Orientological training who were serving in Persia.[18] This intrinsic feature of the scholar's activities was also separately pointed out by Barthold.[19] Thus Zhukovskii received materials from Bravin, Minorsky, Nikitin, Seraia Shapshal, Baranovskii, Girs and many other employees of the Russian Legation and multiple Russian consulates in Persia as well as from military officers-*vostochniki*.[20] In 1906, Zhukovskii's former student and Head of the Russian Loan and Discount Bank in Tehran Leonid Bogdanov succeeded in obtaining Omar Khayyám's manuscripts, which became part of the 246 Persian manuscripts collected and sent by him to St Petersburg during his tenure from 1904 to 1914.[21]

At the same time, using his good relations with the representatives of practical Oriental studies, Zhukovskii would conduct joint scholarly efforts with them (based on the materials they provided) in studying

---

[16] See Seraia Shapshal, "Valentin Alekseevich Zhukovskii," in *Ocherki po istorii Russkogo vostokovedeniia*, ed. Iosif Orbeli (Moscow: Nauka, 1960): 133.

[17] See Viktor Rozen, "Babidskii antikholernyi talisman, 1892," *ZVORAO* 7 (1893): 317.

[18] See Valentin Zhukovskii, "Cherty sovremennogo polozheniia Persii v ee literaturnykh proizvedeniiakh, 1903," *ZVORAO* 16 (1904–5): xvi.

[19] See Bartol'd, "Pamiati V. A. Zhukovskogo," 702–3.

[20] AV, f.17, op. 2, d. 9 (Correspondence with Nikolai Bravin), l. 1, 2, 7, 10, 22. See also Valentin Zhukovskii, "Rossiiskii imperatorskii konsul F. A. Bakulin v istorii izucheniia babizma," *ZVORAO* 24 (1917): 35; Appendix (Shapshal).

[21] AV, f.17, op. 2, d. 9 (Correspondence with Bravin), l. 14.

issues of his own interest, namely aspects of religious life in Persia. As Cambridge researcher Firuza Abdullaeva, albeit in passing, mentions, many of the valuable reports presented by him to various scholarly societies were based on materials recieved from his former students serving in Persia.[22] Based on materials received from Girs, Consul in Mashad, and Baranovskii, Consul in Esfahan, Zhukovskii presented his famous scholarly report "The Features of the Current Condition of Persia in Her Literary Works" at the session of the Oriental Section of the Russian Archaeological Society on 20 November 1903; however, he left it unpublished due to his political reservations.[23] According to Barthold, Zhukovskii's joint works with Colonel Tumanskii on Babism as well as his cooperation with Minorsky on Sufism and the sect *Ahl-e hagh* were sound illustrations of his significant collaborative contribution to Persian studies.[24]

In terms of his administrative activities, using his scholarly prestige and his connections with former students who had already become influential employees of the MID and the War Ministry, he would push forward the realisation of his ideas on the further develop-ment of Russia's Oriental studies and its funding. For instance, from Zhukovskii's correspondence with Minorsky in 1911, it is clear how Minorsky routinely assisted him in liaising with high-ranking minis-terial officials and the representatives of Russia's state Duma.[25] This was during a crucial period for the Educational Section, when its very destiny was at stake. Due to Zhukovskii's efforts and his resulting multi-vector influence, directed through his former students and other influential connections in the key ministries of the Russian Empire, as well as through his scholarly colleagues, not only did he twice succeed in preventing the dismantling of the Educational Section (in 1907 and 1912), but he also elaborated on and successfully introduced the project concerning its extension and long-term development, from which not only Persian, but other areas of Russian Oriental studies benefited, too.[26]

---

[22] See Abdullaeva, "Zhukovskii."
[23] AV, f. 17, op. 1, d. 23.
[24] AV, f. 17, op. 2, d. 37 (Correspondence with Vladimir Minorsky, 1902–4), l. 1, 2, 2ob., 6–8. See also Bartol'd, "Russkie issledovaniia," 332.
[25] AV, f. 17, op. 2, d. 37 (Correspondence with Minorsky, 1911), l. 10.
[26] The number of academics and students was increased. In addition to Persian, Arabic and Turkic, which were traditionally taught in the Section, the Far-East

In 1909, Vasilii von Klemm, an official for special missions of
the Russian MID, wrote in a brief letter to Zhukovskii: 'Your
requests regarding the teaching of Persian – received and executed.
I also managed to have a talk with the Minister with regard to the
[Educational] Section.'[27] From the next page, we see that von Klemm
confirmed that he would receive 'those two young men' Zhukovskii
had told him about.[28] In another letter, we see that, finally, on 5 August
1911, when victory had already become clear (albeit short-lived, as
turned out later) and Zhukovskii had been given *carte blanche* with
regard to the Section, von Klemm returned to St Petersburg from a
party at Zhukovskii's *dacha* and, while thanking him and his wife for
their wonted hospitality, asked Zhukovskii to design and submit a new
curriculum for, this time, a new expanded Educational Section of the
Ministry.[29]

Of course, all this was done by Zhukovskii not merely for the
benefit of scholarship but rather within the patriotic endeavour to
be useful for his Motherland – the discourse which was intrinsic to
the disciples of Rosen, who himself had derived these ideas from the
legacy of his teacher Vasilii Grigor'ev (1816–81)[30] – the emblematic
figure of Russia's troubled relations between scholarship and state
whose life and activities became such a fertile ground for the genesis and flourishing of the debate on Russian Orientalism throughout
almost the last two decades.[31] Rosen 'accepted Grigor'ev's view that
scholarship should serve the interests of a nation to which a particular
scholar belonged'[32] and successfully transferred this postulation to his
disciples, the favourite of whom was Zhukovskii.[33]

languages were added. The one-to-two years fieldwork was also offered by the
    Section's curriculum. See Vigasin and Khokhlov, *Istoriia*, 128–31.
[27] AV, f. 17, op. 2, d. 22 (Correspondence with von Klemm), l. 34–34ob.
[28] 'Those two men' were Zhukovskii's former students for whom he was trying
    to secure jobs in the Ministry (AV, f. 17, op. 2, d. 22 (Correspondence with
    von Klemm), l. 35).
[29] AV, f. 17, op. 2, d. 22, l. 14.
[30] See Tolz, *Russia's Own Orient*, 8–9.
[31] See Chapter 2 for the debate between Knight, Khalid and Todorova which
    took place on the pages of *Slavic Review* and *Kritika: Explorations in Russian
    and Eurasian History*. The debate was then developed in works published in
    the late 2000s. See Kemper, "Integrating"; Schimmelpenninck van der Oye,
    "Imperial Roots"; Tolz, *Russia's Own Orient*.
[32] Tolz, *Russia's Own Orient*, 9.
[33] See Abdullaeva, "Zhukovskii."

Apprehending the crucial importance of the Eastern question for Russian domestic and international affairs, Zhukovskii was even more active and successful in his endeavour to use his scholarly and administrative influence for strengthening his country. Similar to his colleague Barthold, he often stressed 'the greatness of the historical tasks of Russia in application to the Orient' in his scholarly writings and administrative reports.[34] In addition to the apprehension of such a vital question for the Russian Empire as the incorporation of Eastern peoples and their cultures from the peripheries of the Empire, he shared views on Eastern foreign policy which were rather common for the Russian state establishment of the time and were succinctly stated by General Shvedov during the debate over Oriental studies in Russia: 'Now, not only our tasks in the East are equal to those in the West but far outweigh them'.[35]

Therefore, Zhukovskii was indeed part of the Russian civilising mission discourse, which inspired Russia's foreign policy, for instance, towards Persia at that time. However, for him this was only in terms of the promotion of *Russkoe delo*, namely the spreading of Russian prestige and influence outside Russia. When it came to cultural perceptions of the Orient, he, like many other academic colleagues, would disagree with those politicians and military men who believed in the superiority of Russian culture and in the fact ensuing from this regarding the superior rights which the Russian Empire allegedly had over Oriental peoples.[36]

In general, sympathy towards the peoples and cultures they studied was not rare among Russian Orientologists of the *fin de siècle*, as is also pointed out by Knight and Schimmelpenninck van der Oye.[37] Such an approach developed from the belief in the underlying difference between Russian culture and hence Russian scholarship and the West in terms of Russia's cultural affinity to the Orient, which was frequently stressed not only by civilian scholars but also by Russian military Orientologists.[38] This approach was inherent to Zhukovskii,

---

[34] AV, f. 17, op. 1, d. 183 (the manuscript of Ocherk istorii Vostochnogo Otdeleniia, 1907), l. 17; see also Bartol'd, "Russkaia nauka," 534.

[35] Ibid., d. 192 (General Shvedov's Report), l. 34.

[36] Ibid., d. 24 (Review of Belozerskii's Report), l. 4, 11, 14.

[37] Knight, "Grigor'ev," 97; Schimmelpenninck van der Oye, *Russian Orientalism*, 9, 194–5.

[38] AV, f. 115 (A.E. Snesarev), op. 1, d. 70 (The manuscript of "Otnosheniia k aziatskomu miru"), l. 2, 5–7.

as one of his contemporaries, Ol'denburg, confirms in his obituary.[39] This was, of course, added to its ideological armoury by Soviet historiography; however, in an adequately distorted form. Soviet researchers of Zhukovskii hastened to oppose him to Western scholars in terms of their support of their governments' arrogant, colonial attitude towards the East and hence of the exploitation of Eastern peoples, as if not noticing Zhukovskii's indirect but conspicuous participation in Russia's overall colonial presence in Persia.[40]

Indeed, in his correspondence with one of his most favoured disciples, Bravin, Zhukovskii reproached him a few times because of the arrogance and lack of respect towards Persians and their culture that 'suddenly' appeared in Bravin's letters to his former teacher after he went to serve in Persia as a Russian Imperial diplomat. Reminding Bravin that it was not what he had taught him, Zhukovskii calls on him 'to love Iran', in response to which Bravin, like a tricked school pupil, complains that 'in books and your [Zhukovskii's] explanations it [Iran] is one but in reality – another'.[41] This, of course, raises another phenomenon which was more intrinsic to practical Orientologists than, for example, their civilian academic counterparts, namely the very romantic fascination with the Orient that was transferred to Russians from Western Orientalism, depicted by Said in his book.[42] According to Bravin's letters and Minorsky's private diaries,[43] these romantic perceptions would often be followed by disappointment as soon as yesterday's students found themselves in the field. This will be examined in more depth later in this chapter.

In general, the whole spirit of the rather frequent correspondence between Zhukovskii and Bravin, which lasted about seven years, demonstrates that, due to the guidance of his teacher, Bravin looks at Persians not as the object of semi-colonial administration, whose representative he was, but as the equal to Russians, albeit very different from them; people whose culture represents immensely valuable material not only for Orientological scholarship but also in terms of

---

[39] See Ol'denburg, "Zhukovskii."
[40] See Bushev, "Zhizn'," 118.
[41] AV, f.17, op. 2, d. 9 (Correspondence with Bravin), l. 11–11ob.
[42] See Bartol'd, "Russkaia nauka," 541; Said, *Orientalism*, 1–9, 14–123, 222–3.
[43] AV, f. 134, op. 2, d. 39 (The First Trip of the Lazarev Institute Student from Moscow to Persia, 1902).

enriching his own culture.[44] These ideas, rooted in Grigor'ev's perception of the East–West nexus within Russia's nature, later, via his
disciple Rosen, became part of the discourse of a historical fusion of
Western and Eastern civilisations within Russia that prevailed among
civilian scholars of Russia's Oriental studies at the turn of the twentieth century and that was passed over from them to the experts and
scholars of the diplomatic and military domains, albeit with lesser
intensity.[45]

In this respect, Andrew Wachtel points out:

As opposed to the elites of other imperializing nations, whose explicit or
implicit assumption of cultural superiority caused them to view their own
values as universal and as something to be imposed on others, members of
the Russian cultural elite proposed a model that emphasized their nation's
peculiar spongelike ability to absorb the best that other peoples had to offer
as the basis for a universal, inclusive national culture.[46]

However, such a discourse was intended primarily to serve domestic
needs as 'a novel interpretation of the imperial project as a project
of translation of world culture into and through Russia'[47] but immediately spread over to further areas, for two reasons: first, given
the broad specialisation profile of Russian Orientologists, the same
scholars were engaged in dealing with the whole Persianate world,
which comprised both Russia's inner and outer Orient; second,
given the then imperialist expansion, in the perception of the time,
"today's inner Orient" was "yesterday's outer" – as much as "today's
outer Orient" could potentially become "Russia's inner Orient of
tomorrow".

The same approach was characteristic of Barthold's views and
activities since he also belonged to Rosen's 'entirely new school of

---

[44] Ibid., l. 24–7, 53–5. In his criticism of Belozerskii's writings on Persia
Zhukovskii extensively touches upon the spiritual wealth of Persian culture
and the virtues of the Persian character (AV, f. 17, op. 1, d. 24).

[45] See Andrei Snesarev, "Sostoianie Persii," *Golos Pravdy* 1316 (15 January
1910). See also Andrei Snesarev, "Skromnoe, no ochen' vazhnoe delo," *Golos
Pravdy* 1242 (13 October 1909); AV, f. 115 (A. E. Snesarev), op. 1, d. 70,
l. 2–7.

[46] Andrew Wachtel, "Translation, Imperialism, and National Self-Definition in
Russia," *Public Culture* 11/1 (1999): 52.

[47] Ibid.

4.1 K. Smirnov depicts how he received Mohammad-Ali Shah's official request addressed to the Tsar regarding the establishment of Russia's protectorate over Persia, and how, later, he passed on Nicholas II's polite refusal to the Shah in April 1909.
Source: Korneli Kekelidze Georgian National Centre of Manuscripts

Orientology', as Krachkovskii classified it.[48] As early as the 1890s, Barthold declared the principle which was laid into the foundation of

[48] Ignatii Krachkovskii, *Ocherki po istorii russkoi arabistiki* (Moscow: Nauka, 1950): 139.

his methodological approach for the rest of his life: 'It is the same laws of historical evolution that operate in Asia and Europe'[49] – a principle which was still far from being taken for granted at that time. In his work "Istoriia izucheniia Vostoka v Evrope i Rossii" (The History of the Study of the Orient in Europe and Russia) he questioned the approach, widespread in European scholarship at the time, of investigating the difference between the historical laws of the development of European and Oriental societies.[50] Barthold argued: 'For a long time, the apprehension of the history of the Orient … has been hampered by the biased attitude of European scholars towards the object of study. Under the influence of the superiority of European culture that had been defined by that time, since the seventeenth century there has been a neglectful attitude of Europeans towards the peoples of the Orient.'[51]

However, as Schimmelpenninck van der Oye and Tolz point out, the criticism of their European colleagues did not prevent Russian scholars from conscious and active involvement in the colonial policy of their own state in the East.[52] Driven by patriotic motives, they strove to exert their, as they perceived it, scholarly informed influence on Russia's policy in the East for the benefit of their native land, but the final outcome was not as successful as they had been expecting. In this respect, Tolz emphasises: 'When the scholars noticed that their work was disregarded by the government, they were dismayed.'[53]

Indeed, Zhukovskii and Barthold often expressed their dissatisfaction with the inefficiency of the Russian Eastern policy and with the attitude of the state towards Russian Orientological scholarship. This was particularly clearly articulated in Barthold's "Istoriia kul'turnoi zhiz'ni Turkestana", where he expressed his blunt criticism of Russia's military and administrative activities in Central Asia which, according to him, had been executed without any scholarly input, mostly by

---

[49] Vasilii Bartol'd, "Doklad V. V. Bartol'da," *ZVORAO* 11 (1898): 355.

[50] This was Barthold's criticism of Friedrich Christoph Schlosser's work *The History of the Eighteenth Century* (see Bartol'd, "Istoriia izucheniia Vostoka," 226).

[51] Bartol'd, "Istoriia izucheniia Vostoka," 227.

[52] See Tolz, *Russia's Own Orient*, 69–79. See also Schimmelpenninck van der Oye, *Russian Orientalism*, 9–10.

[53] Tolz, *Russia's Own Orient*, 73.

people who did not have the necessary knowledge of the region.[54] In his "Pamiati V. A. Zhukovskogo", Barthold also reports the disappointment expressed by Zhukovskii regarding the fact that the Russian state finally failed to comprehend the right place of Orientological scholarship within its structures.[55] As if drawing a summarising line of hopelessness, just two years before the October coup, Barthold wrote that 'Russian Orientology, eager to work for the benefit of the native land, would meet either repulse or such sympathy that caused it even more to lose heart'.[56]

In general, contrary to Zhukovskii, Barthold often tried, at least in outward appearance, to keep his distance from the institutions of state politics. However, this desire for distance applied to scholarly fieldwork, too. As he acknowledged himself in his autobiography, after his unsuccessful expeditions of 1903–4 to Central Asia he realised that he had 'lacked necessary qualities for the, so to speak, fieldworks on tangible artefacts. I feel comfortable enough only during the work on written sources in a closet.'[57] And so he did, having spent almost all his life teaching at St Petersburg University and working on manuscripts which, of course, coincided well with his upbringing and life aims.[58]

According to the then standard Orientological specialisation, the only one possible at the time, Barthold was trained in the history of the Orient and Persian, Arabic and Turkish languages under the supervision of such professors as Aleksei Veselovskii (1843–1918), Vasilii

[54] See Vasilii Bartol'd, "Istoriia kul'turnoi zhizni Turkestana. Evropeizatsiia upravleniia i tuzemtsy," in *Sobranie sochinenii*, vol. 2, part 1 (Moscow: Nauka, 1977): 350–76.
[55] See Bartol'd, "Pamiati V. A. Zhukovskogo," 700–1. See also Sergei Zhukovskii's brief article-memoirs "Moi otets" (My Father), where he depicted his father's sincere frustration, caused by the complete indifference and incomprehension he had experienced on the part of the Russian government and the Duma's representatives towards Oriental studies in Russia (see Zhukovskii, "Moi otets," in *Ocherki po istorii Russkogo vostokovedeniia*, ed. Iosif Orbeli (Moscow: Nauka, 1960): 128).
[56] Bartol'd, "Russkaiia nauka," 542.
[57] Vasilii Bartol'd, "Autobiography," *Sobranie sochinenii*, vol. 9 (Moscow: Nauka, 1977): 791. In the 1903 expedition Barthold broke his leg while getting off a horse and after that was unable to use a horse, which prevented him from properly carrying out his research in 1904, too. He also found it hard to endure the field hardships of travelling in Central Asia (see also Vasilii Bartol'd, "Otchet o poezdke v Sredniuiu Aziiu," in *Zapiski Imperatorskoi Akademii Nauk* (St Petersburg, 1897): 1–2).
[58] See Bartol'd, "Autobiography," 789.

(Wilhelm Friedrich) Radlov (1837–1918) and, mainly, Viktor Rosen at the Faculty of Oriental Languages. Having spent a year (1891–2) at European universities attending the lectures of August Muller (1848–92) and Theodor Noldeke (1836–1930), according to Rosen's recommendation and on his own account,[59] Barthold realised that at that, rather young, stage of world Orientology, when scholarship so needed primary written sources on the history of the Orient, Russia was in a much more favourable position since it was in immediate geographical and, more importantly, cultural proximity to the Orient.[60]

While emphasising the importance of written sources for the study of the Orient, Barthold propagated the deep academic character of Orientological training and was opposed to introducing components of practical Orientology at universities. Albeit caring about the good of his native land to the same extent as his colleagues Zhukovskii and Ol'denburg, he had a different view from them on the further development of Russia's Oriental studies. Preoccupied with the belief in the supremacy of "pure" scholarship, Barthold was strongly convinced that, in the then situation of Russia, when there was a dearth of necessary specialists and the state was unable to properly fund academic Orientology, it was unjustified to divert energy and funds for any kind of institution for practical Oriental studies.[61] His reluctance in this regard resulted, for example, in the protracted delay of the establishment of the Oriental Institute in Tashkent that had been initiated by military Orientologist Ivan Iagello at the turn of the century.[62]

Indeed, notwithstanding Barthold's endeavour to stay away from any physical involvement in the political activities of state, he could not help using his scholarly prestige for the promotion of "pure"

---

[59] Barthold came from a well-off bourgeois family and was able to afford scholarly trips to Europe, as well as to often buy manuscripts at his own expense, which can be added to the compound of factors that enabled such an enormous scholarly output – more than 650 scholarly pieces (see ibid., 789–90).

[60] See Yuri Bregel, "Barthold and Modern Oriental Studies," *International Journal of Middle East Studies* 12/3 (1980): 386–8; Il'ia Petrushevskii, "Akademik V. V. Bartol'd," in Vasilii Bartol'd, *Sobranie sochinenii*, vol. 1 (Moscow, 1977): 14–16.

[61] See Vasilii Bartol'd, "K proektu vostochnogo instituta," in *Sobranie sochinenii*, vol. 9 (Moscow, 1977): 499–502; Bartol'd, "Po povodu proekta S. F. Ol'denburga"; Vigasin and Khokhlov, *Istoriia*, 73–4, 252

[62] RGVIA, f. 409, op. 2, d. 23872, p/s 313-964a, l. 6. See also Bartol'd, "K proektu," 499.

Orientological scholarship in the way he perceived was right. Having become a professor in 1901, he occupied the post of secretary of the faculty from 1906 to 1910, and as early as 1913 was elected an associated member of the Academy of Sciences. He was a member of almost all the main scholarly societies that in one way or another dealt with the Orient, including the Oriental Section of the Russian Imperial Archaeological Society and the Russian Imperial Geographical Society, among others. However, RKISVA (1903–18) became the main place for the application of his efforts for the advancement of his scholarly interests.

Given the significant full powers of the Committee and the fact that it consisted of representatives from the five main scholarly entities of Russia's Oriental studies, as well as others from the Orthodox Church and the main ministries – namely Foreign Affairs, Interior, Education, the Imperial Court and the War Ministry – the Committee was virtually the culmination of the interconnectedness of all four domains of Oriental studies in late Imperial Russia. Occupying the post of Committee secretary and, in actual fact, being its leading executive,[63] Barthold successfully used his interaction with the other members for organising and funding expeditions, receiving assistance on behalf of Russian legations and consulates, coordinating international activities between Russian scholars and those from other countries, and using reports of the military for scholarly needs.

The Committee's activities covered the whole Persianate world, and the majority of scholarly expeditions and works, which of course did not only included those with a scholarly purpose,[64] were organised by this Committee (for example, the expeditions of Salemann, Zarudnyi, etc.).[65] It should also be noted that the original idea of the establishment of such a compound body was born at the Twelfth International Congress of Orientologists (1899) in Rome with the eventual purpose of facilitating the study of Central and Eastern Asia for European scholars. Thus Barthold's initial idea of taking advantage of Russia's advantageous position in the study of the Orient was realised as well

---

[63] Head of the Committee was Barthold's former teacher, Radlov, who was already sixty-six at the time of its establishment.

[64] All ministries represented on the Committee pursued their own narrowly defined corporate goals in all kinds of activities (see Vigasin and Khokhlov, *Istoriia*, 104).

[65] See Bartol'd, "Russkii Komitet."

as his ideas, inherited from Rosen, on the promotion of the Russian Orientological school within the world of Oriental studies.

The same idea of popularising Russian scholarship on Islam roused Barthold to undertake the responsibilities of chief-editor of the *Mir Islama* scholarly journal in 1912. Notwithstanding the fact that the journal was initially (1907) conceived as a propagandist and missionary anti-Islamic tool by the Sacred Synod, the highest governing organ of the Russian Orthodox Church, and the Department of Clerical Affairs of Foreign Confessions at the Ministry of the Interior in association with a missionary Orientologist, Professor Mashanov (1852–1924), Barthold turned it into a fully fledged, "dry" scholarly journal, dealing with various aspects of the life of Muslim countries.[66]

Noteworthy, detailed research on the history of the foundation of this journal was published in its present-day successor, printed by the Tatarstan Academy of Sciences.[67] According to the author, Mashanov offered the concept of a journal that suggested 'on one hand, to shake Islam and, on the other, to make Muslims closer to Russian Christian culture and, hence, to prepare the ground for the amalgamation of Tatars with Russians'.[68] As it appears from Mashanov's words, the scholars of the missionary domain shared the views of Rosen's school, however with their own approach, inherent to the Orthodox Church – they intended to supersede Muslim culture with the Russian Orthodox one rather than to organically incorporate it into a multi-religion Russia along with simultaneous mutual enrichment. Barthold was inclined to accept neither this militant approach nor the possibility of becoming physically or morally employed by the Ministry of the Interior, which resulted in a rather blunt conversation with the minister about the role of Orientological scholarship in Russia. No Russian scholar was ready to replace Barthold and the journal was eventually closed down.[69]

---

[66] See Vigasin and Khokhlov, *Istoriia*, 261. The project was initially not realised due to financial and bureaucratic encumbrances. The first issue of the journal saw the light of day only in 1912 under Barthold's editorship.

[67] See Ramil' Khairutdinov, "Mir Islama: Iz istorii sozdaniia zhurnala," *Mir Islama* 1/2 (1999): 5–20.

[68] Ibid., 5.

[69] The whole editing board of the journal rejected the "honorary" duty offered to them to also work as Ministry of the Interior informants. During a period of several months after the first issue came out, Russian officialdom became more

The above-mentioned situation highlights another manifestation of Foucauldian power/knowledge relations, namely the resistance of the intellectual and their capability to breakthrough governmentality, which is so well analysed in the works of Herman Nilson, Sara Mills and Jon Simons.[70] Further to their interpretation of Foucault, regarding the specific place of the intellectual and the natural desire of individuals to stay within the limits of the power which endowed them with capacities, hence, creating their own governmentality, Barthold's example appears to be a case in point – an example of an intellectual who exert resistance within their own lot of (scholarly) truth and overcomes their own governmentality.[71] Therefore, the life and activities of Zhukovskii and Barthold once again demonstrate how one-sided and simplified Said's model of 'unanimity of scholarship and politics' is and how cautiously it should be applied, at least to the Russian case.[72]

Officers-*Vostochniki*

Among all the available scholarship on *Russian Orientalism* the issue of the impact of the Russian military on Oriental studies in late Imperial Russia was particularly highlighted only in Marshall's substantial study of the development of Russia's army in relation to its activities in Asia during the period from the beginning of the eighteenth century to 1917. The study also makes clear the underlying role of Miliutin's reforms in the subsequent development of military intelligence in the Asian theatre of activities that, in fact, constituted the core of Russia's military Oriental studies.[73] The same phenomenon is pointed out in Schimmelpenninck van der Oye's "Reforming Military Intelligence".[74]

---

and more disappointed with Barthold's endeavours to keep the journal content at a highly scholarly and objective level; see Appendix (Makarov).

[70] Foucault, *Power*; Foucault, "Two Lectures"; Foucault, *History of Sexuality*; Nilson, *Michel Foucault*; Mills, *Michel Foucault*; Simons, *Foucault*.

[71] Foucault, *Power*, 130–2. See Foucault, *History of Sexuality*, 93; Simons, *Foucault*, 82, 176; Nilson, *Michel Foucault*, 99.

[72] Schimmelpeninck van der Oye, *Russian Orientalism*, 11.

[73] Marshall, *Russian General Staff*, 131–62.

[74] Schimmelpenninck van der Oye, "Reforming Military Intelligence," 141–3.

However, the above-mentioned works examine the interaction between the military and Orientological knowledge in Imperial Russia as a subaltern object of their studies, focusing mainly on purely military aspects, whereas it is such works as "'Applied Orientalism' in British India and Tsarist Turkestan" by Alexander Morrison and *Istoriia otechestvennogo vostokovedeviia s serediny XIX veka do 1917*, edited by Aleksei Vigasin and Aleksandr Khokhlov, which, to a significant extent, focus separately on the contribution of the military to Russia's Oriental studies, particularly during the crucial period of late Imperial Russia's military activities in Central Asia and the Middle East.[75] Leaving aside Russian scholar Vigasin's work – composed with a great deal of the laudation of native achievements still so inherent in Russia's conventional historiography, nevertheless – Morrison's observation of Russia's greater degree of specificity is, instead, worth mentioning since he analysed the impact of late Imperial Russia's Orientologists of different affiliations in a similar context to Western Oriental studies, particularly that of Britain.[76]

This great contribution to Orientological scholarship was mainly provided by individuals who, along with their genuine military status and subsequently acquired Orientological training, were personally interested in carrying out scholarly activities. The secret of their significant impact on scholarship and, arguably, on state policies was hidden in the fact that they succeeded in combining their military and administrative duties with the scholarly quest, which was very often based on their personal endeavour and interest. In this sense, one of the main illustrative examples is Konstantin Nikolaevich Smirnov (1877–1938) who, according to his service record, was trained by the Oriental Languages Officers' Courses (1900–3) and assigned to the Headquarters of the Caucasian Military District as an officer-*vostochnik* of the Russian General Staff.[77]

In 1904, Staff-Captain Smirnov accompanied Colonel Vladimir Liakhov (1869–1920) as an interpreter during his successful reconnaissance trip to northern Kurdistan, which might have been an

---

[75] Alexander Morrison, "'Applied Orientalism' in British India and Tsarist Turkestan," *Comparative Studies in Society and History* 51/3 (2009): 619–47; Vigasin and Khokhlov, *Istoriia*, 134–56.

[76] See Morrison, "Applied Orientalism," 637–8.

[77] GNCM, f. 39 (K. N. Smirnov's Private Collection), d. 3 (Smirnov's Service Record), l. 1ob.–2ob.

essential condition for the later crucial change in Smirnov's professional career.[78] In the wake of this trip, Smirnov received his first
combat bravery awards and in 1906 he became the aide to the Head
of Intelligence of the Caucasian Headquarters.[79] I have been unable
to find direct evidence as to whether Liakhov played an important
role in Smirnov's appointment as a private tutor of the Heir to the
Persian Throne, Ahmad-Mirza (the later Shah of Persia); however,
it is certain that without his approval the appointment would not
have taken place, since in 1907 Liakhov already was the Commander
of the Persian Cossack Brigade. So, as appears from the above,
Smirnov's Orientological training was appreciated from the outset
even by Liakhov, who was experienced enough in Oriental affairs by
that time.

Smirnov's seven-year tenure at the Persian Shah's Court resulted
in the creation of multiple significant scholarly works on the
ethnology and culture, religions and education, and history and
economy of Persia.[80] Among them are Smirnov's diaries or notes, comprising some parts of his reports to the Russian Minister in Persia
and to the Headquarters of the Caucasian Military District as well as
other data on his interaction with Persians which were not included
in his official reports.[81] As the main Israeli researcher of late Imperial
Russia's military and political presence in Persia, Nugzar Ter-Oganov,
points out, the notes

---

[78] See Nugzar Ter-Oganov, "Rapport du Capitaine en Second Constantin Smirnov
sur son Voyage en Turquie en 1904," *Iran and the Caucasus* 10/2 (2006): 209–
29. In addition to the important information on the then relations of Kurds
with the Ottoman state, the report contains a detailed description of Liakhov's
character, so valuable for the historiography of the Russia–Iran nexus.

[79] GNCM, f. 39 (K. N. Smirnov's Private Collection), d. 3 (Smirnov's Service
Record), l. 1ob.–2ob.

[80] Smirnov's articles were extensively published in military journals and the
journal of the Imperial Russian Geographical Society. See, for example,
"Poezdka v Severnyi Kurdistan v 1904 godu," *IRGO* 17 (1904): 282–326;
"Naselenie Persii s voennoi tochki zreniia," *Izvestiia Shtaba Kavkazskogo
Voennogo Okruga* 27 (1910): 20–64; "Naselenie Persii s voennoi tochki
zreniia," *Izvestiia Shtaba Kavkazskogo Voennogo Okruga* 28 (1910): 1–62;
"Messionery v Persii," *Izvestiia Shtaba Kavkazskogo Voennogo Okruga* 23
(1909); "Dervishy i ikh politicheskoe znachenie," *Izvestiia Shtaba Kavkazskogo
Voennogo Okruga* 31–2 (1911). His books include *Persy: Ocherk religii Persii*
(Tiflis, 1916); *Persy: Etnographicheskii ocherk Persii* (Tiflis, 1917).

[81] GNCM, f. 39, d. 11, l. 3.

4.2 Captain Konstantin Smirnov on receiving his appointment as Ahmad Mirza's personal tutor.
Source: Korneli Kekelidze Georgian National Centre of Manuscripts

are a serious document which allows for a deeper and more accurate understanding of the tendencies of the socio-political history of Iran, as well as for the understanding of the Iranian–Russian and of the British–Russian relationships in the epoch of the Constitutional Movement until the very beginning of WWI … [The notes] contain lots of the most interesting information about the British, German and Turkish policies in Iran, about dozens, if not hundreds of political activists, and, undoubtedly, are the most valuable and rather objective eyewitness accounts.[82]

Another researcher of the period, Moritz Deutschmann, rightly notices other dimensions of the work, which Smirnov himself called *Zapiski vospitatelia persidskogo shaha* (The Notes of the Tutor of the Persian Shah). The notes demonstrate how Smirnov's position at the Qajars' Court considerably assisted the better interpenetration of two different cultures and symbolised a rather characteristic tendency in Russo-Iranian relations at that time, namely the increasing, albeit unequal, but mutual influence which was exerted in cultural and political fields between the two countries.

By giving a detailed insight into Ahmad Mirza's education, Smirnov's text documents important transformations in the way the Qajars looked at themselves. He also shows how these transformations were linked to Russian attempts to monopolize their influence on the dynasty at the cost of other groups at the court. Furthermore, Smirnov's role was not an exception, but was part of a broader trend: in fact, many members of the Iranian elites at the time even sent their sons to Russia for education, most importantly to military schools. This role of military education in the Russian empire had a long tradition; it had, for example, played a central role in integrating Muslim elites from the Caucasus into the empire.[83]

It goes without saying that Smirnov's posting at the Persian Court, in addition to gathering relevant political intelligence, was, first of all,

[82] Ter-Oganov, "Zhizn'," 26. Unfortunately, Smirnov did not publish *Zapiski vospitatelia persidskogo shaha, 1907–1914* because of the information given in the manuscript that could be potentially harmful and unpleasant to the characters featured in the notes. The notes were only published in 2002 in Tel-Aviv as a result of the profound efforts of Nugzar Ter-Oganov, who prepared the manuscript for publication.
[83] Moritz Deutschmann, "All Rulers Are Brothers: Russian Relations with the Iranian Monarchy in the Nineteenth Century," *Iranian Studies* 46/3 (2013): 403.

meant to exert cultural influence on the future Shah and his close environment by means of "civilising" them, which implied inculcating the
European "civilised" mentality, however with a simultaneous strong
emphasis on the Russian cultural and political component. In his notes
Smirnov writes of how he adjusted the curriculum of his teaching in
order to give 'a proper European education' to the Heir and to instil
good manners in his charge; however, at the same time, throughout
his whole communication with Ahmad-Mirza and his surrounding,
Smirnov always tried implicitly to behave and speak in a way that
would be for the good of Russian state and culture and to the detriment of other countries – Turkey, Britain and France. He also quite
often points out the witnessed positive outcome of his influence.[84]

His diaries for 1909 also contain a noteworthy depiction of a
successful intelligence micro-operation, aiming at 'civilising *andarun*
in the interests of Russia', which was designed and carried out solely
by him. It resulted in a Russian Muslim governess being "planted"
into the *andarun* of the Shah's Court who was supposed to cultivate
European customs among the women of the Court and, simultaneously, to promote all things Russian.[85] Given the important role the
women of the Qajar Court played in the political life of Persia, which
was also pointed out by Abbas Amanat, one can judge the scale of the
impact of Smirnov's operation.[86]

In his valuable study of the relationships and even of the underlying cultural nexus between the Russian and Iranian monarchies,
as the article claims, Deutschmann characterises Captain Smirnov in
this way: 'Konstantin Smirnov was a typical example of a Russian
"military Orientalist," who combined a career in the military with a
passion for Orientalist scholarship'.[87] Deutschmann, referring to their
significant scholarly impact, implicitly denotes a certain extent of the
specificity of Russian officers-*vostochniki*, however, he immediately

---

[84] GNCM, f. 39, d. 19, l. 51–3 (Annual Report on teaching Soltan Ahmad-
Mirza). See also d. 11, l. 21, 22; d. 12, l. 2ob.–7, 25–6, 65–6, 70–70ob., 75–7,
83ob.–84ob.; d. 13, l. 98–9, 114–114ob.; d. 14, l. 27–32, 50–58ob; d. 15, l. 6–
11ob.; d. 17, l. 35ob.–39; d. 19, l. 3ob.–4ob.

[85] Ibid., d. 12 (Diaries, 1908), l. 53–53ob., 66ob.–69ob., d. 13 (Diaries, 1909),
l. 4ob; d. 19, l. 1–2ob.

[86] See Taj Al-Saltana, *Crowning Anguish: Memoirs of a Persian Princess from the
Harem to Modernity, 1884–1914* (Washington, DC: Mage, 1993), including
Abbas Amanat's introduction and historical notes.

[87] Deutschmann, "All Rulers Are Brothers," 403.

stresses their Saidian Orientalist inward nature, pointing out Smirnov's feeling of an accentuated cultural 'otherness' from Persians.[88] In this context, Smirnov's 'typical Orientalist' status seems debatable since, throughout the whole period from his reconnaissance trip with Liakhov to northern Kurdistan in 1904 until his departure from Persia in 1914, Smirnov's perception of Persians gradually metamorphosed as he witnessed events in Persia and his own country. Therefore, Ter-Oganov's characterisation seems more correct: 'K. N. Smirnov [was] a typical representative of the Russian military intelligentsia, a staunch patriot-monarchist, believing in the paramount predestination of Russia.'[89]

The point is that the officers of the General Staff belonged to the highly educated part of Russian society and, given the interpenetration of all Oriental studies' domains in Russia, they, more or less in the same way, inherited discourses widespread within the civilian scholarly domain. Smirnov sincerely believed in both the beneficial role of Russia for Persia and the possibility of the organic incorporation of Eastern cultures into Russian culture. Smirnov's concern for the promotion of the Russian Cause in Persia, including the protection of Russian interests versus the main European powers – Britain, Germany and France – is, of course, the red thread passing through all his works;[90] however, comparing the Russian revolution of 1905–7 and the Persian one of 1905–11, Smirnov draws conclusions that are not in favour of the Russians. He finally points out that Iranians, due to their ancient culture and moral traits, turn out to be much more "civilised" in the circumstances of the absence of central power that happens during insurgencies.[91]

As far as Smirnov's influence on Russia's policy towards Persia is concerned, the available documents do not provide an unequivocal answer. On the one hand, Smirnov's position at the court, his relations with the Russian mission and his Orientological expertise would allow him to stay in the thick of things during the whole period of his posting in Persia. Being an insider at the court, even in the *andarun*

---

[88] Ibid., 403–4.
[89] Ter-Oganov, "Zhizn'," 7.
[90] GNCM, f. 39, d. 12 (Diaries 1908), l. 47ob.–48, 83ob.–84; d. 13 (1910), l. 103–103ob., d. 24, l. 8ob.
[91] GNCM, f. 39, d. 11, l. 1ob.–2ob; d. 20, l. 39ob.

itself, he had an undoubtedly significant impact on the shaping of the Persian perception of Russia and, at the same time, he was, arguably, the only source of first-hand objective intelligence on the Qajar Court.[92] On the other hand, being a military man and rather modest by nature, Smirnov had no intention of going out of the framework of his above-mentioned nominal role. He neither had nor tried to have (as, for example, Aleksei Domantovich and Kosagovskii did) access to the strategic decision-making level in Russia's policy towards Persia.[93] In addition to that, the then political situation in Persia deprived the Qajars of the necessary grip on power in the country, whereas Russia continued, through inertia, to bet on their preservation and the strategic interaction with this kindred monarchy.[94]

Serving in Tiflis, in the Headquarters of the Caucasian Military District, before coming to Persia, Smirnov had multiple talks with the then commander of the Persian Cossack Brigade, Fedor Chernozubov (1863–1919),[95] who once told him:

You think that Persians need a tutor for the Heir? No way! It is just people in St Petersburg who measure the extent of our influence by facts such as the presence of Russian instructors, of a Russian doctor, etc. Now the Minister thought up a Russian tutor to the Heir and those in St Petersburg will be very happy with him for that.[96]

---

[92] A character that can be compared to Smirnov in terms of his awareness of the court affairs was Seraia Shapshal (1873–1961), one of Zhukovskii's disciples, who had been working with Mohammad-Ali since 1901 and had occupied an influential position at the court. However, not being officially subordinated to the Russian mission, he always prioritised his own personal interest among all others and left Persia in 1908, after the quarrel with the Shah and the court and also fearing an attempt on his life on the part of the Constitutionalists (see GNCM, f. 39, d. 11, l. 17; d. 12, l. 46–46ob., d. 13, 15ob. (Shapshal's corruption)).

[93] GNCM, f. 39, d. 12, l. 52ob., 53ob. On active political games for influence, led by Domantovich, the first Commander of the Brigade, and Charkovskii, his successor, both at the Persian Court and within the Russian mission, see, for example, Nugzar Ter-Oganov, "The Russian Military Mission and the Birth of the Persian Cossack Brigade: 1879–1894," *Iranian Studies* 42/3 (2009): 457, 460; whereas on Kosagovskii's activities in this sense see Ter-Oganov, "Brigada."

[94] On the kinship feelings of the Russian and Persian monarchies see Deutschmann, "All Rulers Are Brothers."

[95] See Appendix (Chernozubov).

[96] GNCM, f. 39, d. 11, l. 5ob.–6.

٤ شهر شعبان ١٣٢٩

بر حسب رای مجلس مقدس اعلان میشود   کسانی که محمد
علی میرزا را اعدام یا دستگیر نمایند یکصد هزار تومان بانها داده میشود
کسانی که شعاع السلطنه را اعدام یا دستگیر نمایند بیست و پنجهز ار
تومان بانها داده میشود
کسانی که سالارالدوله را اعدام یا دستگیر نمایند بیست و پنج هزار تومان
بانها داده میشود
ونیز اخطار میشود که اگر داوطلبان خدمات مزبوره بعد از انجام
خدمت کشته شدند مبلغ های فوق الذکر بهمان نسبت بورثه انها داده خواهد
شد و این مبلغ در خزانه دولت موجود است وبعد از انجام خدمت نقدا بانها
پرداخته میشود   محل امضا حضرت رئیس الوزراء
طهران ، مطبعة تمدن ،

4.3 The Constitutional Government's advert regarding the tangible recompense for either execution or capture of Mohammad-Ali Shah and his two brothers.
Source: Korneli Kekelidze Georgian National Centre of Manuscripts

When in Persia, Smirnov repeatedly remembered Chernozubov's words and came to the conclusion that Russia's "à la Hartwig" support of the Persian Court was a mistake since it did not respond to the condition of Persian society at the time and, in its eventual political outcome, was easily outweighed by the British support of the Constitutionalists.[97]

[97] Ibid., l. 6–8ob.

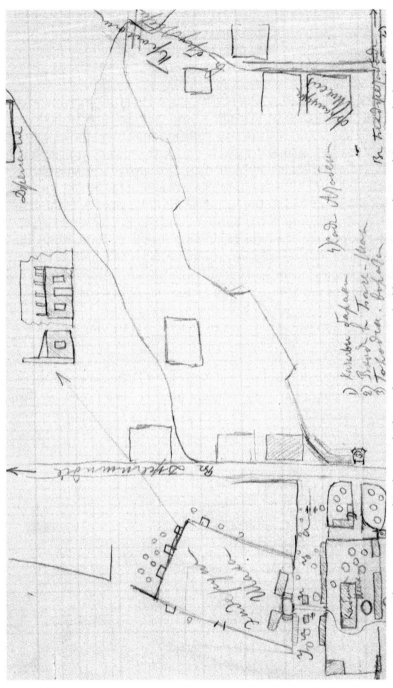

4.4 A croquis of escape in case of Mohammad-Ali's *andarun* was attacked by Constitutionalists and Smirnov had to rescue Mohammad-Ali's children (planned and drawn by Smirnov, 1909). During the revolutionary unrest of 1909, Smirnov refused to carry a weapon, explaining that it could additionally endanger the Shah's children.
Source: Korneli Kekelidze Georgian National Centre of Manuscripts

However, Smirnov's activities and works show that, being a staunch monarchist, he himself could offer nothing but the preservation of the Persian monarchy and criticism of Aleksandr Izvol'skii's policy of losing Russian interests in Persia to the British.[98]

Smirnov's posting in Persia can rightfully be compared to the activities of the fifth commander of His Majesty the Shah of Persia's Cossack Brigade, Major-General Vladimir Kosagovskii, in terms of both his influence in the context of Russo-Persian relations and his impact on Russia's Persian studies.[99] However, given the timing of his posting in Persia and, certainly, his post itself, Kosagovskii's personal activities turned out to be much more conspicuous in the field of Russia's policy towards Persia.[100] During his tenure, he became one of the most influential politicians inside Persia, as well as gaining direct access to the War Minister and the Emperor of Russia. In 1906, during the execution of Kosagovskii's retirement, Nicholas II, who had known Kosagovskii personally because of his Persian activities, consented to grant him the out-of-turn rank of Lieutenant-General for his services in Persia.[101]

According to Kosagovskii, when he took over the Brigade in 1894 it was on the edge of being dismantled.[102] The underlying mistake of the Russian government was that, by establishing the Cossack Brigade (at first it was only a regiment) in Persia in 1879, Russia aimed exclusively at enhancing its own influence over the Shah's court, as well as preventing other European powers such as Great Britain from

---

[98] GNCM, f. 39, d. 11, l. 9, 10ob., 12–15. See also ibid., d. 12, l. 83ob.–84. Aleksandr Petrovich Izvol'skii (1856–1919) was the Russian Minister for Foreign Affairs (1906–10). In Russia at the time his activities were notorious for their excessive orientation towards France and Great Britain.

[99] Though the Soviet and present-day historiographies, for unknown reasons, prefer to spell Kosagovskii with an 'o' in the middle and the main Israeli expert on the Persian Cossack Brigade, Nugzar Ter-Oganov, does the same, I adhere to the way Kosagovskii himself would write his name and so did his direct commander, Head of the Caucasian Military District, General Sergei Sheremetev (for example, RGVIA, f. 446, op. 1, d. 47, l. 6–8, 44). The same spelling with 'a' is also adopted in Baskhanov, *Russkie*, 126–7.

[100] On Kosagovskii's mission in Persia see Nugzar Ter-Oganov, *Persidskaia kazach'ia brigada*, 1879–1921 (Moscow, 2012).

[101] RGVIA, f. 409, op. 2, d. 25711, p/s 317686, l. 21 (Nicholas II's personal instruction).

[102] See Ter-Oganov, *Brigada*, 77–9.

taking a similar step.[103] Its first commander, Domantovich, was even instructed by the War Ministry to try to become one of the Shah's ministers.[104] So real combat training and the creation of a militarily efficient and strong unit in a neighbouring country was by no means part of Russia's plans. At the same time, as a conventional colonial imperialist power, Russia put the whole financial burden of relevant expenses on the Persian government.[105] Naturally, seeing the deplorable condition to which the Brigade had come by the mid 1890s, the Persian War Minister, Naib al-Soltaneh, tried to convince the Shah to replace it with a special personal guard which would, possibly, be trained by German instructors.[106]

Having visited Persia before and being familiar with the culture and the people's character, Colonel Kosagovskii realised what a model military unit should look like in Persia. Already by 1897, the Brigade's new Chief-Instructor had succeeded in making the unit visibly strong and trained: the personnel increased threefold and the Brigade demonstrated properly at parades and at show manoeuvres. Against the backdrop of the general decay of the Persian military, the Brigade looked the strongest national military unit. This helped resolve the lack of funds for the maintenance of the Brigade and allowed Kosagovskii to occupy an influential place at the court, which enabled him to play his own card in the political game with multiple components: the Shah, the Persian ministers, the Russian and the British missions, and the representatives of other countries.

All these efforts aimed at a better promotion of *Russkoe delo* in Persia, which was perceived by Kosagovskii as the main task of his posting. Throughout all his diaries and other writings he emphasises that his activities were dedicated to increasing Russian influence in Persia and counteracting the influence of other powers.[107] However,

---

[103] RGVIA, f. 446, op. 1, d. 47, l. 27–30 (Deputy Minister for Foreign Affairs to the Head of the General Staff, 11 March 1894).

[104] See Ter-Oganov, "Military Mission," 452–3.

[105] RGVIA, f. 446, op. 1, d. 43, l. 28–35 (Contract between Domantovoch and the Persian government).

[106] See Ter-Oganov, *Brigada*, 77–8.

[107] RGVIA, f. 76, op. 1, d. 217 (Diaries, 1899–1909). See also ibid., d. 242 ('The Exclusiveness of the Current Condition of Persia and the Establishment of the Russian Military Intelligence Network in Persia'). See Vladimir Kosogovskii, *Iz tegeranskogo dnevnika polkovnika*, ed. G. M. Petrov (Moscow: Izdatel'stvo vostochnoi literatury, 1960).

in his apprehension, this was not confined to exerting merely political influence, but rather it comprised the component of civilising mission with a strong emphasis on Russian culture. By the virtues which could be seen in the example of the Cossack Brigade and the behaviour of Russian officers, he wanted to make 'the indigenous semi-wild population' familiar with 'the Russian way of life'.[108] He also always forbade, contrary to the insistence of the Persian government, the participation of the Cossack Brigade in the crackdown on bread revolts in Persia and in other punitive actions of the Persian government against the peaceful population, ipso facto stressing the allegedly genuine humane purpose of Russians in Persia.[109]

From the correspondence of the Head of the Caucasian Military District with the War Ministry, it is obvious that Colonel Kosagovskii's Orientological expertise was almost the main decisive factor which led to his final approval as the Cossack Brigade Chief-Instructor among many other candidacies.[110] Such a thoughtful approach on behalf of the state was well paid off. Following the main guideline of Miliutin's views on military intelligence activities and perceiving it as an intrinsic part of his service to the native country, Kosagovskii paid particular attention to gathering all sorts of information about Persia. Being guided by his personal interest in the study of Persia and his perception of promoting Russian interests, Kosagovskii took advantage of his authority as Chief-Instructor and of the influential place he had occupied within the Persian ruling establishment and turned the Cossack Brigade into an exuberant source of Orientological information for Russia: the officers were constantly on missions in various places in Persia, gathering intelligence which, according to Miliutin, was to comprise information of any kind. So, the officers' reports would include the descriptions of towns, villages, routes, local communities, linguistic specificities, customs and traditions, everyday life, etc.[111]

---

[108] RGVIA, f. 400, op. 4, d. 279, l. 9.

[109] *Iran: Political Diaries, 1881–1965* vol. 1 (Slough: Archive Editions, 1997): 640 as quoted in Ter-Oganov, *Brigada*, 102.

[110] RGVIA, f. 446, op. 1, d. 47, l. 4, 6–8 (General Sheremetev to the War Minister Obruchev, 1894).

[111] RGVIA, f. 76 (Kosagovskii's Reports to the Military Learned Committee), op. 1, d. 48 (General Report on Trips around Persia and Kurdistan); d. 255 and 256 (Officers' Reports). Delo 254 (1901) demonstrates that Kosagovskii used to entrust even native agents with composing reports on the local life in their towns and villages.

Kosagovskii would also send his own detailed reports on the geography, ethnography and linguistics of Persia to the Military Learned Committee and was in constant correspondence with the library of the War Ministry.[112]

The amount of area-study materials was so significant that, in 1898, Kosagovskii applied for transfer to the General Staff in order to help process the materials he had sent. Notwithstanding the fact that the then War Minister Kuropatkin, being an active Orientologist himself, realised the high value of Kosagovskii's scholarly reports and the necessity of expediting their processing, he preferred to leave Kosagovskii in Tehran since his importance as a successfully operating agent of Russian political influence in Persia by far overweighed the potential scholarly impact of his materials, even in the eyes of such a scholarship-orientated individual as Kuropatkin.[113]

However, along with the fact that Kosagovskii's contribution to the study of Persia was separately acknowledged by the subsequent generation of Persianists, later on Kosagovskii's writings were also criticised by his younger colleagues such as Smirnov for their lack of objectivity and the sense of superiority of all things Russian towards the Persian.[114] This, of course, also demonstrates Foucault's archaeology of knowledge at play since officers-*vostochniki* were part of Russian society, therefore their views and, consequently, approaches to scholarship, changed in conformity with the main intellectual trends of the time. Kosagovskii intellectually belonged to the 1870s–1880s, the generation of conquerors, whereas Smirnov received Orientological training almost twenty years later and was situated in a row with Minorsky and Snesarev, who were, to a significant degree, influenced by their teachers such as Rosen, Zhukovskii, Barthold and others.[115] This also supports the thesis about the enhanced impact of civilian scholarship of the *fin-de-siècle* on the other adjacent domains of Russia's Orientological knowledge.

Late Imperial Russian Colonels Smirnov and Iagello, and General Snesarev, as well as diplomats Minorsky, Bravin and Vvedenskii

---

[112] RGVIA, f. 76, op. 1, d. 340. See also ibid., d. 374 (Scholarly Report on the Khanate of Maku).

[113] See Ter-Oganov, *Brigada*, 93–5. On the scholarly activities of Kuropatkin, as an Orientologist, see Baskhanov, *Russkie*, 135–6.

[114] GNCM, f. 39, d. 27, l. 75ob. in Ter-Oganov, *Brigada*, 93.

[115] RGVIA, f. 409, op. 2, d. 25711, p/s 317686, l. 70.

constituted a generation of practical *vostochniki* that can be called transitional. In fact, the changes which took place in their perception of the Orient and its scholarship during the last decade of tsarist Russia personified that historical intellectual bridge which concatenated Imperial Russia's sheer colonial mentality of state experts of the 1860s–1890s to the omnipresent critique of imperialism of the first ten to fifteen years of the Bolshevik rule. All the above-mentioned experts made it to the new Soviet era and continued their expert and scholarly activities, having been considerably influenced by the events of 1917 and the following years. In this context, the activities of Andrei Snesarev can be regarded as the most indicative within the military domain.

Snesarev entered the Academy of the General Staff in 1896 when he had already served in the Russian Army for several years, having a doctorate in Abstract Mathematics from Moscow State University and pursuing, at the same time, a professional career as an opera singer at the Bolshoi Theatre. On his graduation from the Academy in 1899, he received an out-of-turn promotion for his excellence in mastering Oriental languages.[116] Having been assigned to the Headquarters of the Turkestan Military District, Snesarev did not have protracted postings to Persia and his main activities were concentrated on Afghanistan and India; however, due to the character of his intelligence service, he carried out several missions in Persia and in 1905 was even bestowed with the Order of Lion and Sun – the highest Persian decoration – on behalf of Mozaffar ad-Din Shah.[117] He authored several works on Babism, the Persian Constitutional Movement and the Russian–British interaction in Persia.[118]

However, his main contribution to scholarship was in his active participation in the activities of various Orientological scholarly societies

---

[116] RGVIA, f. 409, op. 2, p/s 338–604 (Snesarev's Service Record), l. 3. In total, in addition to English, French, German and Latin, Snesarev mastered fourteen Oriental languages, including Persian, Arabic, Urdu, Hindi and Turkish.

[117] Ibid., l. 4.

[118] Andrei Snesarev, *Anglo-Russkoe soglashenie 1907 goda* (St Petersburg, 1908); Andrei Snesarev, "Poslednee politicheskoe dvizhenie v Persii," *Golos Pravdy* 546 (15 June 1907); Andrei Snesarev, "Ot konokrada do Kromvelia," *Golos Pravdy* 1067 (4 April 1909); Andrei Snesarev, "Nizverzhennyi vladyka," *Golos Pravdy* 1260 (1 November 1909); Snesarev, "Sostoianie Persii."

and in the coordination of state entities' activities (Ministry of the Interior, War Ministry, MID, etc.) in the field of Oriental studies. His role can rightfully be compared with that of Zhukovskii, with the difference that Snesarev secured the backward linkage of the practical domains with the academic one. For example, in the period 1905–14 he played the leading role in *Obshestvo Vostokovedeniia* and, in close cooperation with the Ministry of the Interior, represented by General Shvedov, established the Academy of Oriental Studies, where he later taught. Based on Miliutin's Military Statistics, Snesarev elaborated and introduced his own system of practical Orientological training, with the core subject of Military Geography.[119]

Given Snesarev's multifaceted intellectual training and active interaction with the representatives of other intellectual domains of Russian society, including civilian Orientological scholarship, among other officers-*vostochniki* he was particularly subject to the influence of various discourses that were widely spread in educated circles. In his writings from 1900 to 1917, he paid significant attention to the study of the "triptych" of the West–Russia–the Orient and the place of Russian Orientological scholarship therein.[120] The most illustrative, in this sense, work by him is the article "Otnosheniia k aziatskomu miru" (Attitudes towards the Asiatic world) where he, similarly to Rosen, Barthold and Zhukovskii, elaborates on the indebtedness of European civilisation to the East and on Russia's inherently better (than Western cultures) capability to absorb all the best features during interaction with the Orientals.[121]

The following citation can serve as the best illustration that embraces the manifestations of all the main discourses, spread among

[119] AV, f. 115, op. 2, d, 27, 1–2; d. 50, l. 1, 3–7. See also Andrei Snesarev, "K novomu polozheniiu o vostochnykh iazykakh," *Russkii invalid* 235 (2 December 1911).
[120] See Andrei Snesarev, *Indiia kak glavnyi factor v sredneaziatskom voprose: Vzgliad tuzemtsev na anglichan i ikh upravlenie* (St Petersburg, 1906); Andrei Snesarev, *Vostochnaia Bukhara: voenno-geograficheskii ocherk* (St Petersbug, 1906); Andrei Snesarev, "Probuzhdenie Afghanistana," *Tashkentskie Vesti* (31 January 1905); Andrei Snesarev, "V obshestve vostokovedeniia," *Golos Pravdy* (27 October 1909); Andrei Snesarev, "25-letie ofitserskikh kursov vostochnykh iazykov," *Golos Pravdy* 950 (20 November 1908); and many others.
[121] AV, f. 115, op. 1, d. 70 (Manuscript), l. 1–14.

scholars of all Orientological domains of late Imperial Russia. In 1906, Snesarev wrote:

The conquest of Asia was cruel and boorish, particularly in the areas where the purer representatives of Europe came into contact with the local population. Our [Russian] mode of conquest was distinguished by its soft, subdued approach. Thanks to the long presence of Turko-Mongol–Finnish peoples, both on our territory and in the neighborhood, [and] our familiarity with their world and their way of life, we appeared neither arrogant nor disdainful during our conquest, and we differed little from the nations we conquered. Along with our knowledge, we brought leniency and an awareness of some of our Asian neighbors' advantages or at least virtues to our interaction with them. However, wherever pure Europeans, particularly the English, entered the Asian continent, their confident stride signified vicious cruelty, mass theft and undisguised contempt for all things Asian.[122]

The point here is not that the Russians were more merciful and noble than the British, but rather that, similarly to their teachers, Snesarev, Tumanskii, Smirnov, Iagello and the early twentieth century's other military Orientologists, trained and subsequently influenced by Rosen and his civilian disciples, perceived Russia 'as a particular kind of political and cultural space where there was no boundary between the "East" and the "West"'.[123] Accordingly, taking into consideration the political situation in Persia and around her, in the early twentieth century Persia was seen as a potential part of Russia.[124] At least, the northern part of Persia, being under factual Russian occupation with all the conventional colonial institutions from 1911 to 1917 (the public order and security were provided by Russian troops, executive and judicial powers were carried out by multiple Russian consuls, stationed in all significant population aggregates, etc.), had already become a virtual Russian territory by the 1910s.[125]

---

[122] Ibid., l. 5–6.
[123] Tolz, *Russia's Own Orient*, 5.
[124] See Lamzdorf's letter to Nicholas II in Ter-Oganov, "Zhizn'," 6.
[125] In his notes, dated 1908, Smirnov mentioned a certain 'top-secret message', sent through him from Mohammad-Ali Shah to Nicholas II and the latter's response, however, because of the secrecy of the matter he did not reveal the content. Only in 1933 did Smirnov add a comment on his manuscript that it had been a request to accept Persia as Russia's protectorate, similar to Bukhara Khanate, and Nicholas II's polite refusal (see GNCM, f. 39, d. 13, l. 39–39ob; d. 19, l. 13–17).

Diplomats-*Vostochniki*

Russia's military presence in Persia in the early twentieth century went hand in hand with the activities of the Russian late Imperial diplomatic corps. In fact, the activities of the Russian military in the field (except for those aiming to gather strictly military data) were, first of all, subordinated to the Head of Russia's Legation in Tehran and to consuls stationed in other cities and towns of Persia. Marshall argues fairly that, due to this status quo, the diplomats were doomed to play the role of the main bearers of Russian influence in Persia.[126] Given this fact, I would continue that they possessed much more operative autonomy and capability, in comparison with the military, to influence the events and the outcome of Russia's policy towards Persia. In this sense, one of the most representative examples of such diplomats was Vladimir Fedorovich Minorsky (1877–1966).

Having been trained in law at Moscow University, Minorsky converted in 1900 to the course of Oriental studies at the Lazarev Institute of Oriental Languages with the aim of embarking on the career of a diplomat-*vostochnik*. As a senior colleague of his, Andrei Kalmykow, put it in his memoirs, learning Oriental languages could somehow guarantee employability in the most privileged workplace in the Russian Empire – the Ministry for Foreign Affairs – as its European sections were impregnable for students from relatively modest families. This was also indicative of the discursive manifestations of higher Russian society – the opportunity to be permanently engaged in interaction with Western culture was the most desired option for educated Russians.[127]

Given the fact that Minorsky was descended from a very modest family who lived in the small town of Korcheva on the Upper Volga and moreover that his father was a Jew, any prospect of securing a good placement was ruled out, due to the conditions of pronounced anti-Semitism within Russia's state structures at the time. That is why, having succeeded in entering Moscow University merely due to the Gold Medal he had received at secondary school, four years later he decided to convert his Law Course to Persian studies, which was a rather unprestigious area within the Russian Imperial Ministry for

---

[126] See Marshall, *Russian General Staff*, 16, 26–7.
[127] See Kalmykow, *Memoirs*, 12–18.

Foreign Affairs. It should be noted that this unpretentious choice not only allowed Minorsky to penetrate Russia's most hard-to-get-into entity but eventually turned out for the better for his future professional and scholarly career.

Having been employed by the MID in 1903, Minorsky spent four years – 1904–8 – in Russia's General Consulate in Tabriz and the Russian Legation in Tehran. As early as 1966, well before the debates on power/knowledge relations, David Lang separately pointed out that, along with his professional duties, Minorsky dedicated this time to the study of the western and north-western parts of Persia.[128] Precisely during this period he became profoundly interested in the history and culture of the Kurds as part of Iranian culture.[129] Inspired by the writings of Edward G. Browne and the Russian scholars Rosen and Tumanskii, he also used his secondment in Persia for gathering a lot of first-hand material on the Iranian *Baha'is* and the *Ahl-e hagh* sect.[130] It is worth noting that Minorsky's scholarly writings and the reports that he presented to the Russian Imperial geographical, archaeological and other scholarly societies resulted in him being perceived by the MID as someone more than a conventional diplomat and in late 1911 he was assigned to supervise the topographical surveillance of areas in Azerbaijan and Kurdistan, precisely the areas of his scholarly interest.[131]

As early as 1902, while still a student of the Moscow Lazarev Institute, he began to correspond with Zhukovskii, who had by that time authored a number of publications in this field. It was then that they established a close teacher–disciple relationship, which lasted until Zhukovskii's death in 1918. Zhukovskii provided his new disciple with ad hoc guidance and later supervised his work on *The People of Truth* and gathering relevant manuscripts, after Minorsky had embarked on his career as an Imperial diplomat at the Persian Desk on 3 September 1903.[132] This consequently enabled Minorsky

---

[128] See David Lang, "Obituary: Vladimir Fedorovich Minorsky," *Bulletin of the School of Oriental and African Studies* 29/3 (1966): 693.

[129] See Appendix (Minorsky).

[130] On Tumanskii's scholarly activities see Bartol'd, "Iran," 332; Volkov, "Persian Studies," 9–10. On Viktor Rosen see Vasilii Bartol'd, "Baron Rozen i russkii provintsial'nyi orientalizm," in *Sobranie sochinenii*, vol. 9 (Moscow: Nauka, 1977): 589–95.

[131] See Lang, "Obituary," 695.

[132] AV, f. 17, op. 2, d. 37 (Correspondence with Minorsky), l. 1–2ob. See also Vladimir Genis, *Vitse-Konsul Vvedenskii* (Moscow: MYSL', 2003): 255.

to present successful reports at Russia's Orientological societies and to publish his first monograph on the People of Truth (Ahl-e hagh) sect in 1911. The work received the Gold Medal of the Ethnography Section of the Moscow Imperial Society of Natural Sciences and some very positive feedback from a demanding and uncompromising scholar of the time, Barthold, which secured the beginning of their close and protracted scholarly cooperation, which continued even during the early Soviet period, and until Bartold's death in 1930.[133]

Minorsky's above-mentioned scholarly activities highlight a feature that was common for most diplomatic representatives of Oriental studies, namely the endeavour to employ their training and professional postings for the production of scholarly knowledge – a discursive practice propagated by their academic teachers, mentioned earlier in this chapter. Minorsky's activities also demonstrate the immense interconnectedness of the domains in question. On top of that, the professional careers of Minorsky and other such scholars show that the state put additional value on such representatives of practical domains and gave them more operational autonomy, hence opening more opportunities for them to significantly influence the eventual outcomes of its foreign policy.

Minorsky's participation in the activities of the Quadripartite Boundary Commission, established according to the Constantinople Protocol of 1913, can rightly be regarded as the quintessential manifestation of the interplay of power/knowledge relations. The detailed narrative of the Commission spadework and the demarcation of the border itself – both of which, on the whole, took almost four years – are easily reconstructed with the help of Minorsky's unpublished private diaries, kept in the Archive of Orientologists of the St Petersburg Institute of Ancient Manuscripts affiliated with the Academy of Sciences of the Russian Federation, and the accounts of the British officers-members of the Commission which were published in the 1920s.[134]

---

[133] AV, f. 134, op. 3, d. 12, d. 478, d. 479 (Correspondence with Barthold). See also Bartol'd, "Iran," 329–30, 332; Ilya Gershevitch, "Obituary: Professor Vladimir Minorsky," *Journal of the Royal Asiatic Society of Great Britain and Ireland* 1 (1967): 53.

[134] AV, f. 134, op. 1, d. 803 (Notebooks 1 and 2). See also Colonel H. D. Ryder, "The Demarcation of the Turco-Persian Boundary in 1913–1914," *Geographical Journal* 66/3 (1925): 227–37; Arnold Wilson, A. C. Wratislaw

Due to his scholarly prestige and expertise in the region, Minorsky gained the confidence of not only his superiors in the Ministry of Foreign Affairs but also the British Foreign Office, which instructed its officers that Minorsky was the only man competent in the question.[135] This enabled him to retain a lot of areas within the Persian territory, which was in the Russian interest in the context of the discourse of *Russkoe delo*.[136] At the same time, he made use of his strategic position for reaching his personal career goals, deriving tangible benefits for himself.[137] In addition, Minorsky's obsession with collecting area-study data during the spadework of the Commission in 1911–13 and its fieldwork in 1914 resulted in an eventual significant contribution to Russia's Persian studies.

It is worth noting that, in so doing, Minorsky also productively followed the unique institutional practices of Russia's Oriental studies of the time. It was during several months' absence from Istanbul in 1913 that he met his future wife and scholarly assistant for the rest of his life – Tat'iana Shchebunina. Within the period Minorsky was staying in St Petersburg, he succeeded in arranging his marriage and coordinating with the ministry the possibility of his wife accompanying him during the Commission's field activities.[138] This fact is also indicative of his privileged position within the highly bureaucratised diplomatic apparatus of late Imperial Russia.[139] Minorsky did not miscalculate on this account either. Instead of a burden, being the only woman among the almost two-hundred-man party, Tat'iana turned out to be a great scholarly gain. Continuing to master Persian, she was able to establish contacts in those places that were traditionally inaccessible in Muslim societies for male foreigners – almost every time the party made a stop in a village or a nomad winter settlement Tat'iana, properly instructed by Minorsky, would go to *andaruns*, communicating

and Percy Sykes, "The Demarcation of the Turco-Persian Boundary in 1913–1914: Discussion," *Geographical Journal* 66/3 (1925): 237–42.

[135] AV, f. 134, op. 1, d. 803 (Notebook no. 2), l. 7. On the role of Minorsky in the activities of the Commission see also Sir Arnold Wilson's words in Wilson, Wratislaw and Sykes, "Demarcation," 238; and Brigadier-General Sir Percy Sykes' words in ibid., 241.

[136] See Volkov, "Persian Studies," 14, 17.

[137] See AV, f. 134, op. 1, d. 803 (Travel letters; Notebook no. 1), 5–5ob.

[138] See Gershevitch, "Obituary," 56; Lang, "Obituary," 695.

[139] See Kocho-Williams, *Russian and Soviet Diplomacy*, 16–18.

with local women and jotting down necessary ethnographic or linguistic data. Her husband so appreciated her scholarly contribution
that he dedicated his main work, resulting from that protracted trip,
to her, and separately mentioned her productive role in his notes and
published writings.[140]

Therefore, in fact, Minorsky became a successor to the Russian
Orientological tradition that was initially introduced by one of his
teachers, namely Zhukovskii in the 1880s. Later, this phenomenon
became so widespread among Russian Orientologists that it can be
subsumed under the category of an institutional practice adopted by
late Imperial Russia's Oriental studies. Against the backdrop of a dearth
of primary sources and in the context of the discourse of obtaining all
the available information about Russia's Asian neighbours (which was
propagated within military Oriental studies by the War Minister in
the 1860s–1870s and then passed over to the Oriental studies of the
other domains – academic, diplomatic and missionary)[141], such information was supposed to be collected by all means available – military, political and academic. This also included Orientologists' wives
who, due to their conventional high educational background, could
be of great scholarly assistance to their husbands, particularly in those
areas which were impregnable to the men because of strong gender
taboos in Muslim societies. In 1883–6, during Zhukovskii's academic
fieldwork in Persia, his wife, Varvara Karlosheva, mastered Persian
to the extent that she was able to collect and process linguistic data
on Persian folklore that she would receive during her communication
with local women. In the letters to his teacher, Rosen, Zhukovskii
particularly acknowledged her help in his ethnographic studies,
including family relationships and women's everyday life in Persia.[142]
Varvara made friends in the Shah's *andarun* in Tehran and then in
the *andaruns* of the governors of Isfahan and Shiraz – the three cities
where her husband did his fieldwork – and became a valuable source
of ethnographical and political information for Zhukovskii. Later, she

[140] See Vladimir Minorsky, *Kurdy* (Petrograd: Tipografiia Kirshbauma, 1915).
[141] See Volkov, "Persian Studies," 7–10, 16.
[142] ARAN(St.P.), f. 777, op. 2, d. 165 (Rosen's correspondence), l. 14. See also
Valentin Zhukovskii, *Obraztsy persidskogo narodnogo tvorchestva* (St
Petersburg, 1902), 4; Bushev, "Zhizn'," 119, 123–4.

even published an independent scholarly work, *Persidskii enderun*.[143] While in Persia, Captain Smirnov also entrusted his wife, Kseniia, with a similar assignment. In addition to nuanced political intelligence, Smirnov's wife provided him with extensive information on customs and everyday life in the Shah's *andarun*, which was used by Smirnov in his scholarly writings. This phenomenon of the wives' scholarly participation is not observed in the case of European countries' Oriental studies.[144]

In general, it should also be noted that, though Minorsky's impact on the activities of the Commission was enormous, it stayed within the general guidelines of late Imperial Russia's Persian policy, which was determined in St Petersburg. His influence rather had a local bearing within the limited scales of being able to bargain away from the British this or that small territory for its factual inclusion to the zone under Russian control. His suggestions on wresting concessions in the South of Persia from the British or on the severing of Azerbaijan from Persia – which he scholarly substantiated by citing considerable cultural differences between Azeris and Persians – remained unnoticed by the Russian foreign policy establishment, which gave priority to reaching agreements in its Western foreign policy.[145]

Conclusion

Notwithstanding the fact that late Imperial Russia's civilian Orientologists perceived the necessity of their influential involvement in the interaction with the state in different ways, in the 1910s they came to the deplorable conclusion that their protracted efforts to make the state establishment apprehend the importance of Orientological scholarship and to secure the beneficial impact of their knowledge on Russia's present and future had finally suffered a bitter defeat. However, their influence made successful headway in another sphere, namely the formation of their students' perception of the Orient. One

---

[143] Varvara Zhukovskaia, "Persidsky enderun," *Vestnik Evropy* 10 (October 1886): 501–49.

[144] GNCM, f. 39, d. 12, l. 50ob.–51ob; d. 13, l. 75–75ob, 77. See also Ter-Oganov, "Zhizn'," 17.

[145] AV, f. 134, op. 1, d. 803 (Notebook no. 2), 8–9ob. See also GNCM, f. 39, d. 12, 73ob–75; d. 11, l. 3, 16ob. On Minorsky's Azerbaijan Project of 1909 and his efforts to revive it in 1917, see also Aliev, *Istoriia Irana*, 90–1.

of the main features of this perception was that the Orient was not perceived as the Other but rather as something that could successfully interact with Russian culture and even organically supplement it.

It was now them, the former students – the new agents of state power – who were supposed to exert their own influence on the process of policymaking. The late Imperial Russian state valued its diplomats and military officers with special Orientological training, particularly those among them who would productively combine their professional duties with intensive scholarly activities. Such practical Orientologists, as a rule, gained more operational autonomy, which enhanced both their professional efficiency and scholarly productivity. However, although their impact on the realisation of Russian foreign policy towards Persia was enormous at a local scale and their reports did play a part in the shaping of Russia's policy towards Persia, the role of practical Orientologists on the relevant strategic level was neither decisive nor significant. The general guidelines of the Persian policy were drawn up in St Petersburg in the context of the current expediency of Russia's relationships with West European powers by experts in European affairs and, quite often, contrary to the suggestions of experts on Persia.

At the same time, the main impact of the scholars in all four domains turned out to be mostly in making use of their capacities, with which they were endowed by the Russian state, for the promotion of the scholarly institutions in which they were engaged, and for the production of knowledge in their area of interest. The interplay of power relations between scholarly and state institutions, discourses and the various interests of the intellectual eventually resulted in productivity, leading to the accelerated development of Oriental studies.

5 | The Birth and Death of Red Orientalism (1917–41)

Introduction

This chapter presents a study of the activities of the most significant figures of early Soviet Iranology which, as shown in Chapter 3, consisted of three domains: scholarly, diplomatic and military. All three domains included both groups of scholars and experts on Iran: those who were trained and acted before 1917 – the so-called representatives of the *ancien régime* – and those individuals who were completely new to the field and started working on Iran after 1917. So the chapter follows the same criteria as the previous one for choosing the individual subjects to study. It continues to trace the activities of already familiar characters as well as those newcomers who became prominent within their domains and remained scholarly active throughout the period. Along with a new ideology, the latter brought new discourses and institutional practices to the field. This chapter studies the involvement of both groups in the process of shaping foreign policy and the production of scholarly knowledge about Persia. In the examples of the activities of the individuals in question, it also seeks to answer what qualitative and quantitative transformations took place in discourses and practices within the above-mentioned three domains and what continuities can be traced.

The chapter also aims to find out whether there was direct or indirect influence of the scholars and experts in question on the early Soviet foreign policy towards Persia and what was the degree of this influence. In so doing, this research ascertains the approach of the early Soviet state power towards Orientological knowledge and how effectively the state used this knowledge. The analysis in this chapter will demonstrate the grounds on which these scholars and experts cooperated with the state and the character of their relationships with the state. In order to answer these questions, the chapter draws on recent English- and Russian-language scholarship on early Soviet Oriental studies, but mostly on unpublished documents retrieved from Russian and Georgian academic, political and military archives, shedding light on the activities of the individuals in question.

The issue of the significant changes that took place in the activities of individuals engaged in Russian Oriental studies over the boundary of 1917 was particularly dealt with in the Soviet literature of the second half of the twentieth century. In this sense, the importance of works from the 1960s–1980s on the history of Soviet Oriental studies can hardly be overestimated. For instance, *Vostokovedenie v Leningradskom Universitete* (Orientology in Leningrad University) by Andrei Kononov is a case in point that represents a supremely efficient guide to the entanglements of the organisational disruption of the 1920s and 1930s and traces the institutional development of Soviet Oriental studies, particularly of Iranology, up to the late 1950s, though mainly with a rather narrow focus on the Leningrad Orientological school. In addition, it contains a valuable, succinct excursus on the history of St Petersburg Oriental studies in late Imperial Russia. Kononov's endeavour was taken up and developed by such Soviet Iranists as Kuznetsova and Kulagina with their *Iz istorii sovetskogo vostokovedeniia, 1917–1967* (Of the History of Soviet Orientology) and, shortly after, by Ashot Baziants with *Stanovlenie sovetskogo vostokovedeniia* (The Formation of Soviet Orientology). These scrupulous research studies have remained the main comprehensive chronicles of the formation and development of Soviet Orientology, in particular of Iranian studies, including the shaping of multiple national centres of Iranology in various Soviet republics, up to the present.

It is also worth mentioning another influential work whose value is enhanced by its narrow focus on the initial period of the emergence of a new Soviet Iranology formed mainly by the experts of the so-called practical area-study knowledge newly adopted by the Bolshevik state. The book, *Sovetskoe iranovedenie 20-kh godov* (Soviet Iranian Studies of the 1920s) by Semen Agaev, deals with activities and views propagated by the founders of the new Iranology, who all in some way participated in the abortive attempt to organise the Persian Socialist Revolution and in the activities of Iran's Communist Party, namely Pastukhov, Osetrov, Sultanzadeh, Rotshtein, Pavlovich, Gurko-Kriazhin, Tardov and others. The work focuses on the new approaches for Soviet Iranology that were offered by these individuals, which propagated the underlying principle of the practical usage

of Orientological knowledge as a powerful tool in the cause of prolif-
erating social revolution. Given the historical period in which all the
above works were written, and the discourses and self-censorship of
that time, inculcated from the top, they are overwhelmed by the relevant ideological underpinnings and lacking in analysis. If, however,
making use of the Foucauldian tools of archaeology of knowledge,
one disregards or discards the disadvantages determined by the time
the works were created, they can be used as valuable sources of factual historical narrative on the content and forms of the new Soviet
Iranology.

The works by Western researchers of the same period, such as
Vucinich, Frye and Atkin, echo the above-mentioned Soviet scholarship in excessively emphasising the post-1917 shifts.[1] Recently,
however, West European scholarship has begun contemplating the
existence of strong continuities inherited from the late Imperial
period by early Soviet Oriental studies. Although Stephan Conermann
epitomises Said's concept of Orientalism as 'a mode of discourse
with supporting institutions, vocabulary, scholarship, imaginary,
doctrines [...] for dominating, restructuring, and having authority
over the Orient' and argues that 'Soviet studies on the Orient fit very
well into this overall definition',[2] the articles collected in the volume he
edited with Michael Kemper mainly highlight other crucial specificities
of Soviet Orientology. They mostly draw on the interplay of power/
knowledge relations that unfolded within the grid of personal, institutional and state interests and discourses of the Soviet period, which
is significantly broader than merely two-vector relations between a
particular scholarly domain and state power. They demonstrate that
this interplay was inherited from the late Imperial period by Soviet
Oriental studies.

In the introduction to the volume Kemper points out the ambiguity of the relationships of Soviet scholars with the state, which was
also intrinsic to the pre-1917 status quo, as well as in the employment of late Imperial Russia's discursive practices for fighting Islam
by Bolshevik atheist propaganda.[3] In addition, Soviet Orientology

---

[1] See Frye, "Oriental Studies in Russia"; Vucinich, "Structure"; Atkin, "Soviet
and Russian Scholarship."
[2] Conermann, "Foreword," xiii.
[3] See Kemper, "Integrating," 6–9.

'maintained, from the outset, an agenda on liberating the East',[4] embracing it into its own cultural and political entity on equal terms, hence leaving no place for differentiating the Self from the Other – a mind-set rooted in the activities of Kazem-Bek and Grigor'ev. Touched upon in Schimmelpenninck van der Oye's "The Imperial Roots of Soviet Orientology", their views on the organic integration of Russia's Western and Eastern origins were later developed by Rosen and his disciples and constituted the core discourse which existed among the Orientologists of the Russian Academy of Sciences.[5]

The troubled relations that late Imperial Russia's Orientological scholarship had with state power spanned the 1917 watershed and continued into the early Soviet period. In this sense, it is pertinent to mention the article "Profiles under Pressure: Orientalists in Petrograd/ Leningrad, 1918–1956" by Russia-based researcher Mikhail Rodionov, which was published in Kemper and Conermann's above-mentioned edited volume. This focuses on the activities and the Foucauldian resistance of two classical Orientologists of both periods – the specialist in Central Asian studies and Iranist Barthold, and the expert in Arabic studies Krachkovskii – under the rigorous conditions of the Bolsheviks' rule. A notable merit of this work is the detailed periodisation of the gradual destruction of classical Russian Orientological scholarship by the Bolshevik regime. Rodionov also stresses the high importance of work carried out since the 1990s by Marina Sorokina's group of scholars who, based on protracted and painstaking archival research, authored *Liudi i sud'by: Bibliograficheskii slovar' vostokovedov-zhertv politicheskogo terrora v sovetskii period, 1917– 1991* (People and Fates: Bibliographical Dictionary of Orientologists-Victims of Political Terror during the Soviet Period (1917–1991)). In this regard, Rodionov separately touches upon the increasing difficulties which researchers nowadays face in Russian archives regarding restricted access.[6]

The impact of Barthold and Rosen's other disciples, such as Zhukovskii, Marr and Ol'denburg, has been scrupulously studied in the seminal work by Tolz, *Russia's Own Orient: The Politics of Identity and Oriental studies in the Late Imperial and Early Soviet*

---

[4] Ibid., 21.
[5] Schimmelpenninck van der Oye, "Imperial Roots," 34–41.
[6] Rodionov, "Profiles under Pressure," 55–6.

Periods, which dwells upon Russian/Soviet Orientology within the Academy of Sciences and its perceptions of the Orient in the context of Russia's own national discourses existing in those periods. Tolz strongly supports the idea of the great impact of Rosen's disciples, among whom Barthold was one of the main representatives, on the Bolshevik elite's perception of 'various ethnic groups in the Eastern and Southern periphery of the Soviet state in the 1920s'.[7] Tolz engages with the debate on the applicability of Said's model to Russia and argues that his notion of 'Orientalism' is the echo of a larger spectrum of ideas expressed by the above-mentioned *fin de siècle* Russian Orientologists. The advantage of this book is that the author goes beyond the Saidian approach and actively engages with a broader concept of power/knowledge relations which manifested themselves in the interaction of these scholars with state power.[8]

The protagonists of Tolz's book are the members of the Russian Academy of Sciences, which mostly succeeded in preserving the 'pure scholarly' spirit of its activities, as they themselves would perceive it, till the very end of the 1920s. Not sharing Bolshevik ideology, they quite successfully prevented the Academy from being politicised and ideologised for longer than a decade after 1917. However, in spite of their often outward but mostly covert opposition to the Bolsheviks,[9] the old academicians of Russian Oriental studies became consciously and actively involved in the early Bolshevik nationalities policy and turned out in the complete service of the practical needs of the new government.[10] This is explained by the fact that one of the main reasons for scholars' dissatisfaction with the late Imperial government was that it did not duly rely upon their scholarship in policymaking towards Russia's own Orient, as Tolz argues,[11] whereas from the early 1920s they were delighted to discover an affinity with the Bolshevik government on this issue. As Hirsch convincingly maintains, they were allured by the discovery that the Bolsheviks also 'had enormous faith in the transformative power of scientific government and in the idea of progress'.[12]

[7] Tolz, *Russia's Own Orient*, 4.
[8] Ibid., 69–84.
[9] See Rodionov, "Profiles under Pressure," 47.
[10] See Tolz, *Russia's Own Orient*, 75; Hirsch, *Empire of Nations*, 138–44.
[11] Tolz, *Russia's Own Orient*, 73–9.
[12] Hirsch, *Empire of Nations*, 7.

Academic Iranology: New versus Old

A prominent figure of this scholarly community who had become the leading scholar on the whole Persianate world was academician Vasilii Barthold, whose pre-1917 activities have been studied in the previous chapter.[13] Based in Petrograd (Leningrad from 1924), Barthold continued teaching at the Faculty of Oriental Languages, which along with the historic-philological and law faculties, was integrated into the unified Faculty of Social Sciences in 1919.[14] It was based on the academic staff of this faculty that Barthold established *Kollegiia Vostokovedov*, which gathered the so-called *ancien régime* academics who still adhered to the pre-1917 school of Oriental studies and became the virtual scholarly opposition to the new Soviet school of Orientology manifested in Pavlovich's politically influential, Moscow-based VNAV.[15]

Throughout the 1920s, VNAV made multiple efforts to subordinate *Kollegiia* to itself or at least to establish close interaction – efforts which remained mainly ignored by *Kollegiia*. Barthold even refused to write scholarly articles for *Novyi Vostok*, the publishing organ of VNAV.[16] He considered it impossible to cooperate with the new, ideologically driven, illiterate – as he thought – experts on the Orient, who rejected the scholarly practices and methods of the pre-1917 Russian Orientology.[17] This outward stance and reluctance to comply with the new rules of scholarship in the Bolshevik state resulted in the gradual suppression of all activities of *Kollegiia* by the end of the 1920s, a fact which was pointed out by Barthold himself in his letters to Minorsky shortly before his death.[18] This, of course, was not a random coincidence with the purges in the Academy which started in 1929.

Hirsch argues that 'In 1917 Ol'denburg and Vladimir Il'ich Lenin had formed an alliance, bringing together scholars and Bolsheviks; the Academy had provided the regime with expert knowledge and had been granted in exchange funding, protection, and a considerable

---

[13] It should be remembered that Valentin Zhukovskii died in 1918.
[14] See Kuznetsova and Kulagina, *Iz istorii*, 13.
[15] See Chapter 3.
[16] GARF, f. P-1335, op. 1, d. 5 (Pavlovich's correspondence), l. 20.
[17] It should be noted that Pavlovich would pay Barthold with the same coin. For example, in his "Zadachi VNAV" he wrote that there had been no valid study of the Orient in Russia (GARF, f. P-1335, op. 1, d. 23, l. 6).
[18] AV, f. 134, op. 3, d. 479, l. 17ob., 25.

degree of scientific freedom',[19] which manifested itself in the establishment of the Commission for the Study of the Tribal Composition of the Population of Russia (KIPS) composed of the *ancien régime* academics with Ol'denburg himself as its head. This unwritten alliance, achieved mainly after Ol'denburg's famous conversation with Lenin,[20] resulted also in *Sovnarkom*'s decree of 1918 regarding 'The Improvement of Scholar's Wellbeing',[21] also lobbied for by Maxim Gorkii, qualified in Krementsov's work as 'one of the most influential patrons of science'.[22] The decree granted the old scholars who cooperated with the state exceptionally favourable tangible conditions of life in a Russia torn by civil war. As Rodionov points out, for almost all scholars of the time it was a matter of surviving.[23] However, this alliance was not destined to last for long. In the context of the new discourses which were created by the new polity and which questioned the very right of physical existence of any scholarship unable to yield immediate practical returns, the old expert knowledge lost its vital importance. As soon as the main tasks of the Bolshevik nationalities policy were largely solved in the 1920s, the old academics ceased to be, in the new terms, productive for the state. This process became aggravated by the change in the paradigm of political loyalty, which demanded a transition from not committing active resistance and being relatively apolitical to wholehearted devotion, at least outwardly, to the regime and its ideology.

Notwithstanding the fact that after the October coup Barthold continued his endeavours to preserve his work from becoming part of any political ideology or stream, regardless of its affiliation with Bolsheviks or Russian émigrés, there was no longer any place in the new polity for apolitical scholarship. In this sense, his correspondence with the representatives of the Eurasianism movement is worth mentioning. In response to Savitskii's efforts to draw on his ideas for the promotion

[19] Hirsch, *Empire of Nations*, 140.
[20] See Ashot Baziiants, "Dve vstrechi S. F. Ol'denburga s V. I. Leninym i razvitie sovetskogo vostokovedeniia," in *Sergei Fedorovich Ol'denburg*, ed. Georgii Skriabin and Evgenii Primakov (Moscow: Nauka, 1986); Hirsch, *Empire of Nations*, 21–3.
[21] Newspaper *Izvestiia*, 14 December 1921. See also Kuznetsova and Kulagina, *Iz istorii*, 42–3. The materials on the activities of the Central Commission of VTsIK (1921–31) can be found in GARF, f. P-4737.
[22] Krementsov, *Stalinist Science*, 35.
[23] Rodionov, "Profiles under Pressure," 48.

of Eurasianist postulations on Russia's predestination to unite Europe and Asia – a theory predominantly spread among people of letters of the Russian émigré community of the time – Barthold wrote:

I am not the follower of 'eurasianist theories' and would prefer to use the word 'Eurasia' with the former meaning: Europe and Asia. It is absolutely clear that geographical divisions should not be put into dependence on the volatile destinies of political life. In that sense, Asia is not a homogeneous whole, and the Muslim world mainly stands closer to Western Europe than to China.[24]

In addition to Barthold's refutation of what later would be defined as "Orientalist contraposition of the West to the Orient", which was studied in Chapters 2 and 4, this citation confirms his strong belief in the necessity of keeping scholarship beyond politics. The new straight-forward discourse on making scholarship useful to state practical interests secured the exclusion of Barthold and suchlike scholars of Rosen's group not only from the operational grid of interaction with state power but also from national scholarship. Barthold was banned from teaching and would have been arrested, like many others among his *ancien régime* colleagues, had he not died in 1930. Subsequently, his scholarship was denounced as class-alienated and his works became unavailable in libraries.

Barthold's authorised oblivion, as Rodionov argues, continued well into the 1950s.[25] However, contrary to Rodionov's argument, in one of Krymskii's letters to Krachkovskii, dated 20 May 1935, we find the first signs of the state's behaviour towards Barthold's legacy slowly changing. According to Krymskii, while in other cities of the USSR the attitude remained the same, those signs were evident in St Petersburg.[26] Obviously, the process had started by that time and we can witness radical changes as early as a couple of years later. One of Barthold's few disciples, Ivan Umniakov (1890–1976), testifies that the Institute of Orientology of the Soviet Academy of Sciences entrusted him with the codification of Barthold's works and the publication of

---

[24] GARF, f. P-5783, op. 1, d. 418 (Correspondence with Savitskii), l. 37.
[25] Rodionov, "Profiles under Pressure," 51.
[26] A. Krymskii's letter to I. Krachkovskii, 20 May 1935, in Vitalii Naumkin, ed., *Neizvestnye stranitsy otechestvennogo vostokovedeniia* (Moscow: Vostochnaia literatura, 1997): 219–20.

its complete annotation as early as the late 1930s.[27] This, of course, could not have been done without full state authorisation, which can be regarded as the end of the obstruction of Barthold's scholarly legacy. This was done precisely as the state secured its omnipotent ideological grip on domestic scholarship and felt safe inwardly and, on the other hand, as Hirsch argues, at the time when it felt unsafe outwardly because of the re-evaluation of nations issue in Western Europe against the backdrop of the Nazi threat.[28] The Soviet state took into consideration that, as the representatives of Rosen's school believed, World War I had mainly been related to the nationality question, and the Russian Empire had not been prepared for that in terms of scholarly background.[29] Therefore, having learnt from the experience of its Imperial predecessor, on the eve of a new large-scale conflict of a similar character the state felt the necessity of consolidating whatever was available in the scholarly domain.

Curiously enough, as early as 1960 mature Soviet Orientology regarded Barthold as one of the founders of the study of the socio-economic history of Oriental countries in its Marxist terms,[30] although he had never used Marxist methodology in his studies nor supported such an approach in general. For example, the first and only time when Barthold used the term 'feudalism' was in his scholarly paper "To the Question of Feudalism in Iran", presented by him at a session of VNAV in 1929, just several months before his death, and published in its organ *Novyi Vostok* in 1930.[31] It should be noted that, in actual fact, the paper had nothing to do with the study of Marxist postulations in application to ancient Iran. However, scholars were already learning to play their own politics with the state – a phenomenon that became widespread in the 1930s and existed in Soviet scholarship until the late 1980s, as Krementsov and Stephen Fortescue maintain.[32] By including Marxist terminology, quite often far-fetched references to the founders

[27] Ivan Umniakov, *Annotirovannaia bibliografiia nrudov V. V. Bartol'da* (Moscow: Nauka, 1976): 11.
[28] See Hirsch, *Empire of Nations*, 15–16.
[29] Ibid., 45–9.
[30] See Kononov, *Vostokovedenie*, 23.
[31] Vasilii Bartol'd, "K voprosu o feodalizme v Irane," *Novyi Vostok* 28 (1930): 108–16. It was the only time when Barthold participated in the VNAV's activities.
[32] See Krementsov, *Stalinist Science*, 45–6, 80–3; Fortescue, *Communist Party*, 18.

of the ruling ideology and engaging with *novoyaz* in general, Soviet scholars would simply make possible the physical continuation of their scholarly work in the context of an ideologically driven society.[33]

This, of course, did not rescue the old school of Russian Orientology from destruction, which had been accomplished by the early 1930s according to Rodionov.[34] Notwithstanding his active engagement in the state-run project of drawing up the USSR's nationalities map, Barthold and his colleagues merely succeeded in gaining a temporary physical immunity and the relevant operational autonomy in their own scholarly domain. The state used them instrumentally as a source of expert knowledge without granting them the slightest opportunity to access the decision-making area of domestic policy, let alone foreign policy. From the very first days of the new polity, on a scale that increased from year to year, so-called pure academic Oriental studies were gradually substituted with the new "scholarship" of individuals representing a certain symbiosis of practical knowledge and scant theoretical pieces of Orientological knowledge, both of which were being obtained on the move – as they were carrying out their professional duties in the field of Bolshevik policy towards the East while writing their "scholarly" works on the East, based on Marxist ideology.

In the case of early Soviet Iranian studies, this group was represented by individuals such as Gurko-Kriazhin, Pastukhov, Osetrov, Vel'tman-Pavlovich and Tardov. Being staunch apologists for Bolshevism, all of them founded their attitude towards the Orient and their methodology for its study on the writings of Marx, Engels and Lenin.[35] Moreover, acting as the employees of the state entities directly involved in implementing Soviet foreign policy towards Eastern countries, they combined their organisational activities with the ongoing study of the East based on the new methodology, and, vice versa, they immediately integrated their elaborated scholarly approaches and their just-achieved conclusions into their organisational activities, hence securing the conformity of such activities to their scholarly guidelines in practice.

Almost all of them did not have even initial academic Oriental training. The closest any of them came to conventional notions of

[33] See Krementsov, *Stalinist Science*, 27, 49–53.
[34] Rodionov, "Profiles under Pressure," 47, 55–6.
[35] See Vucinich, "Structure," 52.

academic training and scholarly activities was Gurko-Kriazhin, who graduated from the Historico-Philological Faculty of Moscow State University in 1912 and had majored in the ethnography and archaeology of the Caucasus, without mastering a single Oriental language but with a great interest in the history and culture of the Orient. Later, he happened to work in the Lazarev Institute under the supervision of an acknowledged expert on the Persianate world, Aleksandr Freiman (1879–1968). This also influenced Gurko-Kriazhin's overall engagement with Persia.[36]

As Tamazishvili points out, Gurko-Kriazhin's Orientological career began with his public lecture "The White Peril: The West and the East", held in Moscow in 1914.[37] In the lecture, he analysed the colonial expansion of Western powers of the time to the East and emphasised an underlying racist component present in the ongoing submission of the Orient – a thesis that became very popular in the Western critique of Orientalism during the second half of the twentieth century. It is worth mentioning that before 1917 Gurko-Kriazhin did not adhere to any socio-democratic political movement and was, as he later characterised himself, an 'idealistic Orientophile in Tolstoy's style'.[38] Strong sympathy towards Oriental peoples remained evident in Gurko-Kriazhin's activities and scholarly writings throughout his whole life – a rather common feature for all the early Soviet Orientologists, who looked at the "oppressed" Orientals as actual or potential allies in the worldwide struggle of classes.

Given the hectic civil war times and the constantly varying character of the state activities in which they were involved, it is a rather challenging undertaking to assign the above-mentioned Orientologists to a particular domain of the Oriental studies of early Soviet Russia, namely academic scholarship, the diplomatic service or the military. Even Gurko-Kriazhin, who was engaged most consistently and straightforwardly in scholarly academic activities, had time to serve in both the Bolshevik diplomatic serive and the RKKA as an expert

---

[36] GARF, P-1335, op. 1, d. 6, l. 69.
[37] Vladimir Gurko-Kriazhin, "Belaia opasnost'. Vostok i Zapad" [The White Peril: The West and the East], *Russkoe Slovo* (1 February 1914); Tamazishvili, "Gurko-Kriazhin," 34.
[38] Vladimir Gurko-Kriazhin, "V sektsiiu Zarubezhnogo Vostoka Obshestva istorikov-marksistov. Zaiavlenie," *Istorik-marksist* 17 (1930): 89. See also Tamazishvili, "Gurko-Kriazhin," 34.

on the Orient.[39] Of course, one can reason that, beyond the academic sphere, he had neither diplomatic nor military training. However, the others did not, either – this was one of the most unique features of the post-1917 situation: the state would mostly entrust individuals with professional assignments according to their revolutionary zeal and their readiness to undertake new challenges, not by their professional background, hence granting them many more operational capabilities than in Imperial Russia.[40] Yet Gurko-Kriazhin is perceived to belong to the academic domain of early Soviet Oriental studies.

Having wholeheartedly accepted the October coup, and perceiving it as a fully fledged people's revolution with only truthful ideology, he believed in the necessity of establishing a new Orientology that 'would be bearing the burden of the emerging new social psychology.'[41] In his particular case it was an Orientology based on Marxist methodology and aiming at the study of socio-political and economic issues in the modern and contemporary history of the Orient. The study of national liberation movements was supposed to occupy the central place in this quest for new knowledge.[42] Obviously, this approach has much in common with Foucauldian archaeology of knowledge, unearthing the past and comprehending our knowledge about it according to the social context of its time. The difference is that Foucault used this postulation to better understand the knowledge of the past and the practices of its production, whereas Gurko-Kriazhin suggested the transformation of the perception of existing knowledge and of the available ways of its production under the new polity.

Later on, the second part of the new Orientology was perceived as the immediate link to state activities in the East. The social psychology of the time also implied the promotion of worldwide revolution, the future of which mainly lay in the East, according to him.[43] In 1919, Gurko-Kriazhin embarked on service in the General Staff of the Red Army until, in June 1920, he was assigned to the Bolshevik joint

---

[39] GARF, f. P-1335, op. 1, d. 6, l. 69–70.
[40] In this sense, Pavolvich is the most remarkable example, see Appendix (Pavlovich).
[41] Tamazishvili, "Gurko-Kriazhin," 44.
[42] GARF, P-1335, op.1, d. 23, l. 1–10.
[43] See Vladimir Gurko-Kriazhin, "Vostok pri svete revoliutsii," *Vestnik zhizni* 5 (1919): 100–1.

diplomatic mission in Persia and Turkey, which settled in Baku.[44] This happened in the full swing of the abortive Persian Socialist Revolution instigated by the landing of Raskol'nikov's forces in Anzali shortly before. Heading the Information Section of the Bolshevik plenipotentiary mission and the Representation of ROSTA (Russia's Telegraph Agency) in the whole Middle East, Gurko-Kriazhin was subordinated to Rotshtein and fitted well into the team of Pastukhov and Osetrov, forming the core fabric for the production of Bolshevik Persian policy for more than a decade.[45]

Similarly to his above-mentioned colleagues, who used their posts in the new Bolshevik foreign policy structures for integrating their scholarship into their state activities, Gurko-Kriazhin was opposed to the cause that aimed at the organisation of immediate socialist revolution in Persia, which was furiously advocated by actual participants in revolutionary activities in Persia, namely by Sergo Ordzhonikidze (1886-1937), Sultanzadeh, Illarion Mgeladze (pseudonym Il'ia Vardin; 1890–1941) and many other experienced, militant Bolsheviks, who, however, had nothing to do with scholarly activities of the time.[46] Following Marxist methodology, Gurko-Kriazhin considered Persia unprepared for immediate social conversion and believed that Soviet Russia needed to assist Persia in creating and enhancing its nationalist bourgeoisie. Support for the Persian inner communist elements and instigation of the inevitable socialist revolution should take central place in Soviet Persian policy only after the national bourgeoisie had come to power. For the time being, Soviet Russia had to cooperate with the nationalist forces, later clearly represented by Reza Khan, and to unfold a full-scale efficient study of Persia based on the new approaches.[47]

---

[44] See E. V. Gurko-Kriazhina, *Vostokoved Vladimir Aleksandrovich Gurko-Kriazhin*, 1887–1931 (Moscow: INION RAN, 2003): 11.

[45] See the analysis and criticism of their roles in the process of the Persian policymaking in RGASPI, f. 85, op. *Secret Persia*, d. 106 (10 persidskikh pisem Vardina).

[46] GARF, f. P-5402, op. 1, d. 417, l. 1. RGASPI, f. 85, op. *Secret Persia*, d. 11, l. 1–2 (Ordzhonikidze's complaint to Politbiuro on the activities of the Soviet Mission in Persia), l. 7; d. 106 (Vardin's criticism), l. 8–8ob., 16ob.

[47] AVPRF, f. 028, op. 10, d. 11, papka 31, l. 7, 41; RGASPI, f. 532 (KUTV), op. 2, d. 153, l. 17; f. 159, op. 2, d. 51, l. 127(NKID to Politbiuro); f. 85, d. 50, l. 1–2.

In this respect, the article "Red Orientalism" by Kemper, focusing on the activities of Stalin's deputy in *Narkomnats* and the founder of VNAV, Pavlovich, also sheds some light on Gurko-Kriazhin's contribution to the work of VNAV, playing the first role after Pavlovich in terms of its scholarly organisation. Kemper rightly cites Gurko-Kriazhin's words about VNAV, which explicitly testify to the crucial role he ascribed to it, and his work in it, since, according to Gurko-Kriazhin, 'it was meant to be a laboratory of the new revolutionary Orientology'.[48] Indeed, having taken one of the decisive roles in the establishment of VNAV and having become head of its leading politico-economic department after his return from Persia, Gurko-Kriazhin instructed the Soviet missions in the Middle East to submit to him regular analytical reports on the politico-economic situation of the relevant countries.[49] In this area, his cooperation with the Soviet mission in Persia (Osetrov, Pastukhov, Tardov) and the Soviet plenipotentiary in Afghanistan (Raskol'nikov) was particularly fruitful, given their personal drive for scholarly research – a phenomenon totally overlooked in Kemper's works on early Soviet Orientologists, in which he is preoccupied with their straightforward Orientalist link to state power.[50]

Gurko-Kriazhin codified and rigorously processed the area-study information he received for its subsequent usage in composing consolidated reports and in the Orientological training of the students of the Military Academy, KUTV, MIV and Leningrad Institute of Living Oriental Languages. The Military Academy and MIV would apply to Gurko-Kriazhin to obtain his services as a lecturer and as their students' scholarly supervisor.[51] However, Gurko-Kriazhin was almost the only individual based in VNAV of such scholarly significance – the rest, albeit fully fledged members of VNAV, mostly worked in other organisations. So it was not so much VNAV as an institution that granted Gurko-Kriazhin the opportunity to exert his direct influence on early Soviet Persian policy, as it was his own scholarship and the attitude of the early Bolshevik state towards it.

[48] Kemper, "Red Orientalism," 456.
[49] GARF, P-1335, op. 1, d. 6, l. 5, 18, 46, 82.
[50] AV, f. 115, op. 2, d. 29, l. 1; op. 1, d. 156, l. 1.
[51] GARF, P-1335, op. 1, d.5, l. 88, 90, 101.

Separately stressing VNAV's direct affiliation to *Narkomnats* and its founder's status as Stalin's first deputy, Soviet scholarship of the second half of the twentieth century emphasised the great contribution of VNAV as an institution to all Orientological domains of the early USSR,[52] while Western researchers such as Vucinich and Atkin, pointing to certain failures in organisational and scholarly activities, were more reserved.[53] Later in the development of the debate on the applicability of Said's Orientalism mould to Russia, Kemper also emphasised the origins and significant role of VNAV as an Orientalist institution in Saidian terms; however, I argue that, in this case, it was not the organisation which exerted influence or by means of its structure and activities enabled individuals to exert influence on state power, as it, conversely, was in the case of IRGO, and particularly RKISVA, during the late Imperial period.[54]

It is true that all the politically influential Orientologists were members of VNAV, but it was they who gave it more weight to by their individual activities, which were carried out not through VNAV but through the political organisations which employed them. VNAV mostly failed to consolidate the efforts of the representatives of all three Orientological domains within the joint projects from which they all could have benefited. Moreover, during the first years after the establishment of VNAV many of its main members that were affiliated with the Red Army and intelligence services, such as Abikh, Pastukhov, Osetrov, Snesarev, Raskol'nikov among others, had to outwardly withdraw their membership because of the limitations imposed by their main employers on cooperation with civilian entities.[55] These were the individuals who actually shaped the early Soviet Persian policy, of whom more in the following section.

Red Orientalism: NKID as a Mill of Scholarly Knowledge

Pastukhov and Vladimir Osetrov, who had both graduated from the Faculty of Law at Moscow University, went to NKID in 1918 and occupied key positions in the decision-making structures of early

---

[52] See, for example, Kuznetsova and Kulagina, "Vsesoiuznaia."
[53] Vucinich, "Structure," 59–61; Atkin, "Soviet and Russian Scholarship," 229.
[54] See Chapter 2.
[55] GARF, P-1335, op. 1, d. 6, l. 119, 130, 142.

Soviet policy towards Persia. As mentioned above, in the context of the looming worldwide socialist revolution Oriental peoples were perceived by Russian revolutionaries as the nations oppressed by world reaction, and hence potential brothers-in-arms in the class struggle.[56] The affinity of class character which the new Orientologists felt towards the oppressed Orient naturally transformed into plain sympathy – a feeling which had quite often been inherent to late Imperial Russia's Orientologists because of their romanticised Orientalist perceptions and the positivist attitudes inculcated in them by their teachers – the academics of Rosen's family.[57] This even manifested itself in the pseudonyms they took: Pastukhov became Iranskii which can be roughly translated from Russian as 'belonging to Iran', and Osetrov would sign documents as Irandust – 'loving Iran' or 'Iran's friend'.

In his *Russian and Soviet Diplomacy, 1900–1939*, Kocho-Williams maintains a thesis on the multiple continuities inherited from the late Imperial period by the Bolshevik foreign affairs apparatus, whereas I argue that those continuities can mostly be found only in the apprehended necessity to follow conventional rules of diplomatic protocol and to secure routine diplomatic interaction for Bolshevik Russia. This was simply dictated by the existing realities, since otherwise the Bolsheviks would have been excluded from the international field of communication, which the nascent state was undoubtedly unable to afford. Equally, the work *Tak nachinalsia Narkomindel*, notwithstanding all its ideological bias, gives valuable first-hand information on the technicalities of NKID functioning during the first post-1917 years, when it started its activities with a totally new operative personnel of fourteen on 18 November 1917, including Commissar Trotsky and his two deputies.[58] This book demonstrates a different picture to the one depicted by Kocho-Williams.

Indeed, in contrast to the academic and military domains (almost all leading scholars remained in their institutions and many Imperial senior officers joined the Red Army), NKID became a totally new institution as a result of deep ruptures in its personnel and professional

---

[56] See V. I. Lenin, "Letter to Ammanallah-Khan dated 27/05/1919," *Izvestiia TsIK Turkestanskoi Respubliki* 121 (14 June 1919).
[57] AV, f. 17, op. 2, d. 9, l. 3, 5–7ob., 10–11ob.
[58] Zarnitsky and Trofimova, *Tak nachinalsia Narkomindel*, 13–15.

approaches in regards its Imperial predecessor. These ruptures were particularly painful in the field of NKID's Persian activities. In addition to crucial changes in the general political cause and the loss of the relevant experienced, ad hoc trained personnel in St Petersburg, nobody among hundreds of Russian officials in Persia accepted the new power in Russia, except for one diplomat, who will be touched upon later in the chapter.[59]

Given the emerging dearth of experts, it is not surprising that new individuals, who were not even properly trained, succeeded in occupying strategic positions within their professional domain. However, I argue that they would not have been able to retain and to significantly strengthen these positions in the context of new discourses and the attitudes of the new state towards scholarly knowledge had they not quickly gained the necessary scholarly expertise through their own personal drive and the operational capabilities received from state power. For example, Iranskii headed the First Oriental Section of NKID from 1921 to 1933, the year when he embarked on his post as Soviet Ambassador to Iran. Since the first year of his diplomatic service (1918), he had been actively engaged in work and study relating to Iran, arguably combining them with his activities first in (*Ve*)*Cheka* and, later on, in INO (O)GPU and NKVD.[60] Before being appointed Ambassador, he often visited Persia but with short-term assignments, whereas Irandust spent much longer in Persia: 1920–5 and 1928–9, and he was permanently assigned to the same section of NKID.[61]

In this respect Agaev points out: 'The majority of the first Soviet Iranists had not been involved in history studies, in general, nor in Iranian studies, in particular, and came to Orientology from practical activities.'[62] This is fair; however, they embarked on gaining theoretical expertise from the outset: when in NKID, Iranskii undertook Orientological training in the Oriental Section of the Academy of the RKKA, established and turned by Snesarev into the main source of Orientological cadres for NKID and political and military intelligence services.[63] Irandust took language and area-studies lessons from

---

[59] See Dailami, "Bravin in Tehran," 67.
[60] RGASPI, f. 85, op. *Secret Persia*, d. 106, l. 173.
[61] See Vasil'kov and Sorokina, *Liudi i sud'by*, http://memory.pvost.org/pages/osetrov.html.
[62] Agaev, *Sovetskoe iranovedenie*, 7.
[63] GARF, P-1335, op. 1, d. 6, l. 130.

Krymskii's best disciple and expert on Persian literature, Chaikin, who worked as an interpreter in the Soviet mission in Tehran from 1920 to 1926.[64] In 1919–20, before being posted to Persia, the same Chaikin, along with Snesarev, taught Persian and area-studies to Iranskii at the Military Academy.[65]

Given the rupture in applied methodology and the above-mentioned lack of basic Orientological training of new experts on Iran, their first works were, in actual fact, more descriptive essays and superfluous articles, mostly aimed at posing new research questions about contemporary Iran.[66] In addition, a great gain for late Imperial Orientologists such as Minorsky, Tumanskii, Smirnov and other properly trained practitioners – namely direct access to primary sources at site – was not so advantageous for the early Soviet Iranists and often resulted in inferior quality scholarly work because they lacked the ability to rigorously process the abundance of contemporary materials containing local bias. At the same time, it should be noted that these flaws in the nascent Soviet Iranology would later be acknowledged by Gurko-Kriazhin, Iranskii and Pavlovich as their expertise grew.[67] However, quantity had finally turned into quality by the end of the 1920s, and scholarly field activities, heavily mixed up with practical political activities, made their significant contribution to Soviet scholarship on contemporary Iran – the area which had, indeed, received considerably less attention from late Imperial Russia's Persian studies.

Therefore, the symbiosis of revolutionary zeal, of Marxist ideology and of growing Orientological expertise resulted in individuals such as Iranskii and Irandust occupying strategically crucial positions within the grid of power/knowledge relations. Drawing on their own scholarship, they would carry out analysis of the situation in Persia and come to certain conclusions which they implemented in their own practical foreign policy activities and in their analytical reports, determining the decisions of their superiors – Chicherin and Karakhan.[68] Irandust's

---

[64] See Appendix (Chaikin).
[65] GARF, f. 7668, op. 1, d. 2889, l. 5–5ob. See also A. Krymskii's letter to I. Krachkovskii, 3 January 1935, in Naumkin, *Neizvestnye*, 216.
[66] Agaev, *Sovetskoe iranovedenie*, 8–9.
[67] Vladimir Gurko-Kriazhin, "10 let vostokovednoi mysli," *Novyi Vostok* 19 (1927): 35, 43, 44–45; Mikhail Pavlovich, "Zadachi i dostizheniia sovetskogo vostokovedeniia," *Novyi Vostok* 16–17 (1926): 4.
[68] AVPRF, f. 04, op. 18, d. 50691, papka 112, l. 1–3, 38; d. 50749, papka 115, l. 3.

profound work, "Essays on the Economic Polity of Persia",[69] efficiently drawing on the abundant primary material on socio-economic issues that had been accumulated by that time, became the most remarkable – both in terms of length and content – testament of the new Soviet Iranology regarding its standpoint towards the object of study and contemporary and subsequent Soviet foreign policy towards Persia. It contained the perception of Persia as a society unripe for a social conversion similar to the one that had happened in Russia.

The work also expressed a belief in the necessity of supporting the national bourgeoisie and developing all kinds of relationships, particularly economic and political, with 'Reza Khan's government of national dictatorship', as well as of withdrawing Soviet military and political support for various kinds of nationalist armed movements similar to those of Kuchek-Khan, Ehsanollah and Allahverdi-Khan Khadu.[70] As the correspondence of the Soviet mission in Tehran with NKID testifies, these were the main pillars of Soviet policy towards Persia in the period from 1921 to the mid-1930s, which, however, was frequently challenged by the other radical Bolsheviks pursuing the cause of the organisation of immediate revolution in Persia.[71] During the 1920s and early 1930s, Chicherin and his successors were frequently accused of allowing the group of Pastukhov, Osetrov, Tardov and Gurko-Kriazhin to fundamentally shape the USSR's foreign policy towards Persia[72] – a protracted episode in the history of Soviet Oriental studies which can be regarded as the most unequivocal manifestation of Said's plain Orientalism in terms of its straightforward nexus between knowledge and state power.

---

[69] Vladimir Osetrov, "Ocherki ekonomicheskogo stroia v Persii," in *Kolonial'nyi Vostok. Sotsial'no-ekonomicheskie ocherki* (Moscow: Nauka, 1924).

[70] AVPRF, f. 04, op. 18, d. 50750, papka 115, l. 1–71; f. 028, op. 10, d. 11, papka 31, l. 2, 3, 6, 7, 39. The positivist term 'Reza Khan's government of national dictatorship' was first coined by Iranskii (f. 94, op. 5a, d. 1, papka 105, l. 269). RGASPI, f. 159, op. 2, d. 51 (Osetrov on Persia), l. 60–8, 111–13. On Allahverdi-Khan Khadu see Hooshang Nahavandi, *Seh ruidad va seh doulatmard* (Los Angeles: Ketab, 2009): 53–5. See also Bast, "Council for International Propaganda," 174; Bast, "Duping the British and Outwitting the Russians?," 265.

[71] RGASPI, f. 85, d. 14, l. 1–3 (Rotshtein's correspondence with Chicherin). AVPRF, f. Krestinsky, op. 10, d. 81, papka 54, l. 12, 30–6, 44–67, 96.

[72] RGASPI, f. 85, d. 106, l. 170–1, 260, 267; f. 532, op. 2, d. 153, l. 17; on Chicherin seeking Pastukhov's advice see also f. 159, op. 2, d. 51, l. 177; see also Chicherin's response to the accusations in l. 180, 182.

Discontinuities and the Inception of New Institutional Practices

Against the backdrop of all the above-mentioned institutional ruptures and shifts within Russia's new foreign policy structures, the example of tsarist diplomats Nikolai Zakharovich Bravin (1881–1921) and Pavel Petrovich Vvedenskii (1880–1938), used by the Bolshevik foreign policy state entities, can seem more an exception, where this is one of those exceptions that prove the rule. The former was the most controversial figure among the Russian late Imperial diplomatic corps, and he turned out to be the same among the first generation of Soviet diplomats. A gifted diplomat-*vostochnik* of late Imperial Russia[73] and one of the most favoured disciples of Zhukovskii on the one hand,[74] and, on the other, the only diplomat among many dozens of his peers in Persia to recognise the Bolsheviks' power[75] and, subsequently, during the first years after 1917, the first Soviet *polpred* (plenipotentiary) to Persia, Turkestan and Afghanistan, in January 1921 he was assassinated on Moscow's orders following his refusal to return to Russia from Afghanistan.[76]

Both Russian and Western historiography have little on Bravin,[77] mainly because of the restricted access to the relevant documents in Russian archives, a situation which has again been maintained by Russian authorities with new energy since 2000 – the year of Putin's coming to power.[78] Drawing on British and Iranian archival sources, the scarce Western scholarship on Bravin focuses on his failed efforts to take over the representation of Russia's interests in Persia from Russia's acting legation in the period from November 1917 to June

---

[73] AVPRI, f. 159, op. 749/2, d. 1 (Bravin's personal file).
[74] AV contains Bravin's twenty-three letters to Zhukovskii testifying about their close teacher–disciple relations (AV, f. 17, op. 2, d. 9).
[75] AV, f. 134, op. 1, d. 224, l. 1–3 (Minorsky's testimonial for Bravin). GARF, P-5802, op. 1, d. 617, l. 12.
[76] RGASPI, f. 133, op. 1 (Not for Reading Hall), d. 26 (Kobozev's notes), l. 30.
[77] See Dailami, "Bravin in Tehran"; Pezhmann Dailami, "The Bolshevik Revolution and the Genesis of Communism in Iran, 1917–1920," *Central Asian Survey* 11/3 (1992): 51–82; Vladimir Genis, *Nevernye slugi rezhima: Pervye sovetskie nevozvrashentsy (1920–1933)* (Moscow: Informkniga, 2009); Genis, *Vitse-Konsul*. See also Joanna Modrzejewska-Lesniewska, "A Spy or the First Russian Dissident?" [In Polish] *Przeglad Historyczny* 94/4 (2003): 411–18.
[78] See Volkov, "Fearing the Ghosts."

1918, namely from the moment he positively responded from Khoi to Trotsky's cable containing the appeal to all Russian diplomats and went over to Tehran, to the time he left Persia for Moscow.[79] Being preoccupied with the general cause of the Bolshevik foreign policy towards Persia and Bravin's mechanical role therein, France-based researcher Pezhmann Dailami left Bravin's pre-1917 professional and Orientological past beyond the scope of his works, whereas a Russia-based scholar, Vladimir Genis, mainly due to his direct access to Russian archives as a RGASPI employee, carried out more detailed studies of Bravin's activities during the late Imperial and early Soviet periods, predominantly focusing on his biography and emphasising Bravin's excessive career ambitions.[80] Drawing on the valuable, recently declassified collections in the Russian archives, Genis' works have challenged the policing practices conventionally adopted in Soviet historiography and still widely maintained in post-Soviet historiography. In Foucauldian terms, his research on Bravin has become a historiographical breakthrough from the patriotic discourse, widespread in Russia's Iranology, on the necessity to keep expedient silence on the fate of the first Soviet plenipotentiary to Persia and Afghanistan, who eventually became the first high-ranking Soviet diplomat-defector.[81]

Nevertheless, the above-mentioned scholarship on Bravin does not aim in any way at engaging with the interaction of power/knowledge relations in his case. It totally overlooks his contribution to the accumulation of primary material on Persia during the late Imperial period and the role which he had played within Zhukovskii's scholarly intelligence network, which was studied in Chapter 4. Neither does it engage with examining Bravin's activities in the period of more than three years after the Bolshevik coup; whereas, I argue, Bravin's case personifies another indicative example of the interplay of personal and

---

[79] GARF, f. P-4738, op. 2, d. 31, l. 15. See also Dailami, "Bravin in Tehran," 67–70; Dailami, "Bolshevik Revolution," 47–50.

[80] See, for example, Genis, *Nevernye*, 12, 19.

[81] Some of the archival collections, used by Genis, have been either reclassified or relocated to certain distant depositories, which made the retrieval of documents practically impossible. For example, such a destiny has befallen RGASPI's Fond 17, containing documents on the Party's counter-measures against defectors and the Central Committee's orders for OGPU to elaborate preventive and punitive actions on the issue, which later led to the juridical legalisation of the practices, aimed at the extrajudicial physical liquidation of Soviet defectors on the territory of other countries.

institutional interests within the grid of power/knowledge relations. His profound Orientological expertise and his almost thirteen-year professional experience as a diplomat secured him an influential strategic position with considerable operational autonomy within foreign policy activities of the new state.

After he abandoned his post in Persia and went to Moscow, he succeeded in securing his appointment as NKID's plenipotentiary at the Turkestan Revolutionary Government in Tashkent,[82] where he tried to utilise his Orientological expertise in order to improve the new regime's relationships with the local population and to attract the Bukharians' sympathy towards the Bolsheviks.[83] However, he was the only *ancien régime* expert in the government of Turkestan and, under the circumstances of military hostilities, the new power preferred more straightforward methods of coercion and did not take his expertise on board. In addition, not being captivated with the Marxist ideology, by the time he was posted to Afghanistan as Head of the First Soviet plenipotentiary mission he had become rather disappointed with his interaction with the Bolsheviks, which eventually resulted in mutual distrust. When already at the court of the Afghan ruler, Bravin even refused to explain the Bolshevik credenda[84] to Ammanollah-Khan and his entourage, leaving this task to his ideologically driven companions, who could hardly speak Dari. All this was reported to Tashkent and Moscow shortly afterwards, with relevant consequences.[85]

In the early stages of Bravin's rather short-lived Soviet career, he played an underlying role in the successful introduction of the principles of the new Russian state to the Iranians, conquering their hearts by delivering flaming public speeches in excellent Persian in the streets of Tehran and by publishing eloquent articles in Iranian newspapers in praise of the new Russia;[86] however, during its late

---

[82] RGASPI, f. 122, op. 2, d. 41, l. 3.

[83] Ibid., l. 13–15 (Protocol of the Turkestan government meeting).

[84] The military representative and the commissar of the mission, B. N. Ivanov, wrote in his report that Ammanollah-Khan and his government had taken Bravin's mission as the envoys of a certain Prophet Lenin who had proclaimed a new faith. Ivanov also added: 'Finally, he said that he liked our faith since it very much looked like the pure Islam, however the Afghan people were not able to understand it yet.' (AV, f. 115, op. 1, d. 154, l. 3–4).

[85] AV, f. 115, op. 1, d. 154 (The Member of Revolutionary Military Council B. N. Ivanov's Report on his mission in Afghanistan), l. 3.

[86] AV, f. 134, op. 2, d. 304 (Bravin's actions). According to the Iranian historian and diplomat N. S. Fatemi, Lenin's letter and the Soviet policy towards Persia,

stages, Bravin's foreign policy output was *quantité négligeable*. His only tangible impact became his promises to Ammanollah-Khan on behalf of Soviet Russia to start the deliveries of arms for the Afghan army and, more importantly, to give away Kushka to Afghanistan – the future most southern point of the USSR – the two issues which would remain a real headache for Bravin's successors, Soviet plenipotentiaries in Afganistan, Surits and Raskol'nikov, for years.[87]

This diminution can be explained by the fact that, due to the features of his character, Bravin utilised the potential and available capabilities of his strategic position for pursuing his personal interests alone,[88] hence breaking the balance of the equipotent components of the Foucauldian interplay of power relations. In actual fact, Bravin concentrated on solving the issues of his personal wellbeing and squaring his personal accounts with his old enemies, one of whom was Vvedenskii, since the spring of 1917 when Bravin started a whole campaign to discredit him, including sending reports to the official for special missions of the Russian Imperial Minister for Foreign Affairs, von Klemm, which accused Vvedenskii of financial wrongdoing and not observing Russian interests in Persia.[89]

Indeed, only Minorsky, the acting Russian Minister in Tehran, who directly rebuked Bravin in summer 1917 for his libellous behaviour and tried to limit his complaints,[90] as well as the subsequent events of late 1917, prevented Bravin from continuing to ruin his colleagues' reputations – but not for long. When already in Tashkent as NKID's representative at the autonomous government of Turkestan, Bravin

---

successfully introduced to Iranians by Bravin, 'meant more to them than armies and trains with ammunition' (Zarnitsky and Trofimova, *Tak nachinalsia*, 221).

[87] RGASPI, f. 5, op. 1, d. 2179 (Cables of the RSFSR plenipotentiaries in Afghanistan to Lenin), for example, l. 1, 59. These issues were put forward many times by the Afghan authorities throughout the 1920s during negotiations with NKID's representatives with reference to Bravin's promises, whereas Moscow was reluctant to suffer territorial losses and to sell weapons to the Afghans because it feared that the weapons would eventually be shared with the Central Asian Basmatches.

[88] He would say: 'My choice was mercantilistic. Wishing to work, in general, and having spent a part of my life for special education and service, as well as not joining any party, I recognised the Soviet power. I simply do not want to discontinue my service and want to work, regardless of any changes in Russian politics' (Genis, *Nevernye*, 19).

[89] AVPRI, f. 144, op. 489, d. 1022b, l. 106.

[90] Ibid., d. 1023b, l. 33–4.

resumed his attack on Vvedenskii, who had become an advisor to the Amir of Bukhara by that time. By 1919, due to his Orientological expertise and economic enterprise, already successfully demonstrated in Tabriz during the revolutionary unrest of 1905–11,[91] Vvedenskii had succeeded in preventing famine in Bukhara and 'in stopping military hostilities and a bloody massacre [of the Russian population of Bukhara] which had been provoked by an attempt to forcefully sovieticise Bukhara in spring 1918'.[92] As a result, Vvedenskii became the Amir's right-hand man and the de facto head of the heavily populated Russian colony in Bukhara. Naturally, the Turkestan revolutionary authorities saw him as a dangerous rival to Pechatnikov, the official Bolshevik plenipotentiary in Bukhara.

The subsequent abrupt developments were triggered by Bravin alone, who had written a report on Vvedenskii to the government of the Turkestan Republic.[93] He described Vvedenskii's counter-revolutionary activities in Persia during the Constitutional Movement and accused him of current ties with the British and the *ancien régime* Minister in Persia, von Etter (from whom Bravin had failed to take over the mission in Tehran), as well as of receiving financial support from them. In the end, he proposed no less than the physical liquidation of Vvedenskii. 'There should not be hesitations now. Vvedenskii must be liquidated this way or another. Otherwise, in Bukhara there will be constant clandestine British activities and an unequal struggle between Vvedenskii, having the powerful support of the British, and Comrade Pechatnikov, who is far from being versed in the cobwebs of politics in the Orient.'[94]

It should be noted that Bravin's above-mentioned actions, arguably dictated by his implicit, perhaps even unconscious, endeavour to eliminate competing sources of expertise in his pursuit of state attention,[95] determined his mechanical role as a Foucauldian vehicle of power.[96] Eventually, he assisted the inception of a new institutional practice in the context of power/knowledge relations that would remain widespread in different forms, more intense and milder, in the USSR until

[91] AVPRI, f. 144, op. 489b, d. 1022, l. 29–31.
[92] Genis, *Nevernye*, 21.
[93] RGASPI, f. 122, op. 2, d. 41, l. 3–4 (Bravin's report).
[94] Ibid., l. 4.
[95] AVPRI, f. 144, op. 489, d. 1010b, l. 2 (Report to von Klemm).
[96] See Chapter 1.

the virtual collapse of Soviet power in the late 1980s, namely the use of scholars' and scientists' labour in prisons and concentration camps, and other forms of restriction of physical freedom. Shortly after, in April 1919, based on Bravin's accusations, Vvedenskii was kidnapped from Bukhara by the local *Cheka* and imprisoned in Tashkent.

Although the Turkestan *Cheka* could find nothing incriminating about him, except his cooperation with the Amir of Bukhara[97] and Bravin's reports, he was kept in the central prison of Tashkent under suspicion of counter-revolutionary activities. At that very same time, most surprisingly, the Supreme Commission of the VTsIK for Turkestan Affairs entrusted Vvedenskii, while on remand, with the supervision and actual execution of the project on the demarcation of the borders of Turkestan with Persia and Afghanistan. The Commission also allocated a team of topographers who went to Vvedenskii's prison cell to carry out work under his supervision.[98] This allows us to conclude that the phenomenon of the *sharashki* of the 1930s–1940s, studied by Krementsov in his insightful work *Stalinist Science*, which in the 1960s–1970s developed into classified scientific towns and institutes with incarcerated and exiled scientists, in actual fact had its roots in 1919, the very dawn of the Bolshevik state.

The episode of Vvedenskii's imprisoned scholarship, unprecedented in the Imperial period, which unfolded over almost a year, reminds us of a story that would be entertaining were it not about real human lives. However, this time Vvedenskii would have his narrow escape, and it was not until 1938 that he was executed by firing squad – like all his colleagues in Orientology who one way or another participated in foreign policy activities.[99] After the Supreme Commission instructed the authorities of the prison to create all necessary conditions for Vvedenskii's work,[100] he started to play his own game. With each passing week, he produced new demands, which were all satisfied: transfer to a less crowded cell, better nutrition and lighting, a supply of scholarly literature, medical services for his wife, etc.[101] He was also allowed to attend the Turkestan central library under the

---

[97] RGASPI, op. 2, d. 40, l. 815.
[98] Ibid., l. 775–7.
[99] See articles about Chaikin, Pastukhov, Osetrov, Smirnov and Snesarev in Vasil'kov and Sorokina, *Liudi i sud'by*.
[100] RGASPI, f. 122, op. 2, d. 40, l. 775.
[101] Ibid., l. 767, 769, 787, 793, 796, 800.

escort of two armed soldiers.[102] Furthermore – most astonishingly – an archive in Moscow holds the complaints of the head of the prison, written with numerous spelling and grammar mistakes and addressed to the Supreme Commission, regarding the fact that Vvedenskii took his typewriter and '*ne otdaet*' (is not giving it back).[103] It should be remembered that all this was being conducted simultaneously with *Cheka*'s interrogations and over the course of the investigation against Vvedenskii. However, the government of the Republic of Turkestan finally, a year after, opted for efficiency and succeeded in officially forcing *Cheka* to set Vvedenskii free 'since the Section for Foreign Affairs [of the Soviet Turkestan government] needs his services as an Orientologist'.[104]

The eventual inability of *ancien régime* experts like Bravin and Vvedenskii to integrate into NKID supports the thesis on the predominant presence of significant ruptures in institutional practices and discourses in the diplomatic domain over the watershed of 1917, which seriously undermines Kocho-Williams' argument on prevailing continuities. This is also supported by the example of such a crucial figure as Minorsky, who remained in Persia until mid-1919 and became involved in the activities of the White Movement governments, fighting the Bolsheviks.[105] However, Minorsky's subsequent activities during his stay in France and Britain in the 1920s–1930s raise certain questions which still remain to be answered and require additional substantial research in the special archives of France, Britain and Russia. After his move to France, he cooperated with the Soviet diplomatic mission in Paris.[106] Without any doubts, Minorsky was not a conformist, but rather one of the most remarkable examples of an intellectual who skilfully and productively used the capacities with which he was vested by power/knowledge relations.

His private collection in the Archive of Orientologists contains documents indicating that during the 1920s he was one of the most

---

[102] Ibid., l. 790

[103] Ibid., l. 791, 805.

[104] Ibid., l. 764 (Cable N1765 to Head of *Cheka*).

[105] AV, f. 134, op. 1, l. 1; d. 4900; d. 4905. See also Aleksei Bezugol'nyi, *General Bicherakhov i ego kavkazskaia armiia* (Tver: Tsentrpoligraf, 2011), 145–6.

[106] See Mavi Boncuk, "Minorsky and Nikitin," in *Cornucopia of Ottomania and Turcomania*, 22 March 2013, http://maviboncuk.blogspot.ru/2013/03/Minorsky-and-nikitin.html (accessed 12 June 2014).

valuable and reliable sources of political intelligence for NKID.[107] Being handled personally by Chicherin, he would send reports on European domestic and foreign policies, particularly about France, where he lived and worked during this period. According to Chicherin's instructions, Minorsky, using his personal contacts in the upper spheres of the French and British political establishments and, based on his own systematic analysis of events and relevant materials, would cover, 'from the USSR's standpoint', a variety of issues, including France's and Britain's policies in the Middle East, Persia and Afghanistan, policies towards the USSR, domestic politics and the issues related to the situation of the Russian immigrant colony.[108] Equally interestingly, this is also supported by the fact that Minorsky's teacher, Barthold, was aware of his 'special position' and was going to use it for the publication of Minorsky's new scholarly works in 1930, which would have been impossible in the USSR for the scholarly works of ordinary Russian emigrants.[109]

This topic, of course, needs additional research to be carried out in other security services' archives in Russia, France and Great Britain, since the documents available in Minorsky's private collection do not clarify whether this cooperation was voluntary or forced, or whether Minorsky played a double game on behalf of the Russian government in Emigration, the French DST or British MI-5. Minorsky's notes only mention that NKID severed this relationship on its own initiative in late 1927, which leads to the assumption that the Bolsheviks suspected him of supplying disinformation.[110] 'This could have also been influenced by Chicherin's loss of actual power in the NKID by that time because of his sharply deteriorated health problems and his ongoing feud with the factual head of the then NKID, Maksim Litvinov (Vallakh), to whom he just might not have passed his personal contact over.'[111]

---

[107] AV, f. 134, op. 1, d. 396 (Chicherin's assignment), l. 1–3. It is worth noting that the archive authorities at their own discretion banned the photocopying of the materials of this and other files (*delo*) related to Minorsky's cooperation with NKID.

[108] AV, f. 134, op. 1, d. 396, l. 8. See also d. 433 (Reports on the situation in the Russian Embassy in London).

[109] Ibid., op. 3, d. 479 (Correspondence with Barthold), l. 25.

[110] AV, f. 134, op. 1, d. 396, l. 1.

[111] Volkov, "Vladimir Minorsky," 208, 215.

Recent research carried out by the author in several French archives in 2016 and 2017 has yielded further information on Minorsky's voluntary cooperation with Bolsheviks in the 1920s. Minorsky's personal dossier, held by the French Ministry of the Interior, was later stolen by Russian security services.[112] All the above-mentioned episodes of Minorsky's interaction with the state demonstrate the validity of the historically and socially contextualised approach, informed by Foucauldian archaeology of knowledge and the interplay of power/ knowledge relations, where individual and institutional interests and public discourses play equipotent productive roles along with the simplified, Saidian two-vector nexus of state power and knowledge.

'A Nation Does Not Make Mistakes, Does She?'

If in Minorsky's case it is only possible to make assumptions regarding his sincere cooperation with the Soviet state, which might have been grounded in his strong susceptibility to the discourse of *Russkoe delo* and/or in his plans to secure the position of Chicherin's deputy, the cases of Smirnov and Snesarev are more straightforward in this sense, as was the power/knowledge nexus in the military domain of both periods.[113] Like many other Russian military officers in 1917, they both came to the conclusion that they needed to follow the choice of their people, which they perceived had been made in favour of the Bolsheviks: 'It is difficult to immediately understand everything that has happened but if the Russian nation has followed the Bolsheviks I am with her. A nation does not make mistakes, does she?'[114]

In 1918, Snesarev also wrote in his diary: 'what is experienced now by Russia is a great, maybe nationwide, cause, and we must not evade participation as experts'.[115] They both participated in the hostilities of the Civil War at the Caucasian front on the side of the Red Army

---

[112] For further details, see Volkov, *Between Powers, Knowledge and Identities: Vladimir Minorsky as a Diplomat, Scholar and Spy* (in preparation).

[113] See Volkov, "Persian Studies," 3, 14.

[114] Snesarev's letter cited in Mikhail Zakharchuk, "Lichnoe delo generala Snesareva," *Voennoe Obozrenie* (12 December 2012), http://topwar.ru/21778-lichnoe-delo-generala-snesareva.html.

[115] Andrei Snesarev, *Smolenskii dnevnik* (13 November 1918) (www.a-e-snesarev .ru/smolenskiy_dnevnik.pdf).

SCHOOL OF ORIENTAL STUDIES.

VANDON HOUSE,

Telephone : WHITEHALL 4735.
Telegrams : SOSLINST, PHONE, LONDON.

VANDON STREET,

LONDON, S.W.I.

1

9. XII. 1936

Дорогой К. Н., оба письма
получил. Спасибо и за книжку. Издание
всяких документов есть весьма
похвальное. Официальные списки
всегда трудны и требуют долгой
расшифровки. Ваша система вполне
разумная. ...

Что касается до Кенгерлю, то
в Энц. Ислама я очень кратко
упомянул о них под Nakhčivan.
В общем и Ваши документы на
историю их появления не про-
ливают окончательного света.
Это любопытный вопрос. Кенгерлю
были, как кажется, лишь кланом
племени Афшар, и потому историю
их привести за историю Афшар.
Это мягкое племя было сил...

5.1 The first page of Vladimir Minorsky's letter to his best friend Konstantin Smirnov (1936).
Source: Korneli Kekelidze Georgian National Centre of Manuscripts

5.2a A report issued by the counter-intelligence of the Toilers' Army of the Caucasus regarding a search carried out at Smirnov's dacha in Mahinjauri, Georgia, maintaining that different correspondence, documents, photos and the Persian Order of Sun were confiscated from Smirnov (1923).

5.2b A certificate issued by the Military Tribunal of the Trans-Caucasian Military District confirming that the accusation of Konstantin Smirnov was cancelled post-mortem (1959).
Source: Korneli Kekelidze Georgian National Centre of Manuscripts

and then switched to academic activities. Smirnov, who lived in Tiflis, was employed by the Georgian Academy of Sciences as a researcher on ancient Persian manuscripts. He also continued to conduct mostly scholarly correspondence with his old friend Minorsky and continued working on the contemporary issues of Persia, albeit without engaging with Marxist methodology,[116] which altogether was enough to finally determine his fate in 1938.[117]

[116] GNCM, d. 80 (Minorsky's letters). See also Konstantin Smirnov, *Iran: ekonomicheskii spravochnik* (Tiflis: AN GSSR, 1934).
[117] On 13 January 1938 Smirnov was taken away from his home by people from NKVD and disappeared. It was more than twenty-one years later that

Snesarev took a more active approach. In 1919, he played a crucial role in the establishment of the Military Academy of the RKKA and the promotion of the activities of its Oriental section, which provided the necessary area-studies training to Pastukhov, Osetrov, Tardov and the notorious Iakov Bliumkin, who all would play significant roles in Soviet foreign policy towards Persia and Afghanistan.[118] Although Snesarev was not allowed to enter the field of foreign policy practical activities, he was extensively used for the organisation and conduct of Orientological training. As early as the 1900s, Snesarev put forward a thesis of the necessity of developing so-called practical Orientology.[119] He closely cooperated with General Shvedov at the Ministry of the Interior of the time, in course of establishing the Academy of Practical Orientology.[120] However, because of the active counteraction on the part of academic Oriental studies, namely by Zhukovskii and Barthold, and the lack of funding, the enterprise did not receive due development. It was only in 1919 that he succeeded in unleashing fully fledged organisational activities, totally on account of the heightened interest of the new state in the essentially practical component of Oriental studies.

In addition to his posts in the Military Academy, Snesarev became the director of the Moscow Institute of Orientology – the former Lazarev

it became clear that Smirnov was executed on 5 May 1938. During the four years after his arrest, until her death (suicide?), his wife Kseniia pressed the authorities for her husband's release or, at least, any information on him. It was only in May 1939, through her distant relative, that Kseniia got to know that Smirnov had been sentenced to 'ten years without the right of correspondence' – a formula that became apprehensible to Russians only in the late 1980s, after the uncovering of materials on repressions during Stalin's period (GNCM, f. 39, d. 8, l. 1; d. 143 Notebook 2, l. 8ob.). On Kseniia's diaries see also Denis Volkov, "War and Peace in the Other and the Self: Iran through the eyes of Russian spies – The case of Konstantin Smirnov (1877–1938) and Leonid Shebarshin (1935–2012)," *Cahiers de Studia Iranica* 62 (2018): 225–60.

[118] RGVA, f. 11, op. 1, d. 186, l. 2–30ob. AV, f. 115, op. 2, d. 34, l. 1. On the activities of the individual who would nowadays be characterised as a fully fledged professional terrorist – Iakov Bliumkin – see Iurii Sushko, *Deviat' zhiznei Iakova Bliumkina* (Moscow: Tsentrpoligraf, 2012).

[119] See Chapters 2 and 4. See also Snesarev's speech at the Annual Meeting of the Society of Orientologists, 2 May 1910, www.snesarev.ru/trudi/programma .html. See also Evgenii Snesarev, "Prakticheskoe izuchenie Vostoka," *Golos Pravdy* (5 December 1909): 1.

[120] AV, f. 115, op. 2, d. 50, l. 1–3 (Shvedov's letter, 1905).

5.3 Andrei Snesarev with a group of his disciples at the Institute of Oriental Studies. All of them would shortly end up in the Middle East working in various Soviet military and political intelligence stations. The man with a stick is arguably Georges Agabekov, INO OGPU Station-Chief in Tehran (1926–8), Head of Oriental Section of INO OGPU (1928–9), who in 1929 replaced Iakov Bliumkin as Head of OGPU Station-Chief of the entire Middle East.
Source: www.snesarev.ru

Institute – and the Petrograd Institute of Living Oriental Languages – a structure bolshevised from the outset and aimed at counterbalancing the pure academic bastion maintained by Barthold and his colleagues at Petrograd University.[121] He also actively participated in the establishment of VNAV and became a member of its governing board.[122] It was Snesarev who designed the Oriental studies curriculum for all these institutions, which mainly covered such regions as Central Asia, Persia and Afghanistan.[123] Snesarev's activities in this field continued until 1931, when he was arrested and sentenced to death.

---

[121] Ibid., d. 29, l. 1; op. 1, d. 226; d, 231.
[122] Ibid., op. 1, d. 222, l. 2–5.
[123] Ibid., op. 2, d. 63; op. 1, d. 223, l. 1a; d. 202; d. 204; d. 209; d. 220.

5.4 Stalin's note addressed to the USSR's War Commissar, Klimentii Voroshilov (1934): 'Klim! I think that it might be possible to replace the capital punishment with 10 years for Snesarev. I Stalin'.
Source: www.snesarev.ru

However, here again, his past as a scholar and an expert came in handy. Stalin had known Snesarev personally through their joint participation in the Civil War, but mostly through Snesarev's Orientologic activities, which were quite often supervised by *Narkomnats*, which Stalin headed in the 1920s. On a scrap of paper, recently sold at a Sotheby's auction, Stalin "asked" Voroshilov to 'replace capital punishment for 10 years'.[124] This, of course, helped – but only for six years. Given the age of Snesarev, the Gulag conditions undermined his health to the extent that he was set free three years later and died in 1937.[125]

---

[124] A photo of Stalin's note addressed to Voroshilov, www.snesarev.ru/foto/photo19.html.
[125] See Vasil'kov and Sorokina, *Liudi i sud'by*, http://memory.pvost.org/pages/snesarev.html.

Conclusion

The material presented in this chapter allows us to partly confirm the conclusions made in Chapter 3, and, based on the analysis of institutional activities during the period in question, in addition to draw new conclusions which have become feasible only after the study of the particular activities of the above-mentioned key individuals. Similarly to the late Imperial period, early Soviet Oriental studies witnessed the same interplay of power/knowledge relations, comprising the interaction of discourses and personal, institutional and state interests, this time in a more acute form. Furthermore, the presence of the three-fold structure of early Soviet Oriental studies and, in particular, of Iranology has generally been confirmed. However, as it turns out in the case of individuals, the borders between the domains are rather fuzzy, with significant overlaps – the majority of individuals acted in all three domains at different times or simultaneously. This, of course, is explained, first by rather hectic transformation and inception processes which were taking place in general in the new polity after its establishment, and, second, by the discourse on the utilitarianism of Oriental studies. The latter was elevated to an extent that scholarly knowledge lost its primacy over practical knowledge and was replaced by a "scholarship of practice". Therefore, every piece of knowledge in Iranology was expected to be practically useful for the state and the process of Orientological knowledge production had to be directly dependent on various foreign policy activities.

During the 1920s, the *ancien régime* academic scholarship lost even the indirect influence on state foreign policy which academic scholars had before 1917.[126] Because of the lack of engagement with Marxist methodology, their works later in the 1930s were not recognised as trustworthy in the Soviet academic domain either. The most palpable discontinuity, in terms of personnel and hence institutional practices, took place in the diplomatic domain, which, due to new individuals, discourses and the state attitude towards Orientological knowledge, was able to play the leading role in Soviet Iranology of the 1920s–1930s. The military domain witnessed more continuities in terms of its scholarly active experts; however all of them – Snesarev, Smirnov, Iagello, etc. – were pushed into the back-office, namely to the training area.

[126] See Chapters 2 and 4.

Nevertheless, the utilitarianism discourse secured the state's heightened attention to Oriental studies, hence enormously enhancing funding and other operational capabilities for all three domains. Being rightly combined with a personal drive for research and susceptibility to new discourses, it resulted in the enhanced productivity of power/knowledge relations, as the case studies of Iranskii, Irandust, Snesarev and others demonstrate. In addition to this, the examples of Gurko-Kriazhin, Iranskii and Irandust also virtually personify Said's Orientalism; however, only in terms of its most straightforward and strong nexus between state power and scholarly knowledge. These individuals not only influenced and implemented Soviet Persian policy during the 1920s–1930s, but even designed it.

In this respect, Kemper's thesis – that 'Red Orientalism' lost its struggle with classical Oriental studies in Leningrad in the early 1930s after the dismantling of VNAV and with the beginning of the severe criticism of Gurko-Kriazhin's scholarship – seems rather questionable.[127] First, classical Persian studies had died by that time, as was pointed out by its representatives themselves in 1935.[128] Second, the discourse on the gradual grooming of Eastern societies in general, and the Persians in particular, for social conversion, which replaced the late Imperial discourse on the Russian civilising mission and existed as early as 1920, survived well into the 1930s – when its bearers still taught in various Orientological institutions and remained at key posts in connection to Soviet foreign policy towards Iran. In actual fact, 'Red Orientalism' died in the late 1930s, with the demise of all its representatives behind the walls of NKVD torture/execution-chambers and after organisational changes which mostly excluded the opportunity of such an extensive overlapping of the domains.

---

[127] See Kemper, "Red Orientalism," 475.
[128] Krymskii to Krackovskii, 3 January 1935, in Naumkin, *Neizvestnye*, 212–13.

General Conclusion

The involvement of Russia's Orientologists in the intense manifold interactions between the Russian Empire and Persia during the period from the late nineteenth century to 1917 predominantly took place within the main four professional domains, namely academic scholarship, the military, the diplomatic service and the Orthodox Church's missionary activities. Given the nature and historical developments of this interaction, the extent of the involvement of each domain in question was different, as was their impact on Russo-Persian relations of the period. However, there were also easily discernible commonalities in the organisational set-up and practices of these domains, as well as in the roles of individuals involved in them, namely academic scholars and practical experts of Persian studies. In addition, despite the great systemic shift which took place in 1917 and led to significant sequential changes in all spheres of Russian society, there were strong continuities on the structural level in early Soviet Oriental studies and also in the discourses which were widespread among the Orientologists of a new generation.

The four domains of late Imperial Russia's Oriental studies were well institutionalised and professionally self-consistent. At the same time, their organisational structures and institutional activities were closely interconnected, which resulted in the immense productivity of power/knowledge relations due to this deep interconnection at both institutional and individual levels. Based on the character of Russia's presence in the Persianate world, in general, and in Persia, in particular, during the late Imperial period, the four-domain structure is evident in the case of Persianate studies and, especially, of Persian studies therein. The studied scholarly activities of Russian diplomats and of Russian military officers – as well as the missionary activities in addition to those of the academic domain – all support the fourfold organisation of late Imperial Persian studies.

Soviet Iranology of the 1920s–1930s kept the overall pre-revolution organisational structure, with the understandable exception of the missionary domain. The immensely active and overwhelming presence of Soviet trade institutions in Persia/Iran which also productively contributed to Orientological knowledge cannot be singled out into a separate self-consistent domain since there was no relevant Orientological training therein and these institutions were mainly staffed by experts with Orientological expertise, seconded from *Narkomindel*, *Razvedupr* and INO OGPU. Thus early Soviet Oriental studies comprised three domains, namely academic scholarship, the military and the diplomatic service, where the first domain consisted of the "old" and "new" schools, and other two were profoundly intertwined at both institutional and individual levels, particularly throughout the 1920s.

During the early Soviet period, the emphasis of Orientological training radically changed. Stressing the crucial importance of the practical usefulness of Oriental studies to state needs, the Bolsheviks replaced the former emphasis on gathering linguistic, ethnographic and cultural information for the study of Persia with an enhanced focus on political and, particularly, economic areas. Though, similarly to the late Imperial period, academic Oriental training was shared by all domains, during the 1920s, it was the Military Academy of the RKKA that played the leading role in the Oriental training of practical experts on Persia, where formerly Russia's Imperial MID had taken this role.

With the stipulated goals and the nature of the new regime in mind, the efficiency of Orientological training and the state's ability to bring scholars and experts into play was much higher in the early Soviet period than in the case of late Imperial Russia where, on the contrary, in practical domains there was an excessive emphasis on the study of allegedly irrelevant Classics and the ancient history and texts of the Persianate world. The excessive academicism eventually led to the War Ministry withdrawing its students from the officers' courses at the Foreign Ministry and to the establishment of courses in Oriental languages affiliated with local military headquarters on the periphery of the Russian Empire in 1911.

This institutional practice of the late Imperial military domain became a continuity, taken up and extrapolated onto all the Orientological domains by the Bolsheviks, who later set up various kinds of Orientological institutions in the republics of (Trans)Caucasus and Central Asia, which led to the unseen institutional expansion of Persianate studies and eventually to the significantly increased production of Orientological knowledge. However, in general, research demonstrates that the contribution of the practical domains to Russia's Orientology of both periods was enormous, due to their physical proximity to first-hand materials and artefacts and being inside the culture – a strategic position which was particularly beneficial at the incipient stages of both Iranologies, pre-1917 and post-1917, and which was successfully exploited by practical and, indirectly, by academic Orientologists, for contributing to Oriental studies due to the relevant discursive manifestations of the time.

The late Imperial academic scholars of Persian studies exerted indirect influence on Russia's Persian policy through their significant impact in shaping their current students' attitude of mind towards Persia – the future executors of this policy. It was precisely those scholars who passed over their professional discourses to their disciples, who embraced the interested attitude towards the Orient and the encouragement to continue carrying out scholarly research alongside the duties of professional postings. This was underpinned by broader inner Russian discourses on *Russkoe delo* and on building a multi-national state with Russian culture at its head but enriched and strengthened by Oriental cultures which, of course, also served the colonial expansion of the Russian Empire. In actual fact, late Imperial Orientologists, in the context of the importance which the East had for the state interests of the Russian Empire, promoted contributions to Orientological – in this particular case, Persian studies – knowledge to the rank of forwarding Russian national interests, equal to the straightforward professional activities of diplomats and the military in the Persianate world.

This later became conventional institutional practice within practical domains and carried over to the early Soviet period, albeit in a transformed way. The continuity of friendly teacher–disciple relations through regular correspondence on mainly scholarly issues and staying in personal contact gave way to orders, instructions and political expediency. In addition to their professional duties, the new practical Orientologists were expected to contribute to the class struggle in the East through the gathering and scholarly systematising of contemporary area-study data to bring them into academic circulation.

As the research maintains, almost immediately after 1917, *ancien régime* Persian studies not only became deprived of even its indirect influence, which it had had through academic training and its influential activities in various joint multi-organisational Orientological societies, but was also gradually marginalised by the scholarship of the new Soviet Iranology. Put as an aphorism, early Soviet Iranists created their scholarship on site, while designing and conducting foreign policy towards Persia/Iran, and, vice versa, they designed and conducted this policy based on their scholarship on Persia/Iran, while producing it.

This, of course, was not a case in point for the late Imperial period. Although experts were able to crucially influence events on site and quite often they were granted great operational autonomy on site by their ministries, this impact can be regarded as of tactical character. Despite rare exceptions (Zinov'ev and von Klemm), Persian studies experts could not directly access strategic decision-making levels. More importantly, late Imperial Russia's Persian foreign policy was defined by designers and executors of Russia's Western foreign policy and mainly sacrificed to that, regardless of what was expertly advised or suggested in the official reports and notes of Minorsky, Smirnov, Kosagovskii and others. Their suggestions on showing a tough stance towards Britain and on a gradual taking over of Persia, or, at least, separating off Persian Azerbaijan (proposed by Minorsky and Smirnov), did not have any effect whatsoever, whereas their impact on the technicalities of on-site execution of the general guidelines of Russia's Persian policy and the upholding of Russian interests in the context of the discourse of *Russkoe delo* was enormous.

The high degree of Kosagovskii's political influence on the Shah's court and the government's affairs, and that of Smirnov on shaping the Qajar family's expedient attitude of mind towards the Russian Empire, in particular, and all things Russian, in general, as well as that of Minorsky on counteracting the British and preserving more territory for Persia as Russia's current ally and her potential integral part, is evident. This was achieved through the interplay of power/knowledge relations in which Orientological expertise played an underlying role. Therefore, as the research shows, the late Imperial Russian state valued this expertise in practical domains, granting more tangible and moral capacities, hence power, to those experts. The same was inherent to the state's interaction with the academic domain. Although academic (or the so-called "pure") scholars were denied direct access to the decision-making space and their official advice was seldom heard, the state completely relied on their expertise in terms of the organisation of Orientological training throughout all four domains. In this field, these scholars were autonomous enough and exerted direct impact on the relevant activities with the only constraints being of a purely financial character.

Drawing on the Foucauldian concept of power/knowledge relations has enabled this monograph to ascertain a reciprocal, productive multi-vector interaction between the knowledge, chasing new resources for self-reproduction and endowing its agents with new capacities, and the state, represented by its own practices, institutions and individuals, all these being Foucault's equipotent vehicles of power. This interaction was productive during both periods in question. Late Imperial and early Soviet academic scholars acted in an identical way, as did scholars from other domains. Regardless of whether their influence on state policies was successful or unsuccessful, they all, consciously or unwittingly, carried out the following enthusiastically and productively. They exploited those capacities with which they were endowed within the grid of power relations for the eventual advancement of knowledge itself, in the given case – Persian studies.

This process was productively influenced by two main factors. The first one is the overwhelming political, military, economic and cultural importance of the Persianate world for Russia in both periods. The second is the compound of multiple sophisticated discursive components, widespread in the field in question, the main ones of which, during the late Imperial period, were:

(a) the trivial European Orientalist civilising mission, passed through the sieve of Russia's alleged much more receptive interaction with the Orient; (b) the protection of Russian interests versus Western powers; (c) the promotion of all things Russian, including its own scholarship. The latter was patriotically seen as being "for the benefit of the native land" in its rivalry with the West.[1]

It is precisely these three components that constituted the discourse of *Russkoe delo* throughout the entire field of Russia's Oriental studies.

---

[1] Volkov, "Persian Studies," 17.

During the early Soviet period, the first two transformed into the proliferation of revolution in Persia and then into the grooming of Persians for social conversion, with the same condescending approach as before 1917; however, this time not as a country, representing "the civilised world", but rather as the first in the world polity of victorious socialist revolution. The third component, with the interchangeable words "Russian" and "Soviet", has made it through the whole Soviet to post-Soviet period. Regardless of whether it was consciously or unwittingly, throughout all the three periods Russian Iranists have been seeing their scholarship in expedient compliance with their country's so-called national interests. In practice, the representation of such interests in Russia is conventionally usurped by the political institutions of the ruling power. Therefore, on the surface, it may seem that this status quo eventually resulted in the instrumental use of knowledge in the interests of the current political regimes in Russia, whereas it was all the participants of this interplay of power/knowledge relations that played on this state of affairs for their own interests, namely individuals, various institutions and the state itself. Due to the eventual Foucauldian productivity of power relations, it was knowledge that, possessing the nature of self-agency, reproduced and extended itself, ultimately overcoming the constraints of the governmentality inevitably created by such continuous patriotic discourses.

A major finding of the analysis of the organisational set-up of Russian Oriental studies is that Persianate studies and Persian studies therein occupied the leading positions in Imperial Russia's Orientology from its institutional inception in the first quarter of the nineteenth century. This continuity made its way to the early Soviet period. A second, rather astonishing finding is that the discursive institutional practice involving the Soviet state's use of imprisoned scientists and scholars, which is depicted by Krementsov as established in the 1930s, in actual fact emerged in 1919. And third, the evidence also compels us to conclude that in the case of early Soviet Iranology there was an utterly straightforward two-vector, reciprocal link between Orientological knowledge and foreign policy, very much in the sense of what one might term "vulgar" Saidism. We must further note the great individual impact of late Imperial military Orientologists on the process of establishing early Soviet military Oriental studies, in contrast to the remaining two domains which, in this sense, demonstrate discontinuity. A fifth finding is the discursive institutional practice, invented by Rosen and fully developed by Zhukovskii, of handling a scholarly intelligence network, consisting of agents-disciples who supplied academic Oriental studies with scholarly processed first-hand materials. In so doing, the former students, who had become diplomats and military officers, were encouraged by the discourse of promoting national scholarship, hence eventually contributing to *Russkoe delo* – the discourse inculcated in them by their former teachers. The sixth is the Orientologists' practice of employing their own wives to obtain additional area-study information; these women eagerly engaged with such tasks and were able to penetrate areas traditionally inaccessible for male foreigners in the Muslim East, such as *andaruns*, etc. The seventh is that the studied individuals, as the diaries, private notes and memoirs of Kosagovskii, Smirnov, Minorsky and others maintain, quite often were guided not so much by the imperatives of the relevant discourses but rather by their personal – sometimes very tangible – interests, such as career, better living conditions, state rewards, scholarly fame, etc.

Archival Findings

The archival research carried out for this monograph has also unearthed a number of hitherto completely unknown documents, some of which directly challenge well-established views within the scholarship or shed a totally new and rather unexpected light on the biographies of some of the individuals studied here. These archival findings have helped to reveal new, previously unknown dimensions of the activities of individuals such as Valentin Zhukovskii, Vladimir Minorsky, Nikolai Bravin, Pavel Vvedenskii, Vladimir Kosagovskii, Konstantin Smirnov, Andrei Snesarev and others. Thus Minorsky's secret cooperation with NKID during the 1920s, never mentioned before in relevant works, requires further separate, thorough research in Russian, British and French archives, potentially including those of SVR-FSB, MI-5 and DST. A second discovery is Bravin's correspondence with Zhukovskii during 1905–11 (twenty-three letters from Bravin), revealing that Bravin was Zhukovskii's most favoured disciple. Given Bravin's pre-1917 and crucial post-1917 activities and his notorious status in the context of the Soviet and post-Soviet politics of history, still maintained by the Ministry for Foreign Affairs of Putin's Russia, this archival finding, never mentioned in the relevant works either, is of great importance in terms of shedding more light on Bravin's fate and the apprehension of present Russia's regime of truth.

A third discovery is that there is evidence in correspondence between Chicherin and Lenin that suggests that of those who orchestrated the Soviet invasion of Persia in May 1920, namely Chicherin and Trotsky, the former entertained rather more serious hopes as to the feasibility of a forced sovietisation of Persia than was allowed for by Genis, who argued that Chicherin, like Trotsky, had never seriously contemplated trying to turn Iran into a Soviet Republic but had been solely after scaring the British. A fourth discovery are archival documents that show that there was Soviet military assistance in cracking down on Kuchek-Khan's forces as well as the other militant nationalist groups in 1921, authorised by Rotshtein, and the consideration by the Bolsheviks of Kuchek-Khan's liquidation in October 1920. A fifth and final one concerns a hitherto completely unknown, recently declassified archival file, containing the so-called "Ten Persian letters of Vardin", shedding light on the process of shaping early Soviet foreign policy towards Persia and the activities of its main designers and perpetrators.

Another curious and rather illustrative finding which seems worth stating in the end is that two high-ranking Russian intelligence officers-*vostochniki* of two very different epochs, namely Konstantin Smirnov, whose activities in the early twentieth century have been discussed above, and Leonid Shebarshin (1935–2012), who was the KGB Station-Chief in Iran during the crucial period 1979–83, with a gap of almost one hundred years between their writings, did not differ one iota in their respective judgments of the moral qualities of their own people in comparison to those of the people about whom they had become experts. Indeed, they both stated that, during the years of revolutionary unrest caused by the Constitutional Movement and the Islamic Revolution, which saw the greatest failure of central state power in the modern history of Iran, criminal manifestations remained at low levels and Iranians revealed hardly any tendency to violent robbery or homicide for personal gain, contrary to Russians during their own periods of unrest. Hence, according to these officers-*vostochniki*, Iranians turned out to be much more civilised than the people of the country that was trying to carry out a civilising mission for them, believing it could thus incorporate them into its own "greater culture".[2]

---

[2] See Volkov, "War and Peace in the Other and the Self," 251; Leonid Shebarshin, *Ruka Moskvy: Razvedka ot rastsveta do razvala* (Moscow: Algoritm, 2012), 121–3. GNCM, f. 39, d. 22. l. 1–1ob.

Appendix
Biographical Notes

Abikh, Rudol'f Petrovich (1901–40), (Chapter 3, footnote 103). Abikh worked in the Soviet military in Persia in 1920–1. In 1924 he graduated from the Oriental Faculty of the Military Academy. Majored in Iran, he worked in NKID and the Intelligence of the Red Army. In 1926 he was appointed the head of the Oriental Section of the Intelligence Department of the Red Army Headquarters. In 1927 he was recalled from Tehran because of the quarrel with Ambassador Iurenev. He was a member of VNAV and taught in MIV. During the 1930s he was arrested a few times and then executed in 1940 (GARF, P-1335, op. 1, d. 6, l. 55).

Barthold, Vasilii Vladimirovich (1860–1930), (Introduction, footnote 14). Baron Rosen's disciple, Professor of St Petersburg University (1901), Member of Russia's Academy of Sciences, Secretary of the Russian Committee for the Study of Central and Eastern Asia (1903–18). He authored more than 650 scholarly works on Central Asian, Persian and Islamic studies.

Beneshevich, Vladimir Nikolaevich (1874–1938), (Chapter 1, footnote 67). Beneshevich was a leading Russian specialist on Byzantine Church Law and a corresponding member of the Russian Academy of Sciences until his scholarly field was abolished by the Bolsheviks. He faced constant harassment from the authorities, was arrested three times, de facto deprived of employment and was executed in 1938 as a Polish spy.

Bertel's, Evgenii Eduardovich (1890–1957). An Iranist and Turkologist as well as later one of the main "big wigs" of Soviet Iranology. He graduated from the Oriental Languages Faculty in Petrograd in 1920. He taught at Leningrad State University and became a professor in 1928. In 1925 he was arrested by OGPU but was shortly after released, having started to cooperate with them. He played a fatal role

233

in the destinies of many colleagues, reporting on them.[1] Starting from the late 1920s his works became highly ideologised, paving his steep career in Soviet Iranology. During the 1930s–1950s he was the field's main "spokesman" in its interaction with the Soviet state, receiving numerous state commendations and awards, including the Stalin award in 1948.[2]

Chaikin, Konstantin Ivanovich (1889–1938), (Chapter 3, footnote 115; Chapter 5, footnote 64). Zhukovskii's disciple, Chaikin graduated from the St Petersburg Faculty of Oriental Studies in 1916. Based on his graduation paper, which was the translation of Jami's *Selaman and Ebsal* in verse, he was retained at the university to prepare for a professorship in Persian literature. In 1920–6 he worked in the Soviet diplomatic representation in Persia as an interpreter. After returning to the USSR he worked in various Oriental studies institutions authoring a number of influential scholarly works on Persian poetry. Throughout the 1920s and 1930s he was used from time to time by NKID as a linguist at the highest level until he was executed in 1938 under the accusation of espionage.[3] Besides a considerable number of works on Persian literature and language, in the mid-1930s, he authored a book on Persian literature and a number of translations of Persian classic poetry, which were the only works of this kind for decades. On 27 April 1938, Chaikin was executed by NKVD as a foreign spy during Stalin's purges. Based on archival documents it appears that it was Evgenii Bertel's who played the fatal role in Chaikin's destiny, having reported on him.[4]

Chernozubov, Fedor Grigor'evich (1863–1919), (Chapter 4, footnote 95). Lieutenant-General of the Russian General Staff. An

---

[1] See Appendix (Chaikin); see also Vasil'kov and Sorokina, *Liudi i sud'by*.

[2] See Vasil'kov and Sorokina, *Liudi i sud'by*; see also Volkov "Individuals, Institutions, Discourses: Knowledge and Power in Russia's Iranian Studies of the Late Imperial, Soviet and Post-Soviet Periods," *Middle East – Topics & Arguments* 4 (2015): 74; see also Volkov, "Fearing the Ghosts," 903–4, 918; for details related to academic activities see Edmund Herzig and Paul D. Wordsworth, eds, *E. E. Berthels, The Great Azerbaijani Poet, Nizami: Life, Work and Times* (London: Gilgamesh, 2017).

[3] AVPRF, f. 08 'The Secret Archive of NKID. Karakhan', op. 10, papka 33, d. 190, l. 22.

[4] See Volkov, "Individuals, Institutions, Discourses," 74; see also Volkov, "Fearing the Ghosts", 903–4, 918.

officer-*vostochnik*, he graduated from the Academy of the General Staff, where, at the Officers' Courses of Oriental Languages, he mastered Persian, Turkish and Arabic. From 1902 to 1907 he was Chief-Instructor (Commander) of His Majesty the Shah of Persia's Cossack Brigade, coordinating intelligence activities in Persia. He authored a number of scholarly works, including those on the ethnography of Persian Kurdistan, Azerbaijan and Armenians.[5]

Ehsanulla (transliteration from Russian), or **Ehsanollah-Khan, Dustdar** (1884–1939), (Chapter 3, footnote 103). A member of the Revolutionary Committee, one of Kuchek-Khan's fellow-fighters. In July 1920, according to a plan designed by Bliumkin, he took over command of the troops and leadership from the ousted Kuchek-Khan. After the defeat of the Persian Socialist Revolution, he spent the rest of his life in the USSR (he was executed in 1939). In 1933, he took up Abikh's case to defend him against repressions, having written a letter to Ordzhonikidze.[6]

Frunze, Mikhail Vasil'evich (1885–1925), (Chapter 3, footnote 34). At the time of the October coup, he was already an active Bolshevik with the experience of combat activities. During the Civil War he occupied various commanding posts in the Red Army, including Chief Commander of the Turkestan Army and Chief Commander of the Southern Front. The Red troops under his command defeated Kolchak's and Vrangel's White troops as well as capturing Khiva and Bukhara emirates. He was enormously popular in the Red Army. In 1925 during routine medical surgery he died – allegedly murdered under Stalin's plot. This version is supported by some historians and contemporaries, including Boris Bazhanov, a personal assistant to Stalin, who in 1928 defected to the West, escaping via Iran.[7]

Gamazov, Matvei Avelevich (1812–93), (Chapter 2, footnote 138). He dealt with translations from Persian and Turkish languages, including scholarly materials and manuscripts. He was in charge of publishing historical and literary texts and diplomatic documents. Gamazov also

[5] See Baskhanov, *Russkie*, 260–1.
[6] See Genis, "Rudol'f Abikh," 153.
[7] Boris Bajanov, *Avec Staline dans le Kremlin* (Paris: Editions de France, 1930). See also Persits, *Zastenchivaia interventsiia*, 27.

authored the military-technical Russian-French-Turkish-Persian dictionary, published in 1887 for the War Ministry.[8]

Grigor'ev, Vasilii Vasil'evich (1816–81), (Chapter 2, footnote 34). A historian-Orientologist, associated member of the Russian Academy of Sciences, active member of the Russian Geographical Society and specialist on Central Asia. He spoke Arabic, Persian, Kazakh, Kirghiz and Mongolian. In Western scholarship Grigor'ev has become famous because of his idealistic 'walkings into state power' for exerting enlightened scholarly influence on it. Between teaching at universities, he was Head of the Orenburg Border Commission (1854–9), Head of the Department of Kirghiz Affairs (1859–62), Head of the Chief-Directorate of Press Affairs of the Russian Empire (1874–80). He was a staunch apologist for embracing the cultures of the peoples on the periphery of the Russian Empire into Russian culture, including the use of local scholars in Russian scholarship.

Kolomiitsev, Ivan Osipovich (1896–1919), (Chapter 3, footnote 57). Soviet historiographers argued that on 21 August 1919 Colonel Starosel'skii sent a telegramme to the then Prime Minister of Persia, Vosugh-od-Douleh, informing him about the arrest of Kolomiitsev and the Prime Minister ordered that the arrested Kolomiitsev be brought to Tehran. So, the execution of Kolomiitsev was not authorised. However, no possible reasons for the Cossacks' behaviour were given; they were disciplined enough not to commit such a serious crime without solid grounds. An interesting explanation was offered by Father Superior Aleksandr Zarkeshev, based on his research in AVPRF in the late 1990s. Kolomiitsev was carrying the so-called Bolsheviks' hard currency – the Orthodox Church's sacred golden articles and vessels – expropriated by the Bolsheviks and officially allocated to him by NKID to cover mission expenses. During the first post-revolution years the Bolsheviks regularly officially confiscated gold from churches and used it in export-import trade operations. The Cossacks were traditionally very religious, especially those who served under General Baratov – an ardent Orthodox believer. Shocked by such sacrilege, they decided to try and execute the Bolsheviks' representative themselves.[9] This is also supported by the documents kept in RGASPI: new Soviet money was

---

[8] See Bartol'd, "Iran," 327; ARAN, Fond 68.
[9] See Zarkeshev, *Tserkov'*, 111–14, 120–1.

not accepted abroad and the state did not have a sufficient amount of foreign currency, so the conventional practice was to provide the agents being sent abroad, in this case to Persia, with "Bolshevik hard currency", namely golden ritual articles, expropriated from Russian Orthodox churches.[10]

Kosagovskii, Vladimir Andreevich (1857–1918), (Chapter 2, footnote 14). Between 1894 and 1902, Colonel Kosagovskii was Chief-Commander of the Persian Cossack Brigade and in 1905–8 he served as Head of the Transcaspian region. He is the author of multiple works on the economy, finance, governmental set-up, history, geography and military forces of Persia. He retired in 1909 as Lieutenant-General and lived on his private country estate. After 1917 he had to resort to farming and, after the October Revolution, the Bolsheviks burdened him, a 'class-alienated landowner', with extremely high taxes, which would have bankrupted him had they not been voluntarily paid by the peasant population of five neighbouring villages as a mark of respect towards their former landlord. They also saved him from being arrested by the Bolsheviks several times, but, allegedly, he finally had to commit suicide in 1918 to avoid being seized by Bolsheviks.[11]

Krachkovskii, Ignatii Iulianovich (1883–1951), (Chapter 2, footnote 109). Professor of Arabic studies (1918). He was a member of the Russian Academy of Sciences (1921) and knew Arabic, Persian and Turkish. In the 1920s he produced a translation of the Qur'an that remained the only reputable one throughout the whole Soviet period.

Kuropatkin, Aleksei Nikolaevich (1848–1925), (Chapter 2, footnote 6). War Minister of the Russian Empire (1898–1904), Lieutenant-General, eminent Russian Orientologist (including works on Persia) and full member of the Imperial Russian Geographic Society; in different periods, he served in Turkestan, and was Head of the Asian Department of the General Staff, Head of the Transcaspian Region, War Minister and Governor-General of Turkestan. In 1895 Kuropatkin was sent to Tehran as a special envoy of the Tsar at the Persian court. As War Minister he took an active part in establishing Tashkent

---

[10] RGASPI, f. 454, op. 1, d. 8, l. 28, 29, 30, 243, 290, 292.
[11] His diaries are kept in RGVIA, f. 76; see also Baskhanov, *Russkie*, 126–7; Ter-Oganov, "Brigada," 69–79.

Officers' School of Oriental Languages and the Officers' Faculty at the Oriental Institute.[12]

Lebedeva, Ol'ga Sergeevna (1854–1909), (Chapter 2, footnote 87). Literary translator and Orientologist. She authored the first Russian translation of "Kabus-nameh" from Persian. While living in Turkey, she translated works by Pushkin, Lermontov and Tolstoy into Turkish. She was a famous public figure and one of the founders of the Society of Oriental Studies in 1900. She also was an active promoter of Muslim women's emancipation in Russia.

Lobachevskii, Nikolai Ivanovich (1792–1856), (Chapter 1, footnote 26). A prominent Russian mathematician and geometer, the founder of non-Euclidean (Lobachevskian) geometry.

Lomonosov, Mikhail Vasil'evich (1711–65), (Chapter 1, footnote 48). In pre-revolutionary Russian intellectual circles Lomonosov was considered as a symbol of emerging Russian scholarship and an active propagator of the so-called "nationalisation" trend in Russian science. Whereas, having made of him the "founder" of this and that field of scientific knowledge and the "refuter" of some others, 'the first scientist to study ... to describe ... to discover', and even a fighter of the injustices of Imperial Russia, the Soviet regime took full advantage of his personality for ideological purposes.[13]

Makarov, Aleksandr Aleksandrovich (1857–1919), (Chapter 4, footnote 69). At the end of 1912 the Minister of the Interior Aleksandr Makarov summoned Barthold for a conversation, during which, in response to Barthold's argument regarding the importance of Russian Orientological scholarship for Russia itself, he said that it was Western scholars whom he preferred to consult on scholarly issues about the Orient.[14]

Marr, Nikolai Iakovlevich (1864–1934), (Chapter 3, footnote 68). Russian and Soviet Academician, Orientologist, linguist and historian. Vice-President of the Soviet Academy of Sciences. He spoke Persian and many other Oriental languages. The founder of the New Doctrine

[12] See Baskhanov, *Russkie*, 135–6.
[13] See Graham, *Science in Russia*, 20–4; Vucinich, *Empire of Knowledge*, 16–18.
[14] Khairutdinov, "Mir Islama," 12–16.

about the inception of languages. He also authored works on Iranian languages.

Mendeleev, Dmitry Ivanovich (1834–1907), (Chapter 1, footnote 26). A prominent Russian chemist and inventor, the creator of the first version of the periodic table of elements.

Mikaelian, Avetis Sultanovich (1888–1938), (Chapter 3, footnote 103). Pseudonym Sultanzadeh. He was a Bolshevik from 1912. In 1919 he was sent to Tashkent to work at the Council for International Propaganda. He became one of the founders of the Persian Communist Party. In 1920–1 he was the head of its left (extremist) wing. In 1920–3 he was the Persian representative at the Executive Committee of Komintern. In 1925 he became the Chief-Editor of the journal 'Economic Development'. He authored a number of research works on Iran. In 1938, on the accusation of espionage, he was executed.[15]

Miliutin, Dmitrii Alekseevich (1816–1912), (Chapter 2, footnote 18). Professor of the General Staff Academy, Minister of War (1861–81).[16] On Miliutin's activities see his memoirs: *D. A. Milyutin. Dnevnik. 1876–1878. 1879–1881* (Moscow: ROSSPEN, 2010). Also see the relevant literature: A. M. Nikolaeff, "Universal Military Service in Russia and Western Europe," *The Russian Review* 8/2 (1949): 117–26; Bruce W. Menning, *Bayonets before Bullets: The Imperial Russian Army, 1861–1914* (Bloomington: Indiana University Press, 2000).

Minorsky, Vladimir Fedorovich (1877–1966), (Introduction, footnote 15; Chapter 4, footnote 129). A diplomat-*vostochnik* and an outstanding Russian scholar of Persian history, historical geography, literature and culture. He graduated from the Lazarev Institute of Oriental Languages. From 1903 he visited Persia on various secondments on behalf of the Russian MID, in 1915–19 worked as Russia's *Chargé d'Affaires*, and he was acting head of the Russian mission after 1917. Having refused to subordinate the mission to the Bolsheviks, he left for France in 1919. In the period 1932–44 he was Professor of Persian studies at SOAS, London (evacuated to Cambridge, 1941–4). He spent his retirement (1944–66) in Cambridge.[17]

---

[15] GARF, f. 7668, op. 1, d. 2449 (MIV, 1935), l. 4, 11.
[16] RGVIA, f. 224 (1860–83), d. 1–6.
[17] *Encyclopaedia Iranica*, www.iranicaonline.org/articles/Minorsky-vladimir (accessed 17 April 2014).

Osetrov, Vladimir Petrovich (1893–1938), (Chapter 3, footnote 104). Pseudonym Irandust. A historian of Iran. In 1918–38 he worked for NKID. In 1920–5 and 1928–9 he worked in the Soviet diplomatic mission in Iran. Throughout the 1920s and 1930s, he was a member of VNAV and MVK. He taught in the Moscow Institute of Oriental Studies (MIV). In 1938, while deputy head of the second section of the Oriental Department of NKID, he was accused of being a spy – a common accusation at the time – and he was arrested and executed.

Pastukhov, Sergei Konstantinovich (1887–1940), (Chapter 3, footnote 104). Pseudonym Iranskii. A historian of Iran. In 1918–39, he worked in NKID. He was the head of the Middle Eastern Department, the head of the first Oriental Section and the Soviet Ambassador to Iran (1933–5). He also taught in MIV and was a member of VNAV. In 1939, accused of being a spy, he was arrested and in 1940 he was executed.

Pavlovich (real surname Vel'tman), **Mikhail Pavlovich** (1871–1927), (Chapter 5, footnote 40). A journalist by practice, with an incomplete higher education in law and without any kind of Orientological training nor speaking a single Oriental language, he became the most influential figure on the nationalities issue after Stalin and "the main Orientologist" of the early USSR.[18]

Raskol'nikov (real surname Il'in), **Fedor Fiodorovich** (1892–1939), (Chapter 3, footnote 25). By the October coup, was already an experienced Bolshevik. He actively participated in the organisation and realisation of that coup. From January 1918, he was the Vice People's Commissar for Maritime Affairs. In the period of December 1918–May 1919 he was in British captivity. From June 1919 to June 1920, he was the Chief Commander of the Red fleet on the river Volga and the Caspian Sea. After the successful Anzali operation, he was appointed the Chief Commander of the Baltic Sea fleet. In 1921 he retired from the military and became the Soviet diplomatic representative to Afghanistan. Between 1924 and 1928 he was the Head of the Oriental Section of the Communist International Executive Committee. He was a member of the All-Union Scientific Association of Orientologists (VNAV). He taught Middle Eastern studies at Moscow State University. In 1930–8 he was the Soviet representative

---

[18] See Kemper, "Red Orientalism."

to a number of European countries. In 1938, under the threat of arrest, he defected to the West and wrote an open letter to Stalin, protesting against the purges. One year after, he was murdered by NKVD in France.[19]

Rotshtein, Fiodor Aronovich (1871–1953), (Chapter 3, footnote 79). Pseudonym Mirza. He became a member of the Bolshevik Party in 1901. During World War I he worked in the British Foreign Office and the British Ministry of Defence. He was one of the founders of the British Communist Party. In 1920–1 he was the Soviet representative to Persia and Turkey, and was among those who prepared and signed the 1921 Soviet–Persian Treaty. In 1924 he was appointed a director of the Institute of World Economy and Politics. In 1939 he became a member of the Soviet Academy of Sciences.

Rosen, Viktor Romanovich (1849–1908), (Chapter 1, footnote 114). Professor of Arabic and Persian studies. He was a member of the Russian Academy of Sciences (1890), Dean of the Faculty of Oriental Languages of St Petersburg University (1893) and Head of the Oriental Section of the Russian Archaeological Society (1885). Barthold, Zhukovskii, Marr and Ol'denburg were among his disciples.[20]

Shapshal, Seraia Markovich (1873–1961), (Chapter 4, footnote 20). After graduating from the St Petersburg Faculty of Oriental languages, Shapshal, due to Zhukovskii's connections with the Qajar Court, was hired as a tutor of the Persian Crown Prince Mohammad-Ali and in 1907 became a minister of the Persian government. Edward Browne refers to him as a 'Russian spy', whereas Konstantin Smirnov's notes, which say in several places that Shapshal worked in Persia exclusively in his own interests that even very often contradicted Russian ones, refutes this assumption.[21]

Smirnov, Konstantin Nikolaevich (1877–1938), (Chapter 2, footnote 126). A military Orientologist, Colonel Smirnov authored a considerable number of works on Persian history, ethnography, geography and economics. Having graduated from the Officers' Courses of Oriental

---

[19] Vasil'kov and Sorokina, *Liudi i sud'by*, http://memory.pvost.org/pages/index2.html. See also Genis, *Krasnaia Persiia*, 65–6.
[20] See also Bartol'd, "Baron Rozen," 589.
[21] Edward Browne, *The Persian Revolution of 1905–1909* (Cambridge: Cambridge University Press, 1910): 214, 419.

Languages he served in the Intelligence Unit of the Caucasian Military
District Staff and was appointed as personal tutor to Soltan Ahmad
Mirza, later Ahmad Shah Qajar (serving from 1907 to 1914). He
participated in World War I and after the Russian Civil War he worked
as an interpreter in the Red Army in the Caucasus. In the 1920s and
1930s he worked as a research associate in the Academy of Sciences of
Georgia, before he was executed in 1938.[22]

Snesarev, Andrei Evgen'evich (1865–1937), (Introduction, footnote
16). Pseudonym Mosafer. Lieutenant-General of the Imperial Army.
By 1917 he was an acknowledged Orientologist and had authored
works on Persia, Afghanistan, India and China. He spoke Persian,
Dari, Uzbaki, Hindi, etc. After 1917 he joined the Red Army and
participated in the Civil War. In 1919, he was appointed the Head
of the Soviet Military Academy and its Oriental Section. He made an
underlying contribution to the organisation of Soviet military Oriental
studies.

Surits, Iakov Zakharovich (1882–1952), (Chapter 3, footnote 125).
In their work *Iz istorii sovetskogo vostokovedeniia* Kuznetsova and
Kulagina mention that in 1922 Surits was the Soviet diplomatic representative to Afghanistan when it was Raskol'nikov who was the Soviet
representative to Afghanistan in the period of 1921–3. The mistake
must have been caused by Soviet censorship (1970), trying to hush
up Raskol'nikov's name after he defected to the West in 1939. Surits
was an experienced Bolshevik by 1917. In 1919–21 he was the Soviet
diplomatic representative to Afghanistan. In the period 1921–2 he was
the Soviet plenipotentiary in Turkestan and Central Asia.

Tageev, Boris Leonidovich (1871–1938), (Chapter 2, footnote 99).
Pseudonym Rostam-Bek. An officer-*vostochnik*, a scholar and a writer,
Tageev had a remarkable destiny, worthy of his epoch: after his military service in Turkestan and Afghanistan and his alleged severance
from the Russian army he took part in the Russo-Japanese War of
1904–5 and was taken prisoner by the Japanese in 1904. Having
been released, he did not come back to Russia and had time to serve
in the British Army and to work as a *Daily Express* front-line correspondent during World War I. After the war he struck up a close

[22] Vasil'kov and Sorokina, *Liudi i sud'by*.

acquaintance with Henry Ford and worked for his newspaper syndi-
cate, simultaneously cooperating with the weekly *Soviet Russia*, which
was published in the USA. In 1920 he returned to Russia and worked
in structures affiliated with the Revolutionary Military Council of
the Republic (*Revvoensovet*) and other state entities, before he was
executed in 1938 on the charge, common for that time, of working for
foreign intelligence services.[23]

Tardov, Vladimir Gennadievich (1879–1938), (Chapter 3, footnote
104). A journalist, poet, historian and Iranist. In 1909–11, he worked
in Persia as a correspondent for the newspaper *Russkoe slovo*. In his
reports he would criticise the activities of Russian troops in Persia.
He would send some reports to the *Manchester Guardian* because of
Imperial Russia's censorship. He initially learnt Persian by taking private lessons from Persian students in St Petersburg. In 1917 he joined
the Bolsheviks. He worked in the Soviet military and NKID and was a
member of VNAV. In 1928 gifted a large collection of Persian artefacts
to the Soviet state. After 1928 he taught Persian history and economy
at MIV and the Military Academy. Accused of being a spy, in 1938 he
was arrested and executed.

Teimurtash, Abdolhosein (1883–1933), (Chapter 3, footnote 101).
Teimurtash was Reza Shah's Court Minister and the effective leader of
Persian foreign policy of the late 1920s–early 1930s. At the time, there
was a great deal of distrust and fear towards the USSR because of
Article 6 of the Soviet–Iranian Treaty of 1921, which allowed military
invasion of Iran on the part of the USSR if Iranian territory was used
in some way against the USSR. In 1935 after joining the League of
Nations by the Soviet Union, Iran took considerable but unsuccessful
measures to try to abolish this article through the League. Reza Shah
also personally distrusted the Bolsheviks and feared their intelligence
services. This was particularly aggravated after Teimurtash's cooperation with the USSR was revealed by Stalin's secretary, Bazhanov, who
defected to the West via Persia in 1928.[24] Afterwards, this and other

---

[23] See V. Abramov and V. Frolov, "Voennyi uchenyi-vostokoved Tageev. Ob'ezdil
polmira, a rasstrelian v Moskve", *Voenno-istoricheskii zhurnal* 4 (2002), 77–
80; Baskhanov, *Russkie*, 231–2; Marshall, *Russian General Staff*, 145–6, 227;
Volkov, "Persian Studies," 8–9.
[24] Boris Bazhanov, *Vospominaniia byvshego sekretaria Stalina* (Moscow: SP
Sofinta, 1990).

factors finally led to Reza Shah arresting and secretly ordering the murder of Teimurtash in prison.[25] The SVR archives naturally keep silence on the issue. Indirect evidence of Teimurtash's close relations with the Soviet Ambassador and the INO OGPU Station-Chief Davtian can be found in the recently declassified collections of RGASPI – copies of NKID's correspondence, which is still classified in AVPRF.[26]

Trutovskii, Vladimir Konstantinovich (1862–1932), (Chapter 2, footnote 77). Trutovskii graduated from the Lazarev Institute of Oriental Languages and the Educational Section of Oriental Languages of MID. The title of his thesis was "Mazdak and his doctrine". In 1898 he was appointed Head of the Kremlin Armoury. He actively participated and supervised the study of the museum artefacts. He also was Head of Moscow Numismatic Society and was one of the founders of the Oriental Commission.

Zhukovskii, Valentin Alekseevich (1858–1918), (Chapter 2, footnote 63). Professor of Persian language and literature at the Faculty of Oriental Languages of St Petersburg University. He was an associated member of the Russian Academy of Sciences, Head of the Section of Oriental Languages at the Foreign Ministry(1905–18) and also Head of the Translation Section at the Foreign Ministry (1915–17). During the 1880s, 1890s and 1900s he undertook scholarly missions to Persia. He was an active promoter of Oriental studies within scholarly and state power institutions.[27]

---

[25] See Aliev, *Istoriia Irana*, 171–3; Mamedova, "Istoriia," 161.
[26] For example, RGASPI, f. 159, op. 2, d. 51, l. 178 (Chicherin to Kamenev), 190 (Chicherin to Karakhan).
[27] See Bartol'd, "Pamiati V. A. Zhukovskogo," 689.

Bibliography

In addition to the unpublished archival materials (see the List of Archives), the following published sources were used.

Abdullaeva, Firuza, "Zhukovskii Valentin Alekseevich," *Encyclopaedia Iranica* (15 August 2009), www.iranicaonline.org/articles/zhukovskii-valentin-alekseevich.

Abramov, V., and V. Frolov, "Voennyi uchenyi-vostokoved Tageev. Ob'ezdil polmira, a rasstrelian v Moskve," *Voenno-istoricheskii zhurnal* 4 (2002): 77–80.

Agaev, Semen, *Sovetskoe iranovedenie 20-kh godov* (Moscow: Nauka, 1977).

Aliev, Saleh, *Istoriia Irana. XX vek* (Moscow: IVRAN – Kraft+, 2004).

Al-Saltana, Taj, *Crowning Anguish: Memoirs of a Persian Princess from the Harem to Modernity, 1884–1914* (Washington, DC: Mage, 1993).

Andreeva, Elena, *Russia and Iran in the Great Game: Travelogues and Orientalism* (New York: Routledge, 2007).

Arabajan, A. Z., "O nachal'nykh etapakh izucheniia ekonomiki Irana v Sovetskoi Rossi ii SSSR (1920–1956)," in Kulagina, *Iranistika v Rossii i iranisty*, 74–5.

Atkin, Muriel, "Soviet and Russian Scholarship on Iran," *Iranian Studies* 2/4 (1987): 223–71.

Bajanov, Boris, *Avec Staline dans le Kremlin* (Paris: Editions de France, 1930).

Bartol'd, Vasilii, "Autobiography," in *Sobranie sochinenii*, vol. 9 (Moscow: Nauka, 1977): 789–94.

"Baron Rozen i russkii provintsial'nyi orientalism," in *Sobranie sochinenii*, vol. 9 (Moscow: Nauka, 1977): 589–95.

"Doklad V. V. Bartol'da," *ZVORAO* 11 (1898): 341–56.

"Iran: Istoricheskii obzor," in *Sobranie sochinenii*, vol. 7 (Moscow: Nauka, 1977): 230–336.

"Istoriia izucheniia Vostoka v Evrope i Rossii," in *Sobranie sochinenii*, vol. 9 (Moscow: Nauka, 1977): 199–484.

"Istoriia kul'turnoi zhizni Turkestana. Evropeizatsiia upravleniia i tuzemtsy," in *Sobranie sochinenii*, vol. 2, part 1 (Moscow: Nauka, 1977): 350–76.

"K proektu vostochnogo instituta," in *Sobranie sochinenii*, vol. 9 (Moscow: Nauka, 1977): 499–502.

"K voprosu o feodalizme v Irane," *Novyi Vostok* 28 (1930): 108–16.

"Obzor deiatel'nosti fakul'teta vostochnykh iazykov," in *Sobranie sochinenii*, vol. 9 (Moscow: Nauka, 1977): 24–198.

Otchet o poezdke v Sredniuiu Aziiu s nauchnoiu tsel'iu, 1893–1894 (St Petersburg: Tipografia Imperatorski Akademii Nauk, 1897).

"Pamiati V. A. Zhukovskogo," in *Sobranie sochinenii*, vol. 9 (Moscow: Nauka, 1977): 689–703.

"Po povodu proekta S. F. Ol'denburga," in *Sobranie sochinenii*, vol. 9 (Moscow: Nauka, 1977): 492–5.

"Proekty spetsial'nykh shkol. Vostokovedenie v S.-Peterburge," in *Sobranie sochinenii*, vol. 9 (Moscow: Nauka, 1977): 52–66.

"Russkii Komitet dlia izucheniia Srednei i Vostochnoi Azii v istoricheskom, arkheologicheskom, lingvisticheskom i etnographicheskom otnosheniiakh, 1903–1909," in *Sobranie sochinenii*, vol. 9 (Moscow: Nauka, 1977): 503–9.

"Vostok i russkaia nauka," in *Sobranie sochinenii*, vol. 9 (Moscow: Nauka, 1977): 534–45.

Baskhanov, Mikhail, *Russkie voennye vostokovedy* (Moscow: Vostochnaia literature RAN, 2005).

Bast, Oliver, "The Council for International Propaganda and the Establishment of the Iranian Communist Party," in *Iran and the First World War*, ed. Touraj Atabaki (London: I. B. Tauris, 2006): 163–76.

"Duping the British and Outwitting the Russians? Iran's Foreign Policy, the 'Bol'shevik Threat', and the Genesis of the Soviet–Iranian Treaty of 1921," in *Iranian–Russian Encounters: Empires and Revolutions since 1800*, ed. Stephanie Cronin (New York: Routledge, 2013): 261–97.

Bateman, Aaron, "The KGB and Its Enduring Legacy," *Journal of Slavic Military Studies* 29/1 (2016): 23–47.

"The Political Influence of the Russian Security Services," *Journal of Slavic Military Studies* 27 (2014): 380–403.

Bazhanov, Boris, *Vospominaniia byvshego secretaria Stalina* (Moscow: SP Sofinta, 1990).

Baziiants, Ashot, "Dve vstrechi S. F. Ol'denburga s V. I. Leninym i razvitie sovetskogo vostokovedeniia," in *Sergei Fedorovich Ol'denburg*, ed. Georgii Skriabin and Evgenii Primakov (Moscow: Nauka, 1986): 14–27.

"Iz istorii Sovetskogo vostokovedeniia v 1917–1922 gg.," in *Stanovlenie Sovetskogo vostokovedeniia*, ed. Ashot Baziiants (Moscow: Nauka, 1983): 29–84.

Beer, Daniel, *Renovating Russia: The Human Sciences and the Fate of Liberal Modernity, 1880–1930* (Ithaca, NY: Cornell University Press, 2008).

Belozerskii, Evgenii, "Pis'ma iz Persii ot Baku do Ispagani, 1885–1886," *Sbornik geograficheskikh, topograficheskikh i statesticheskikh materialov po Azii* 25 (1887): 1–108.

Bezugol'nyi, Aleksei, *General Bicherakhov i ego kavkazskaia armiia* (Tver: Tsentrpoligraf, 2011).

Birstein, Vadim J., *The Perversion of Knowledge: The True Story of Soviet Science* (Cambridge, MA: Westview Press, 2001).

Boncuk, Mavi, "Minorsky and Nikitin," in *Cornucopia of Ottomania and Turcomania* (22 March 2013), http://maviboncuk.blogspot.ru/2013/03/Minorsky-and-nikitin.html (accessed 12 June 2014).

Borshevskii, Iurii, "K kharakteristike rukopisnogo naslediia V. A. Zhukovskogo," in *Ocherki po istorii russkogo vostokovedeniia*, ed. Iosif Orbeli (Moscow: Nauka, 1960): 5–44.

Bregel, Yuri, "Barthold and Modern Oriental Studies," *International Journal of Middle East Studies* 12/3 (1980): 385–403.

Bromberger, Christian, *Milda, une pasionaria rouge: De la Baltique à la Caspienne, enquête sur une destinée hors du commun* (Paris: CREAPHIS, 2018).

Brown, James, "A Stereotype, Wrapped in a Cliché, inside a Caricature: Russian Foreign Policy and Orientalism," *Politics* 30/3 (2010): 149–59.

Browne, Edward G., *The Persian Revolution of 1905–1909* (Cambridge: Cambridge University Press, 1910).

Bushev, Petr, "Zhizn' i deiatel'nost' V. A. Zhukovskogo," in *Ocherki po istorii russkogo vostokovedeniia*, ed. V. Avdiev (Moscow: Izdatel'stvo vostochnoi literatury, 1959): 116–36.

Cohen, Stephen F., *Rethinking the Soviet Experience: Politics and History since 1917* (New York: Oxford University Press, 1985).

Conermann, Stephan, "Foreword," in *The Heritage of Soviet Oriental Studies*, ed. Michael Kemper and Stephan Conermann (Abingdon: Routledge, 2011): xiii–xv.

Cronin, Stephanie, ed., *Iranian–Russian Encounters: Empires and Revolutions since 1800* (London: Routledge, 2013).

Dailami, Pezhmann, "The Bolshevik Revolution and the Genesis of Communism in Iran, 1917–1920", *Central Asian Survey* 11/3 (1992): 51–82.

   "Bravin in Tehran and the Origins of Soviet Policy in Iran," *Revolutionary Russia* 12/2 (1999): 63–82.

Deleuze, Gilles, *Foucault*, trans. Sean Hand (Minneapolis: University of Minnesota Press, 1988).

Deutschmann, Moritz, "All Rulers Are Brothers: Russian Relations with the Iranian Monarchy in the Nineteenth Century," *Iranian Studies* 46/3 (2013): 383–413.

Dostoevskii, Fedor, *Dnevnik pisatelia, 1881*, http://az.lib.ru/d/dostoewskij_
f_m/text_0530.shtml (accessed 21 August 2012).

Engelstein, Laura, "Combined Underdevelopment: Discipline and the Law
in Imperial and Soviet Russia," in *Foucault and the Writing of History*,
ed. Jan Goldstein (Oxford: Blackwell, 1994): 220–36.

Ezhov, Georgii, "Polveka tomu nazad v Tegerane (Otryvki iz vospominanii
sovremennika)," in *Iran. Istoriia, ekonomika, kul'tura* ed. Nina
Mamedova and Liudmila Kulagina (Moscow: Institut vostokovedeniia
RAN, 2009): 78–94.

Fedorchenko, V. I., *Imperatorskii Dom. Vydaiushiesia sanovniki*, vol. 2
(Moscow: Olma Press, 2003).

Fortescue, Stephen, *The Communist Party and Soviet Science* (London:
Macmillan, 1986).

Foucault, Michel, *The Archaeology of Knowledge* (London: Routledge, 1972).
   The Archaeology of Knowledge and the Discourse on Language (New
   York: Pantheon, 1972).
   The History of Sexuality: An Introduction, trans. Robert Hurley
   (Harmondsworth: Penguin, 1978).
   "The Order of Discourse," in *Untying the Text: A Post-Structuralist
   Reader*, ed. Robert Young (London: Routledge, 1981): 48–78.
   The Order of Things: An Archaeology of the Human Sciences (London:
   Routledge, 1989).
   Power, ed. James D. Faubion (New York: New Press, 2000).
   Power/Knowledge: Selected Interviews and Other Writings, 1972–1977,
   ed. Colin Gordon (Brighton: Harvester, 1980).
   "Prison Talk," in *Power/Knowledge*, ed. Colin Gordon (Brighton: Harvester,
   1980): 37–54.
   "Truth and Power," in *Microfisica del potere: interventi politici*, ed.
   Alessandro Fontana and Pasquale Pasquino, trans. C. Lazzeri (Turin:
   Einaudi, 1977): 3–28.
   "Two Lectures," in *Power/Knowledge*, ed. Colin Gordon (Brighton:
   Harvester, 1980): 78–108.

Frye, Richard N., "Oriental Studies in Russia," in *Russia and Asia: Essays
on the Influence of Russia on the Asian Peoples*, ed. Wayne S. Vucinich
(Stanford, CA: Hoover Institution Press, 1972): 30–52.

Genis, Vladimir, *Krasnaia Persiia: Bol'sheviki v Giliane, 1920–1921*
(Moscow: MNPI, 2000).
   Nevernye slugi rezhima: Pervye sovetskie nevozvrashentsy (1920–1933)
   (Moscow: Informkniga, 2009).
   "Rudol'f Abikh – istorik Gilianskoi revoliutsii," in Kulagina, *Iranistika v
   Rossii i iranisty*, 145–56.
   Vitse-Konsul Vvedenskii (Moscow: MYSL', 2003).

Geraci, Robert, *Window on the East: National and Imperial Identities in Late Tsarist Russia* (Ithaca, NY: Cornell University Press, 2001).

Gerasimov, Ilya, Jan Kusber and Alexander Semyonov, eds, *Empire Speaks Out: Languages of Rationalization and Self-Description in the Russian Empire* (Boston: Brill, 2009).

Gershevitch, Ilya, "Obituary: Professor Vladimir Minorsky," *Journal of the Royal Asiatic Society of Great Britain and Ireland* 1 (1967): 53–6.

Geyer, Dietrich, *Russian Imperialism: The Interaction of Domestic and Foreign Policy, 1860–1914* (Oxford: Berg, 1987).

Graham, Loren, *Science in Russia and the Soviet Union* (Cambridge: Cambridge University Press, 1993).

Gurko-Kriazhin, Vladimir, "Belaia opasnost'. Vostok i Zapad," *Russkoe Slovo* (1 February 1914).

"Vostok pri svete revoliutsii," *Vestnik zhizni* 5 (1919): 100–1.

"V sektsiiu Zarubezhnogo Vostoka Obshestva istorikov-marksistov. Zaiavlenie," *Istorik-marksist* 17 (1930).

"10 let vostokovednoi mysli," *Novyi Vostok* 19 (1927): 20–45.

Gurko-Kriazhina, E. V., *Vostokoved Vladimir Aleksandrovich Gurko-Kriazhin, 1887–1931* (Moscow: INION RAN, 2003).

Herzig, Edmund, and Paul D. Wordsworth, eds, *E. E. Berthels, The Great Azerbaijani Poet, Nizami: Life, Work and Times* (London: Gilgamesh, 2017).

Hirsch, Francine, *Empire of Nations: Ethnographic Knowledge and the Making of the Soviet Union* (Ithaca, NY: Cornell University Press, 2005).

Hodgson, Marshall, *The Venture of Islam: The Expansion of Islam in the Middle Periods* (Chicago: Chicago University Press, 1974).

Horrocks, Chris, and Zoran Jevtic, *Introducing Foucault* (New York: Totem Books, 1998).

Ironside, Lord, ed., *High Road to Command. The Diaries of Major-General Sir Edmund Ironside, 1920–1922* (London: Leo Cooper, 1972).

Ivanov, M. S., and V. N. Zaitsev, eds, *Novaia istoriia Irana* (Moscow: Nauka, 1988).

Ivanova, M. V., *Vvedenie v regionovedenie. Iz istorii sovetskogo vostokovedeniia* (Tomsk: Izdatel'stvo TPU, 2006).

Kalmykow, Andrew D., *Memoirs of a Russian Diplomat: Outposts of the Empire, 1893–1917* (New Haven, CT: Yale University Press, 1971).

Kazemzadeh, Firuz, *Russia and Britain in Persia: Imperial Ambitions in Qajar Iran* (London: I. B. Tauris, 2013).

Kelle, Vladislav, "Introduction," in *Nauka i tekhnika v pervye desiatiletiia sovetskoi vlasti: sotsiokul'turnoe izmerenie, 1917–1940*, ed. Elena Muzrukova and Liudmila Chesnova (Moscow: Academia, 2007): 7–12.

Kemper, Michael, "Integrating Soviet Oriental Studies," in *The Heritage of Soviet Oriental Studies*, ed. Michael Kemper and Stephan Conermann (Abingdon: Routledge, 2011): 1–25.

"Red Orientalism: Mikhail Pavlovich and Marxist Oriental Studies in Early Soviet Russia," *Die Welt des Islams* 50 (2010): 435–76.

"The Soviet Discourse on the Origin and Class Character of Islam, 1923–1933," *Die Welt des Islams* 49 (2009): 1–48.

Khairutdinov, Ramil', "Mir Islama: iz istorii sozdaniia zhurnala," *Mir Islama* 1/2 (1999): 5–20.

Khalid, Adeeb, "Russian History and the Debate over Orientalism," *Kritika: Explorations in Russian and Eurasian History* 1/4 (2000): 691–9.

Khanykov, Nikolai, *Ekspeditsiia v Khorasan* (Moscow: Nauka, 1973).

Kheifets, A. N., and P. M. Shastiko, "V. I. Lenin i stanovlenie sovetskogo vostokovedeniia," in *Stanovlenie Sovetskogo vostokovedeniia*, ed. Ashot Baziiants (Moscow: Nauka, 1983): 3–28.

Kistiakovskii, Bogdan, "V zashitu prava. Intelligentsiia i pravoznanie," in *Vekhi: Sbornik statei o russkoi intelligentsii* (Moscow, 1909) www.vehi .net/vehi/kistyak.html (accessed 25 September 2013).

Kneen, Peter, *Soviet Scientists and the State* (London: Macmillan, 1984).

Knight, Nathaniel, "Grigor'ev in Orenburg, 1851–1862: Russian Orientalism in the Service of Empire?," *Slavic Review* 59/1 (2000): 74–100.

"On Russian Orientalism: A Response to Adeeb Khalid," *Kritika: Explorations in Russian and Eurasian History* 1/4 (2000): 701–15.

Kocho-Williams, Alastair, *Russian and Soviet Diplomacy, 1900–1939* (Basingstoke: Palgrave Macmillan, 2012).

Kolpakidi, A. I., and D. P. Prokhorov, *Imperiia GRU. Ocherki istorii Rossiiskoi voennoi razvedki* (Moscow: Olma Press, 1999).

Kononov, Andrei, "Introduction," in Vasilii Bartol'd, *Sobrane sochinenii*, vol. 9 (Moscow: Nauka, 1977): 5–22.

Vostokovedenie v Leningradskom Universitete (Leningrad: Izdatel'stvo Leningradskogo Universiteta, 1960).

Kosogovskii, Vladimir, *Iz tegeranskogo dnevnika polkovnika,* ed. G. M. Petrov (Moscow: Izdatel'stvo vostochnoi literatury, 1960).

Kotkin, Stephen, *Magnetic Mountain: Stalinism as a Civilization* (Berkeley: University of California Press, 1995).

Krachkovskii, Ignatii, *Ocherki po istorii russkoi arabistiki* (Moscow: Nauka, 1950).

Krementsov, Nikolai, *Stalinist Science* (Princeton, NJ: Princeton University Press, 1997).

Kriazhin, Vladimir, "Retsenziia na Troianovskii K. Vostok pri svete revolutsii," *Sovetskaia strana* 1 (27 January 1919).

Krivonosov, Iurii, "Partiia i nauka v pervye gody Sovetskoi vlasti," in *Nauka i tekhnika v pervye desiatiletiia sovetskoi vlasti: sotsiokul'turnoe izmerenie, 1917–1940*, ed. Elena Muzrukova and Liudmila Chesnova (Moscow: Academia, 2007): 13–32.

Kulagina, Liudmila, ed., *Iranistika v Rossii i iranisty* (Moskva: Institut vostokovedeniia RAN, 2001).

"Iz istorii rossiiskoi iranistiki," in Kulagina, *Iranistika v Rossii i iranisty*, 18–36.

"Moskovskaia shkola iranistiki: izuchenie istoricheskikh problem," in Kulagina, *Iranistika v Rossii i iranisty*, 45–52.

Rossiia i Iran (XIX – nachalo XX veka) (Moscow: Izdatel'skii Dom 'Kliuch-S', 2010).

Kulagina, Liudmila, and Elena Dunaeva, *Granitsa Rossii s Iranom. Istoriia formirovaniia* (Moscow: Institut Vostokovedeniia RAN, 1998).

Kullanda, M., and N. Sazonova, "Zabytoe imia (V. G. Tardov)," in Kulagina, *Iranistika v Rossii i iranisty*, 127–44.

Kuznetsova, Nina, and Liudmila Kulagina, *Iz istorii sovetskogo vostokovedeniia, 1917–1967* (Moscow: Nauka, 1970).

"Vsesoiuznaia Nauchnaia Assotsiatsiia vostokovedeniia, 1921–1930," in *Stanovlenie Sovetskogo vostokovedeniia*, ed. Ashot Baziiants (Moscow: Nauka, 1983): 131–63.

Lang, David, "Obituary: Vladimir Fedorovich Minorsky," *Bulletin of the School of Oriental and African Studies* 29/3 (1966): 694–9.

Lenin, V. I., "Letter to Ammanallah-Khan, dated 27/05/1919," *Izvestiia TsIK Turkestanskoi Respubliki* 121 (14 June 1919).

"Rech ob otnoshenii k Vremennomu pravitel'stvu na Pervom Vserossiiskii s'ezde Sovetov rabochikh i soldatskikh deputatov, 3–24 iiunia 1917 g.," in *Sobranie sochinenii*, vol. 32 (Moscow: Progress, 1970): 263–76.

Lunin, B. V., "Vostokovedenie v respublikakh Srednei Azii posle Velikoi Oktiabr'skoi Sotsialisticheskoi revoliutsii," in *Stanovlenie sovetskogo vostokovedeniia*, ed. Ashot Baziiants (Moscow: Nauka, 1983): 85–130.

Mamedova, Nina, "Issledovanie sotsial'no-politicheskikh problem Irana i iranskogo obshestva," in Kulagina, *Iranistika v Rossii i iranisty*: 53–60.

"Istoriia Sovetsko-Iranskikh otnoshenii (1917–1991)," in *Iran: Istoriia, ekonomika, kul'tura*, ed. Nina Mamedova and Liudmila Kulagina (Moscow: Institut Vostokovedeniia RAN, 2009): 157–70.

Marshall, Alex, *The Russian General Staff and Asia, 1800–1917* (London: Routledge, 2006).

Marten, Kimberly, "The 'KGB State' and Russian Political and Foreign Policy Culture," *Journal of Slavic Military Studies* 30/2 (2017): 131–51.

Melville, Firuza, "Zhukovskii Valentin Alekseevich," *Encyclopaedia Iranica*, www.iranicaonline.org/articles/zhukovskii-valentin-alekseevich (accessed 15 August 2009).

Menning, Bruce W., *Bayonets before Bullets: The Imperial Russian Army, 1861–1914* (Bloomington: Indiana University Press, 2000).

Miller, B. V., "Trudy russkikh uchionykh v oblasti iranskogo iazykoznaniia," *Uchionye zapiski MGU* 107/3/2 (1946): 71–85.

Mills, Sara, *Michel Foucault* (London: Routledge, 2005).

Milyutin, Dmitrii, *Dnevnik. 1876–1878. 1879–1881* (Moscow: ROSSPEN, 2010).

Minorsky, Vladimir, *Kurdy* (Petrograd: Tipografiia Kirshbauma, 1915).

Modrzejewska-Lesniewska, Joanna, "A Spy or the First Russian Dissident?" [In Polish] *Przeglad Historyczny* 94/4 (2003): 411–8.

Morrison, Alexander, "'Applied Orientalism' in British India and Tsarist Turkestan," *Comparative Studies in Society and History* 51/3 (2009): 619–47.

Nahavandi, Hooshang, *Seh ruidad va seh doulatmard* (Los Angeles: Ketab, 2009).

Naumkin, Vitalii, ed., *Neizvestnye stranitsy otechestvennogo vostokovedeniia* (Moscow: Vostochnaia literatura, 1997).

    ed., *Neizvestnye stranitsy otechestvennogo vostokovedeniia* (Moscow: Vostochnaia literatura, 2008).

Nikolaeff, A. M., "Universal Military Service in Russia and Western Europe," *Russian Review* 8/2 (1949): 117–26.

Nilson, Herman, *Michel Foucault and the Games of Truth*, trans. Rachel Clark (London: Macmillan, 1998).

Ol'denburg, Sergei, "Pamiati M. P. Pavlovicha," *Novyi Vostok* 18 (1927): 23–6.

    "Pamiati V. P. Vasil'eva i o ego trudakh po buddizmu," *Izvestiia Rossiiskoi Akademii Nauk* 7 (1918): 438–9.

    "Valentin Alekseevich Zhukovskii, 1858–1918," *Izvestiia Rossiiskoi Akademii nauk* 2 (1919): 2039–68.

Orishev, A. B., *Iranskii uzel. Skhvatka razvedok. 1936–1945 gg.* (Moscow: Izdatel'skii dom Veche, 2009).

Osetrov, Vladimir, "Ocherki ekonomicheskogo stroia v Persii," in *Kolonial'nyi Vostok. Sotsial'no-ekonomicheskie ocherki* (Moscow: Nauka, 1924).

Pasquino, Pasquale, "Michel Foucault (1926–84): The Will to Knowledge," in *Foucault's New Domains*, ed. Mike Gane and Terry Johnson (London: Routledge, 1993).

Pavlovich, Mikhail, "Zadachi i dostizheniia sovetskogo vostokovedeniia," *Novyi Vostok* 16–17 (1926): 2–20.

"Zadachi Vserossiiskoi nauchnoi assotsiatsii vostokovedeniia," *Novyi Vostok* 1 (1922): 3–15.

Persits, Moisei, *Zastenchivaia interventsiia. O sovetskom vtorzhenii v Iran i Bukharu v 1920–1921* (Moscow: Izdatel'skii Dom 'Muravei-Gaid', 1999).

Petrushevskii, Il'ia, "Akademik V. V. Bartol'd," in Vasilii Bartol'd, *Sobranie sochinenii*, vol. 1 (Moscow: Nauka, 1977): 14–21.

Popovskii, Mark, *Science in Chains*, trans. Paul S. Falla (London: Collins and Harvill Press, 1980).

Ravandi-Fadai, S. M., "Vneshnepoliticheskie problemy Irana v rabotakh rossiiskikh uchenykh," in Kulagina, *Iranistika v Rossii i iranisty*, 61–4.

Roberg, Jeffrey, *Soviet Science under Control: The Struggle for Influence* (London: Macmillan, 1998).

Rodionov, Mikhail, "Profiles under Pressure: Orientalists in Petrograd/Leningrad, 1918–1956," in *The Heritage of Soviet Oriental Studies*, ed. Michael Kemper and Stephan Conermann (Abingdon: Routledge, 2011): 47–57.

Romaskevich, Aleksandr, "V. A. Zhukovskii i persidskaia narodnaia poeziia," *ZVORAO* 25 (1921): 399–419.

Rozen, Viktor, "Babidskii antikholernyi talisman, 1892," *ZVORAO* 7 (1893): 311–18.

Ryder, Colonel H. D., "The Demarcation of the Turco-Persian Boundary in 1913–1914," *Geographical Journal* 66/3 (1925): 227–37.

Rzaev, A. K., *Muhammed Ali M. Kazem-Bek* (Moscow: Nauka, 1989).

Said, Edward, *Orientalism* (London: Routledge & Kegan Paul, 1978).

Schimmelpenninck van der Oye, David, "Mirza Kazem-Bek and the Kazan School of Russian Orientology," *Comparative Studies of South Asia, Africa and the Middle East* 28/3 (2008): 443–58.

"Reforming Military Intelligence," in *Reforming the Tsar's Army: Military Innovation in Imperial Russia from Peter the Great to the Revolution*, ed. David Schimmelpenninck van der Oye and Bruce W. Menning (Washington, DC: Woodrow Wilson International Center for Scholars, 2004), 133–50.

Russian Orientalism: Asia in the Russian Mind from Peter the Great to the Emigration (New Haven: Yale University Press, 2010).

"The Imperial Roots of Soviet Orientology," in *The Heritage of Soviet Oriental Studies*, ed. Michael Kemper and Stephan Conermann (Abingdon: Routledge, 2011): 29–46.

Schlosser, Friedrich Christoph, *The History of the Eighteenth Century and of the Nineteenth Till the Overthrow of the French Empire*, trans. D. Davison (London: Chapman and Hall, 1845).

Shapshal, Seraia, "Valentin Alekseevich Zhukovskii," in *Ocherki po istorii Russkogo vostokovedeniia*, ed. Iosif Orbeli (Moscow: Nauka, 1960): 131–3.

Shahvar, Soli, Gad Gilbar and Boris Morozov, eds, *The Baha'iis of Iran, Transcaspia and the Caucasus: Letters of Russian Officers and Officials* (London: I. B. Tauris, 2011).

Shebarshin, Leonid, *Ruka Moskvy: Razvedka ot rastsveta do razvala* (Moscow: Algoritm, 2012).

Shirokorad, Aleksandr, *Rossiia-Angliia: Neizvestnaia voina, 1857–1907* (Moscow: AST, 2003).

Persiia – Iran: Imperiia na Vostoke (Moscow: Veche, 2010).

Shishov, Aleksandr, *Persidskii front (1909–1918)* (Moscow: Izdatel'skii dom Veche, 2010).

Simbirtsev, Igor, *Spetssluzhby pervykh let SSSR, 1923–1939* (Moscow: Tsentrpoligraf, 2008).

Simons, Jon, *Foucault and the Political* (London: Routledge, 1995).

Slezkine, Yuri, *Arctic Mirrors: Russia and the Small Peoples of the North* (Ithaca, NY: Cornell University Press, 1994).

Smirnov, Konstantin, "Dervishy i ikh politicheskoe znachenie," *Izvestiia Shtaba Kavkazskogo Voennogo Okruga* 31–2 (1911).

Iran: ekonomicheskii spravochnik (Tiflis: AN GSSR, 1934).

"Messionery v Persii," *Izvestiia Shtaba Kavkazskogo Voennogo Okruga* 23 (1909).

"Naselenie Persii s voennoi tochki zreniia," *Izvestiia Shtaba Kavkazskogo Voennogo Okruga* 27 (1910): 20–64.

"Naselenie Persii s voennoi tochki zreniia," *Izvestiia Shtaba Kavkazskogo Voennogo Okruga* 28 (1910): 1–62.

Persy: Etnographicheskii ocherk Persii (Tiflis, 1917).

Persy: Ocherk religii Persii (Tiflis, 1916).

"Poezdka v Severnyi Kurdistan v 1904 godu," *IRGO* 17 (1904): 282–326.

Snesarev, Andrei, *Anglo-Russkoe soglashenie 1907 goda* (St Petersburg, 1908).

Snesarev, Andrei, *Indiia kak glavnyi factor v sredneaziatskom voprose: Vzgliad tuzemtsev na anglichan i ikh upravlenie* (St Petersburg, 1906).

Snesarev, Andrei, "K novomu polozheniiu o vostochnykh iazykakh," *Russkii invalid* 235 (2 December 1911).

"Nizverzhennyi vladyka," *Golos Pravdy* 1260 (1 November 1909).

"Ot konokrada do Kromvelia," *Golos Pravdy* 1067 (4 April 1909).

"Poslednee politicheskoe dvizhenie v Persii," *Golos Pravdy* 546 (15 June 1907).

"Probuzhdenie Afghanistana," *Tashkentskie Vesti* (31 January 1905).

"Skromnoe, no ochen' vazhnoe delo," *Golos Pravdy* 1242 (13 October 1909).

Smolenskii dnevnik (13 November 1918) www.a-e-snesarev.ru/ smolenskiy_dnevnik.pdf (accessed 12 June 2014).

"Sostoianie Persii," *Golos Pravdy* 1316 (15 January 1910).

"A Speech at the Annual Meeting of the Society of Orientologists," (2 May 1910), www.a-e-snesarev.ru/trudi/programma.html (accessed 12 June 2014).

"V obshestve vostokovedeniia," *Golos Pravdy* (27 October 1909).

Vostochnaia Bukhara: voenno-geograficheskii ocherk (St Petersbug, 1906).

"25-letie ofitserskikh kursov vostochnykh iazykov," *Golos Pravdy* 950 (20 November 1908).

Snesarev, Andrei, "Prakticheskoe izuchenie Vostoka," *Golos Pravdy* (5 December 1909).

Sukhorukov, Sergei, *Iran mezhdu Britaniei i Rossiei. Ot politiki do ekonomiki* (St Petersburg: Aleteia, 2009).

Sushko, Iurii, *Deviat' zhiznei Iakova Bliumkina* (Moscow: Tsentrpoligraf, 2012).

Tamazishvili, Aleksandr, "Vladimir Aleksandrovich Gurko-Kriazhin: Sud'ba boitsa 'vostokovednogo fronta,' " in *Neizvestnye stranitsy otechestvennogo vostokovedeniia*, ed. Vladimir Naumkin (Moscow: Vostochnaia literatura, 2008): 32–136.

Ter-Oganov, Nugzar, *Persidskaia kazach'ia brigada, 1879–1921* (Moscow: IVRAN, 2012).

Ter-Oganov, Nugsar, "Persidskaia kazach'ia brigada: period transformatsii (1894–1903 gg.)," *Vostok: Afro-aziatskie obshchestva: istoriia i sovremennost'* 3 (2010): 69–79.

Ter-Oganov, Nugzar, "Pis'mo N. G. Gartviga K. N. Smirnovu kak tsennyi istochnik dlia kharakterisiki anglo-russkikh otnoshenii v Irane v nachale XX veka," in *Iran: Istoriia, ekonomika, kul'tura*, ed. Nina Mamedova and Liudmila Kulagina (Moscow: Institut vostokovedeniia RAN, 2009): 207–16.

"Rapport du Capitaine en Second Constantin Smirnov sur son Voyage en Turquie en 1904," *Iran and the Caucasus* 10/2 (2006): 209–29.

"The Russian Military Mission and the Birth of the Persian Cossack Brigade: 1879–1894," *Iranian Studies* 42/3 (2009): 445–63.

"Zhizn' i deiatel'nost' Konstantina Nikolaevicha Smirnova," in *Zapiski vospitatelia persidskogo shaha*, ed. K. N. Smirnov (Tel-Aviv: Irus, 2002): 4–14.

Todorova, Maria, "Does Russian Orientalism Have a Russian Soul? A Contribution to the Debate between Nathaniel Knight and Adeeb

Khalid," *Kritika: Explorations in Russian and Eurasian History* 1/4 (2000): 717–27.

Tolz, Vera, "European, National, and (Anti-)Imperial: The Formation of Academic Oriental Studies in Late Tsarist and Early Soviet Russia," *Kritika: Explorations in Russian and Eurasian History* 9/1 (Winter 2008): 53–82.

"Orientalism, Nationalism and Ethnic Diversity in Late Imperial Russia," *Historical Journal* 48/1 (2005): 127–50.

Russian Academicians and the Revolution: Combining Professionalism and Politics (London: Macmillan, 1997).

"Russia: Empire or a Nation-State-in-the-Making?" in *What Is a Nation? Europe 1789–1914*, ed. Timothy Baycroft and Mark Hewitson (Oxford: Oxford University Press, 2006): 293–311.

Russia's Own Orient: The Politics of Identity and Oriental Studies in the Late Imperial and Early Soviet Periods (Oxford: Oxford University Press, 2011).

Umniakov, Ivan, *Annotirovannaia bibliografiia trudov V. V. Bartol'da* (Moscow: Nauka, 1976).

Vashurina, Z. P., and A. I. Shishkanov, "Rodoslovmaia voennykh perevodchikov," *Voennoe Obozrenie Nezavisimoi Gazety* (19 May 2000) http://nvo.ng.ru/notes/2000-05-19/8_interpreters.html (accessed 15 November 2011).

Vasil'kov, Iaroslav, and Marina Sorokina, eds, *Luidi i sud'by: Bibliograficheskii slovar' vostokovedov-zhertv politicheskogo terrora v sovetskii period, 1917–1991* (St Petersburg: Peterburgskoe vostokovedenie, 2003).

Veniukov, Mikhail, "Rossiia i Vostok," in *Sbornik geograficheskikh i politicheskikh trudov* (St Petersburg, 1877): 155–212.

Vigasin, A., and A. N. Khokhlov, eds, *Istoriia otechestvennogo vostokovedeniia s serediny XIX veka do 1917 goda* (Moscow: Institut vostokovedeniia RAN, 1997).

Vladislavlev, Mikhail, "The Letter of the Rector of the St Petersburg University M. Vladislavlev to the Minister of Education," in *Materialy dlia istorii Facul'teta Vostochnykh Iazykov*, vol. 2 (St Petersburg: Tipografiia A.A. Stasiulevicha, 1905): 182–5.

Volkov, Denis V., "Fearing the Ghosts of State Officialdom Past? Russia's Archives as a Tool for Constructing Historical Memories on its Persia Policy Practices," *Middle Eastern Studies* 51/6 (2015): 901–21.

"Individuals, Institutions, Discourses: Knowledge and Power in Russia's Iranian Studies of the Late Imperial, Soviet and Post-Soviet Periods," *Middle East – Topics & Arguments* 4 (2015): 61–79.

"The Iranian Electric Power Industry after the Islamic Revolution: Nuclear Developments and Current Conditions," *New Middle Eastern Studies* 2 (2012): 1–8.

"Persian Studies and the Military in Late Imperial Russia (1863–1917): State Power in the Service of Knowledge?" *Iranian Studies* 47/6 (2014): 915–32.

"Rupture or Continuity? The Organizational Set-up of Russian and Soviet Oriental Studies before and after 1917," *Iranian Studies* 48/5 (2015): 695–712. [special issue, ed. Stephanie Cronin and Edmund Herzig]

"Vladimir Minorsky (1877–1966) and the Iran–Iraq War (1980–1988), or The Centenary of 'Minorsky's Frontier'," in *Russians in Iran: Diplomacy and Power in Iran in the Qajar Era and Beyond*, ed. Rudolph Matthee and Elena Andreeva (London: I. B. Tauris, 2018): 188–216.

"War and Peace in the Other and the Self: Iran through the eyes of Russian Spies – The case of Konstantin Smirnov (1877–1938) and Leonid Shebarshin (1935–2012)," *Cahiers de Studia Iranica* 62 (2018): 225–60.

Vucinich, Alexander, *Empire of Knowledge: The Academy of Science of the USSR (1917–1970)* (Berkeley: University of California Press, 1984).

Science in Russian Culture 1861–1917 (Stanford, CA: Stanford University Press, 1970).

Vucinich, Wayne S., "The Structure of Soviet Orientology: Fifty Years of Change and Accomplishment," in *Russia and Asia: Essays on the Influence of Russia on the Asian People*, ed. Wayne S. Vucinich (Stanford, CA: Hoover Institution Press, 1972): 52–134.

Wachtel, Andrew, "Translation, Imperialism, and National Self-Definition in Russia," *Public Culture* 11/1 (1999): 49–73.

Werth, Paul, *At the Margins of Orthodoxy: Mission, Governance, and Confessional Politics in Russia's Volga-Kama Region, 1827–1905* (Ithaca, NY: Cornell University Press, 2002).

Wilson, Arnold, A. C. Wratislaw and Percy Sykes, "The Demarcation of the Turco-Persian Boundary in 1913–1914: Discussion," *Geographical Journal* 66/3 (1925): 237–42.

Zakharchuk, Mikhail, "Lichnoe delo generala Snesareva," *Voennoe Obozrenie*, 12 December 2012, http://topwar.ru/21778-lichnoe-delo-generala-snesareva.html (accessed 12 June 2014).

Zakharova, Larisa, "Autocracy, Bureaucracy, and the Reforms of the 1860s in Russia," *Soviet Studies in History* 29 (1991): 6–33.

Zarkeshev, Father Superior Aleksandr, *Russkaia Pravoslavnaia Tserkov' v Persii-Irane (1597–2001)* [The Russian Orthodox Church in Persia-Iran (1597–2001)]. (St Petersburg: Satis, 2002).

Zarnitsky, S. V., and L. I. Trofimova, *Tak nachinalsia Narkomindel* (Moscow: Politizdat, 1984).

Zhukovskaia, Varvara, "Persidsky enderun," *Vestnik Evropy* 10 (October 1886): 501–49.

Zhukovskii, Sergei, "Moi otets," in *Ocherki po istorii Russkogo vostokovedeniia*, ed. Iosif Orbeli (Moscow: Izdatel'stvo vostochnoi literatury, 1960): 125–30.

Zhukovskii, Valentin, "Cherty sovremennogo polozheniia Persii v ee literaturnykh proizvedeniiakh, 1903," *ZVORAO* 16 (1904–5): 11–18.

Drevnosti zakaspiiskogo kraia. Razvaliny Starogo Merva (St Petersburg: Ministry of the Imperial Court, 1894).

Obraztsy persidskogo narodnogo tvorchestva (St Petersburg, 1902).

"Rossiiskii imperatorskii konsul F. A. Bakulin v istorii izucheniia babizma," *ZVORAO* 24 (1917): 33–90.

Index

For EU product safety concerns, contact us at Calle de José Abascal, 56–1°,
28003 Madrid, Spain or eugpsr@cambridge.org.